T0287060

Praise for Ayman Ibrahim's
A Concise Guide to the Quran

"An important resource for non-Muslims seeking to understand the Quran in the light of Islamic tradition and critical academic scholarship."

—**Gabriel Said Reynolds**, University of Notre Dame

"A wonderful introduction to the sacred text of Islam. I will be recommending this book for any person who wants to understand Islam and the Quran better and more correctly."

—**Daniel L. Akin**, Southeastern Baptist Theological Seminary

"An eminently accessible and lucidly written introduction. For those embarking on their first Quranic journey, *A Concise Guide to the Quran* is a beacon and a road map."

—**A. J. Droge**, author of *The Qur'an: A New Annotated Translation*

"A handy-yet-comprehensive overview of Islam's most sacred text. Skeptical yet respectful, this book will equip Christians and other non-Muslims to be well-informed about one of the most influential books in world history."

—**Mark Durie**, Arthur Jeffery Centre for the Study of Islam

"Ibrahim has struck the perfect balance between rigor and accessibility. This book is a must-read."

—**Peter G. Riddell**, Australian College of Theology

A
Concise Guide
to the Life of
MUHAMMAD

A
Concise Guide
to the Life of
MUHAMMAD

ANSWERING THIRTY KEY QUESTIONS

Ayman S. Ibrahim

Baker Academic
a division of Baker Publishing Group
Grand Rapids, Michigan

Published by Baker Academic
a division of Baker Publishing Group
PO Box 6287, Grand Rapids, MI 49516-6287
www.bakeracademic.com

Printed in the United States of America

Library of Congress Cataloging-in-Publication Data
Names: Ibrahim, Ayman S., 1973– author.
Title: A concise guide to the life of Muhammad : answering thirty key questions / Ayman S. Ibrahim.
Description: Grand Rapids, Michigan : Baker Academic, a division of Baker Publishing Group, 2022. | Includes bibliographical references and index.
Identifiers: LCCN 2021042018 | ISBN 9781540965073 (paperback) | ISBN 9781540965592 (casebound) | ISBN 9781493436613 (ebook) | ISBN 9781493436620 (pdf)
Subjects: LCSH: Muḥammad, Prophet, –632—Biography. | Islam—Origin.
Classification: LCC BP75 .I338 2022 | DDC 297.6/3 [B]—dc23
LC record available at https://lccn.loc.gov/2021042018

Baker Publishing Group publications use paper produced from sustainable forestry practices and post-consumer waste whenever possible.

22   23   24   25   26   27   28   7   6   5   4   3   2   1

Contents

Part 2: Muhammad's Message

Acknowledgments

I am indebted to Gabriel Said Reynolds, who read the first draft of this book and offered outstanding observations and helpful comments. His remarks have elevated the value in this resource. I am also thankful to my friend Brent Neely, who suggested some questions to be covered in the book. At Baker Academic, I thank Dave Nelson and Julie Zahm. They are supportive, professional, and dedicated to exceptionalism.

At Southern Seminary, I am grateful to my supervisors and colleagues, who constantly encourage me in my writing. My students are an inspiration. Through their diligence in research and questions in the classroom, they open new dimensions for me and give me direction for avenues to pursue in my books. Among these students, I am particularly grateful to my team at the Jenkins Center for the Christian Understanding of Islam. They are always seeking more knowledge in Islamic Studies. I wrote this book with them in mind, as well as for learners like them. I am so thankful for the resources of the Jenkins Center and the constant support my research receives from the leaders at Southern Seminary.

My wife is the hero behind all this. Her love, encouragement, and constant support for me and my work allow me time and space to write. To all, with gratitude, I say *shukran*!

Chronological Events in Muhammad's Life

555: Khadija's birth
570: The Year of the Elephant and the defeat of Abraha by Allah's army at Mecca
570: Muhammad's birth
576: Muhammad's mother, Amina, dies
581: Muhammad travels with his uncle Abu Talib to Syria and meets Bahira, a Syrian monk who foretells his prophethood
595: Khadija proposes to Muhammad, and they marry
599: Khadija delivers Muhammad's first child, a daughter, Zaynab
610: Muhammad receives the first revelation from Allah, through Gabriel
610: Waraqa, a Christian, confirms to Muhammad the divine revelation, emphasizing to him that he is the long-awaited prophet
610: Waraqa dies, and Muhammad's inspiration pauses
610: Early propagation of Islam in secret
610: Ali and Abu Bakr accept Islam, becoming among the earliest converts
613: Public proclamation of Islam begins
613: Meccan persecution of Muslims begins
616: First hijra (emigration) to Ethiopia
619: Muhammad's uncle Abu Talib dies
619: Khadija dies, and Muhammad calls this year "The Year of Sorrow"
619: Muhammad marries Sawda (she is almost fifty)
619: Muhammad is betrothed to Aisha (she is six or seven)
619: Satanic verses incident
620: Muhammad's night journey to Jerusalem and his ascension to heaven
622: The hijra, Muhammad's emigration from Mecca to Medina

622: Starting point of the Islamic Hijri lunar calendar
622: Muhammad consummates his marriage with Aisha (she is nine)
623: Muhammad launches first raid against the Meccans and their caravans
624: Battle of Badr, a major conflict in which Muhammad defeats the Meccans
624: Raid against the Jews of Qaynuqa
624: Muhammad orders the murder of the Jewish poet Ka'b, who insulted him
625: Battle of Uhud; Meccans are revenged and defeat the Muslims
625: Raid against the Jews of Nadir
626: Aisha is accused of adultery but declared innocent by Muhammad and Allah
627: Battle of the Trench, or of the Confederates
627: Raid against the Jews of Qurayza
628: Raid (or Treaty) of Hudaybiyya
628: Raids against the Jewish settlements at Khaybar and Fadak; Muslim victory
629: Conversion of Khalid ibn al-Walid and Amr ibn al-As, two shrewd Meccan commanders
629: Battle of Mu'ta, initiated by Muslims against the Byzantines and their allies from the Arab Christian Ghassanids
630: Conquest of Mecca; Muhammad declared victorious over most of Arabia
630: Battle of Hunayn, initiated by the Muslims against Arab pagans
630: Battle of Tabuk, initiated by Muhammad against the Byzantine Empire
630: Muhammad's daughter Umm Kulthum dies
631: Muhammad's son Ibrahim dies
632: Muhammad's farewell pilgrimage and farewell sermon
632: Ghadir Khumm, the designation of Ali as Muhammad's successor, according to Shiites
632: Muhammad dies
632: Abu Bakr appointed as Muhammad's caliph, successor
632: Apostasy Wars begin, lasting for two years

Introduction

Why Should One Learn about Muhammad's Life?

As I grew up in Cairo, Egypt, the name Muhammad quickly became familiar to me. Many of my neighbors and classmates were named Muhammad, as Muslims greatly cherish the name and what it represents. If one had the name Muhammad, we all knew he was Muslim. Because it is the name of the prophet of Islam, it is the most valued, respected, and honored name among Muslims. In most Muslim families, there is usually one member named Muhammad—the name reflects devotion to Islam and invites Allah's favor on the one who holds it. Islam's prophet was also known by other names, including Ahmad and Mustafa. These are also often used as personal names among Muslims. The point is clear: Muhammad is the most loved among Muslims, and anything referring to him is of highest value.

I have always been amazed by the astounding way Muslims respect Muhammad. Whenever they mention his name, it is always followed by an honoring phrase, "Salla allahu alayhi wa sallam," which means, "May Allah send prayers and peace upon him." Even Muslims who do not speak Arabic know the phrase and usually repeat it in Arabic. It means a great deal to devoted Muslims. It can be repeated numerous times in one short conversation, sermon, or speech. It does not matter how many times one repeats it, because it is expected. The ample repetition is not viewed as redundant, as it reflects devotion and respect to Muhammad.

As a Coptic Christian, I always wondered about the phrase. What does it mean for Allah to send prayers upon Muhammad? If Allah prays upon Muhammad, who listens to the prayer? I understood that Muslims treat this phrase as a salutation of honor and respect to Muhammad given by those who admire him. But I wondered whether I was supposed to use this honorific statement in front of my Muslim friends when his name was mentioned. This led to awkward moments any time the name Muhammad was mentioned in a public setting.

At an early age, I became aware of Muhammad's pivotal role in Islam. If anyone asks what is the foundation of Islam, it is not difficult to answer. The foundation is built of two parts: the Quran and Muhammad. The former is, for Muslims, Allah's perfect word, while the latter is Allah's final prophet and perfect example for humankind. But the Quran is often too sophisticated for cultural—and even many religious—Muslims to comprehend. Muhammad's sayings, on the other hand, are straightforward, clear, specific, and accessible. For almost every situation in life, Muslim clerics have at least one saying attributed to Muhammad to address it. In fact, the vast majority of Muslims, past and present, believe that the Quran cannot be understood apart from the statements of Muhammad. They interpret the Quran against the background of Muhammad's life—every verse in the Quran, we are told, should be understood against the backdrop of the biography of Muhammad. Muslims claim that no man can ever apply the Quran better than Muhammad did.

Moreover, every practicing Muslim wants to follow Allah's sharia—that is, his path, laws, and will. There is no way for a Muslim to learn this sharia apart from its two major sources: the Quran and Muhammad's example. If the Quran is the most authoritative text in Islam, the next two are Muhammad's sayings (hadiths) and Muhammad's biography (sira). This reflects Muhammad's centrality in Islam and in the lives of the adherents of this faith. If we want to understand the Muslim worldview, we should learn the importance of the Quran and Muhammad to the Muslim community. In the end, Muslims are a community of believers united around a sacred text and following it as exemplified in Muhammad's pattern of conduct. Thus, it is crucial to examine Muhammad's life, his deeds, and his teachings in order to understand Islam and our Muslim neighbors properly.

Non-Muslims are usually confused by the strong devotion Muslims have for Muhammad. Throughout history, non-Muslim writers have identified him in various ways, including trader, shepherd, king, conqueror, false prophet, lustful Arab, and so on. You can see how this deviates significantly from the traditional Muslim beliefs about him. Although a few non-Muslims have viewed him positively, as a hero, reformer, revivalist, and monotheist preacher, many have identified him as a deceiver who sought only power and wealth. Some medieval Christians viewed him as a Jewish or Christian heretic who distorted biblical accounts in order to conquer Arab tribes. Of course, this multifaceted non-Muslim portrayal has been completely dismissed by Muslims throughout history. There is no question about Muhammad among Muslims: he is the most pious man who ever lived, the final prophet to humankind, and his message is the decisive and definitive divine truth, which surpassed and superseded all previous faiths. For these reasons, Muhammad is honored, venerated, and praised above all other humans.

Here lies an important reason why one should study Muhammad's life. Muslims currently make up about 20 percent of the world population; thus, it is imperative to understand and evaluate the life of the man whom they revere. This one man directly influences the lives of one-fifth of humankind and, indirectly, a significant portion of non-Muslims all around the world. If Islam and Muslims have been unknown in Western circles for a period until now, this must end. Consider this: Muslims believe that Muhammad's example has something to teach about every aspect of life, including family, education, laws, politics, economics, abortion, slavery, homosexuality, and, of course, religion. In order to understand and examine Muhammad's impact, it is crucial for non-Muslims to learn what Muhammad did and said, based on trusted Muslim sources. This is precisely the heart of this book. Because knowledge of Muhammad is fundamental to so many people, the importance of studying his life cannot be overstated. In a previous book, *A Concise Guide to the Quran*, we examined Islam's scripture. In this book, we study the life of Muhammad. While I highly recommend that readers begin with *A Concise Guide to the Quran*, as it provides foundational information on Islam's sacred text in its relationship to Muhammad, I attempt to treat this book as an independent resource.

Now, I will provide a few remarks on the style and structure of this book.

First, my target audience is primarily non-Muslims, but I write with Muslims in mind. I appreciate the richness and diversity among Muslims. In my life, I have known cultural Muslims who knew very little about their religion. I have also met with religious Muslims, some of whom were conservative whereas others were progressive. I learned that some progressives self-identify as devoted Muslims in their own way. I also know some Muslims who could be considered extremist or radical in their interpretation and application of Islam. Yet overall, cultural and conservative Muslims make up the majority of Muslims. While I acknowledge the existence of various kinds of Muslims and a variety of visions within Islam, I ask questions as an academic. The questions I ask in this book focus on episodes, events, and teachings in Muhammad's life. Although the questions are likely familiar to scholars and students of Islamic studies, some Muslims may have never discussed such issues, especially as I examine them critically.

Second, the book follows the form of questions and answers. This is meant to help the reader who has little to no familiarity with matters of Islamic studies. The book consists of two main parts: (1) Muhammad's history and (2) Muhammad's message. In the first, I highlight major events in Muhammad's life and career and provide critical observations about them. My discussion of Muhammad's life events follows a chronological order as found in the Muslim sources. My aim is to help the reader become familiar with the biography of Muhammad as Muslims wrote it. In the second part, I focus on topics related to Muhammad's teachings and statements on important subjects. Each question and answer was written to stand independently. This gives readers the option to skip around according to their interests. However, as I cover many topics related to Muhammad, there might be some overlap from one question to another. This was unavoidable because some information discussed in earlier questions needed to be incorporated in later questions. In this case, I covet your patience as I attempt to explain to those who might not have read earlier selections. Finally, there is one more observation concerning the book's structure. Some questions needed more discussion than others, which resulted in lengthier answers. Overall, every answer aims to present various Islamic perspectives, which sometimes contradict each other. While I strive for thoroughness, these answers should not be viewed as exhaustive.

Third, in this book I aim to introduce the reader to the most trusted Muslim sources. I rely heavily on authoritative Muslim sources—the earlier the better—in presenting the information on Muhammad's life. I hope to equip the reader to learn where to obtain reliable reports on Islam and Muhammad. I believe that a Muslim primary source takes the highest priority in telling the reader what Muslims believe and say about Muhammad. In my analysis, I avoid speculations about Muhammad, as there is much confusion about him in today's world. Rather, I consult Muslim sources—both the Sunni and Shiite traditions—about Muhammad and seek to present them together when this is possible. While most Western studies rely on the Sunni accounts, as Sunnis are the majority among Muslims, I value the Shiite voice and consider it crucial to any serious study on Islam. Moreover, I understand that some available secondary studies, particularly in the West, present Muhammad unfavorably, focusing only on negative accounts about him. I am also aware that many recent Western studies on Muhammad seek to present his life and teachings quite favorably by emphasizing some accounts while ignoring others. I do not follow either of these two trends. In this book, I seek to be as charitable as possible, knowing what Muhammad means to Muslims and how information can be interpreted in different ways. I do not want to show Muhammad in a dark light, nor do I aim to proselytize Muslims. My goal is to present an informative book, an introduction about Muhammad's history and teachings, to non-Muslims in the West. In the end, he is one of the most important figures in human history.

Fourth, while I rely heavily on Muslim primary sources, I also interact with recent scholarly research on Islam's origins. There is value in asking critical questions and building on recent academic scholarship. Islamic studies as a field of research is flourishing as never before. This is almost undeniable—just consider the growing discussion about Islam in academia in the past four decades. This book is one piece in this discussion. In my answers to critical questions, I introduce the reader to recent scholarly arguments by both Muslims and non-Muslims. One should be thankful for non-Muslim scholars and their questions, and equally amazed at the diversity among Muslim scholars. Among self-identified Muslim scholars, there are both conservatives, who utilize strict traditional interpretations, and progressives, who revise classical claims and present Islam in a nonconventional way. These are not completely distinct; it is more like a marvelous spectrum of scholars. We should acknowledge and cherish this diversity. By including these scholars in the discussion, I hope to add nuance to our conversation.

Fifth, in order to help the reader learn where to locate information about Muhammad in Muslim primary sources, I provide several tools. I present a list of Muslim primary sources already published in English translations (see appendix A). These sources are fundamental to our understanding of Islam and Muhammad. I want the reader to have access to the sources that form the bulk of the Muslim history, dogma, and identity. These sources are accessible in most major libraries in the West, and some are now available online since they were published many decades ago. In addition to the English translations of Muslim primary sources, we have a wealth of knowledge at our fingertips. Appendix B provides a list of excellent websites that direct us to more Muslim primary sources. Some of these websites include a search feature, which helps tremendously in research. Furthermore, since I discuss various events in Muhammad's life, I provide two more tools: a chronology and a glossary. The chronology highlights major events and figures in Muhammad's life, and the glossary explains important words found in the text. Both serve as informative tools on Muhammad and Islam in general.

Sixth, I made three stylistic choices to make the book easy to read for nonspecialists. While scholars render Arabic names in transliterated English forms to indicate phonetics, I do not follow this pattern. So instead of transliterations like Muḥammad and ʿUthmān, I simply use Muhammad and Uthman, except in footnotes citing Arabic sources. Similarly, I do not use Kaʿba or Kaʿba, but simply Kaʾba. This suffices to serve the goals of this book as readers at this level of study do not need to be concerned with the nuances of the meaning of these symbols. The second choice relates to the footnotes. I rely on numerous scholarly studies, but I do not use exhaustive footnotes. While some supplementary resources are provided in the notes, most of the secondary literature on the topics for each chapter can be found in the Sources Consulted section at the end of this book. The third choice relates to the dates of events. In Islamic studies, scholars use two dates to refer to an event. For example, it is understood that the Battle of Badr took place in 2/624, which makes it AH 2, or year 2 in the Islamic Hijri calendar (lunar), and AD 624 or 624 CE in our familiar Gregorian calendar (solar). For simplicity, I primarily use the latter, although when relevant I will sometimes mention both dates. These choices, I hope, make the text more accessible and easily readable.

In this concise introduction to Muhammad's life and teachings, it is impossible to be exhaustive. This is not one of my goals. Moreover, the book reflects my thoughts and interpretations of historical accounts. I understand and expect that some will disagree with my writing. This is acceptable and commendable. It is important to encourage discussions about diverse opinions, as long as they are supported by evidence. My goal in writing this book is threefold. I want the English-speaking reader to receive a significant amount of information on Muhammad—as we find it in the Muslim sources—in a concise way. I also want to introduce my reader to the diversity of interpretations among Muslims. For instance, some Muslims insist that Muhammad performed miracles, while others deny this. Islam is not monolithic, and Muslims are not all the same in their approach to Islam and Muhammad. It is important not only to understand and value the conservative traditional interpretation of Islam but also to appreciate the various progressive arguments advanced by Muslims—especially in the West. This creates a better understanding of today's Islam. Finally, I hope that this book encourages you to do more research about Muhammad. Many topics discussed in this study can stand alone as books on their own. This book can serve as a delicious appetizer before your main course begins.

PART 1

MUHAMMAD'S HISTORY

1

Who Was Muhammad?

In world history, Muhammad is known as the founder of the religion of Islam. He reportedly lived in Arabia between 570 and 632, being born in Mecca and dying in Medina. Muslims believe he was a prophet sent by the deity to the Arabs to exhort them to abandon idolatry and to bring them to monotheism. Muslims claim that before becoming a prophet, he, like most Bedouins, traveled throughout Arabia as a trader. Islam is unique among world religions in that we know a great deal about its founder. The credibility of this information is questionable, but this is what Muslims generally believe about their prophet. Some two centuries after Muhammad's death, numerous Muslim authors began claiming precise details about Muhammad: his height, appearance, habits, wives, and even specific conversations he had behind closed doors. While most scholars are skeptical of these traditions, as they appear religiously and politically driven, Muslims tend to trust their reliability. In answering this question, we will focus on what Muslims claim about their prophet before we analyze the various traditions critically in later questions.

Muhammad was born in 570 in Mecca in the western region of the Arabian Peninsula known as the Hijaz. His mother, Amina, gave birth to him months after his father, Abdullah, died. Muhammad was from a well-known family in Mecca, Banu Hashim. The Arabic word *banu* means "sons of," while Hashim is the surname of the head of this family or clan. In Arabia, a man is usually identified as a member of the "Banu" so-and-so in order to refer to his larger family. Banu Hashim is rendered in English as the Hashimite clan. This clan was part of the prestigious and prosperous Quraysh tribe. The Quraysh was a powerful merchant tribe that held significant power in Mecca. Not only did the Quraysh control the trade routes that allegedly passed through Mecca, but they also managed the idol worship in the Ka'ba—the holy pagan shrine that generated ample wealth as a well-known destination for idol worshipers performing rituals and pilgrimage. While Muhammad's family and tribe are important due to their prestigious status and role in Mecca, they are less important than is indicated by the Muslim claim that Muhammad is a descendant of Ishmael, the son of Abraham. For Muslims, Muhammad not only is a descendant of Abraham through Ishmael but also serves as a clear sign of the fulfillment of the divine promise for Ishmael to have a great nation.

In his youth and early adulthood, Muhammad worked as a shepherd and merchant. Muslims say he was known for his honesty and trustworthiness, to the extent that he was called al-Sadiq al-Amin, meaning "the honest and the faithful." In his early twenties he worked for a wealthy and noble widow, Khadija, who needed someone to manage her reputable business, especially to lead her merchandise caravans between Mecca and Syria. Her wealth not only was obtained through her trade caravans but also came from an inheritance passed along from her previous two husbands, with whom she had several children. Because of Muhammad's truthfulness, according to Muslim sources, she asked to marry him. They married when Muhammad was twenty-five and she was forty. Some suggest that Khadija was Christian because of her close connection to her cousin, Waraqa, who was a Christian priest with exceptional knowledge of Scripture. Muhammad and Khadija had four daughters as well as one or two sons who did not live long.

Muhammad was not satisfied with idolatry in Mecca. He did not subscribe to the pagan worship and its immoral lifestyle popular during his day. Muslim sources claim that Muhammad would isolate himself in a cave in Mount Hira and worship the true deity. When Muhammad was forty, during one of his visits to the cave, the angel Gabriel appeared to him. Muhammad was terrified and tried to climb the mountain to throw himself to his death. Gabriel rescued him and affirmed that Allah appointed him to be his messenger to the Arabs.[1] With his heart beating rapidly in fear, Muhammad ran to Khadija and asked her to cover him until his fear was gone. She took him to her Christian cousin, Waraqa, who was an expert in Hebrew and the Christian gospel. Muhammad described to Waraqa what he had seen. Waraqa assured Muhammad that what he saw in the cave was the angel Gabriel, who was also sent by Allah to Moses of the Israelites. Waraqa prophesied that the Meccans would be hostile toward Muhammad and those who believed his message and that they would be expelled from Mecca. Muslims believe that this was a confirmation of Muhammad's prophetic mission, designating him as the Prophet of the Arabs. From then on, Muhammad allegedly received divine inspirations from Allah through Gabriel. When a word came down, Muhammad would immediately proclaim it to the Meccans, who abused, persecuted, and mocked him.

For thirteen years, Muhammad continued to live in Mecca and persistently sought to proclaim what Gabriel told him. This is what became the message of Islam. The term *Islam* refers to devotion and submission to Allah. The followers of its message are "Muslims," which reflects their submission to Allah. The proclamations came to be known as the Quran. Muhammad's years in Mecca were colored by hostility and persecution toward his message and his young and newly believing community. Very few Meccans believed Muhammad's message. Due to this harassment and abuse, Muslims claim, Allah instructed Muhammad to emigrate from Mecca to Medina, which was a small oasis about 250 miles northwest of Mecca. This move was later called the hijra, meaning "emigration," and became significant for Muslims and the solidification of their new community of believers under Muhammad's leadership.

For ten years, Muhammad lived with his community in Medina and continued to teach them the basics of Islam. Here, Muhammad became known as a commander and statesman. Muslim sources portray him as a skillful warrior and a clever leader who mastered the creation of tribal alliances and also knew when to break political treaties. He knew when

1. Ibn Hisham and Ibn Ishaq, *Life of Muhammad*, 106; and Sahih al-Bukhari, vol. 1, book 1, hadith 3 (hereafter Bukhari, 1.1.3). Unless otherwise indicated, all hadith references in this book are from https://sunnah.com, which includes original Arabic texts and English translations of the hadith collections that are, according to Sunni Islam, the most trusted.

to fight his enemies and when to withdraw. From Medina, Muhammad and his companions launched raids and expeditions to consolidate their political power in Arabia. Some raids targeted the Meccan pagans, whereas others dealt with Arab and Jewish tribes and settlements throughout Arabia. As time passed, Muhammad grew in power and military prowess. His enemies grew weaker, while he grew stronger. Eight years into his time in Medina, Muhammad successfully led a campaign of about ten thousand of his believing warriors to conquer Mecca, his homeland, from which he was earlier forced to emigrate. After his successful raid against Mecca, he became the sole leader of West Arabia. Some of his enemies called him the King of Arabia.[2] Muslims believe that this turning point marked Islam's victory since all Arabs submitted to Muhammad and his religious message. Before his death in 632, he organized military expeditions against Mu'ta and Tabuk—two strategic locations on the frontier of the Christian Byzantine Empire—but these campaigns were less successful.

Muhammad died in 632 in Medina. He was poisoned, according to the most trusted Sunni and Shiite traditions—although they differ regarding who actually poisoned him. Sunni traditions accuse a Jewish woman of poisoning Muhammad because he killed her husband, father, and uncle; Shiite reports point to Muhammad's close companions and his young wife Aisha as conspirators who murdered Muhammad to gain power. The choice of the Sunnis to blame the Jewish woman may reflect a recurring pattern in Muslim tradition of accusing the Jews of a crime to cover up the ambiguity of a specific historical incident. The Shiite preference to accuse Muhammad's companions and his wife is also understandable because it follows the major Shiite claims that Muhammad was betrayed by his own people, who stole power from the rightful heir, Ali. Since martyrdom is valued and revered in religious terms, both Sunni and Shiite Muslims still insist on depicting Muhammad as a martyr who gave his life for the sake of Islam.[3] It should also be noted that the Sunnis' favored tradition indicates that before Muhammad finally felt a deadly pain—described in the sources as the cutting of his aorta—the poison remained in his blood for three or four years, and then he died.

2. Ibn Hisham and Ibn Ishaq, *Life of Muhammad*, 515; and Tabari, *History*, 8:122.
3. Ibn Hisham and Ibn Ishaq, *Life of Muhammad*, 210, 516; and Shoemaker, *Death of a Prophet*, 301–2.

This claim is usually dismissed by secular scholarship, which rejects the unreasonable time interval. The favored narratives of the Shiites, on the other hand, portray a conspiracy to poison Muhammad immediately prior to his painful death.[4]

After Muhammad's death, Abu Bakr's succession as the first caliph in Islam was controversial. Shiite Muslims believe that Ali should have been the immediate successor to lead the Muslim community politically and religiously. They reject Abu Bakr and his elevation, describing it as a coup. According to Muslim sources, many abandoned Islam after Muhammad's death and refused to submit to Abu Bakr. Consequently, he launched the so-called Apostasy Wars to fight the apostates and the Arab tribes who abandoned Islam. Since wars lead to wars, the Apostasy Wars served as the launching pad for more conquests, which reached beyond Arabia. Within a few decades, the Arab Muslim warriors had conquered major lands in today's Middle East, North Africa, and Asia. During the first century of Islam, the Muslim empire stretched from Central Asia to the Iberian Peninsula.

This is a summary of Muhammad's life and career. However, it is important to note that the accuracy and reliability of its details are questionable. While it is the traditional story accepted by Muslims, most of the information provided above has been contested by many thinkers, Muslim and non-Muslim alike. Before we examine the major problems in the Muslim sources, we should first identify literature that claims to provide the story of Muhammad's life. What are the major Muslim sources? Where can one begin to study Muhammad's life? We discuss these matters in the next question.

4. Bukhari, 5.59.713; and Sunan Abi Dawud, book 40, hadith 4499 (hereafter Sunan Abi Dawud, 40.4499).

2

What Are the Major Muslim Sources for Muhammad's Life?

Most of what we know about Muhammad comes from Muslim sources written over a century after his death. Not one Muslim source can be traced to his generation, nor do we have any eyewitness testimonies from his time. Some Muslim reports were recorded several decades after Muhammad's death, but none are extant. They were either lost or destroyed by later political leaders who sought to advance their views against those of their rivals. Nonetheless, in the second century of Islam (over one hundred years after Muhammad's death), Muslims were the rulers in a vast region of conquered lands where most of the population was still non-Muslim. Muslim rulers—also known as caliphs—realized the need to establish a distinct religious identity unique to Islam. They sought to present Islam to non-Muslims, especially Christians and Jews who had already established solid traditions and had used their religious texts for centuries. Because Christians and Jews had Jesus and Moses, respectively, Muslims felt the need to introduce Islam's prophet to Muslims and non-Muslims in their growing territory. This triggered the writing of numerous works in the second century of Islam.

Under the instruction of powerful caliphs, Muslim writers began to document what they claimed to be statements said by and reported about Muhammad. The statements were projected back in time, more than a century earlier, and were collected in volumes called the hadith traditions. A *hadith* (saying or statement) is a Muslim tradition about Muhammad, describing something he supposedly said or did. Sometimes it is called a prophetic hadith. The volumes became known as hadith collections. Of course, these hadith traditions aligned with the desires of the political power of the day and sought to advance political claims or settle religious disputes: the Abbasid caliph, for instance, wanted the hadith traditions about Muhammad to advance Abbasid claims of legitimacy against their Umayyad rivals. Similarly, there were huge religious disagreements among various Muslim groups. Sunni Muslims adopted, supported, and trusted different hadith collections than their Shiite counterparts. Every Muslim group claimed numerous hadiths to support their religious opinions. For example, Shiites believe that Ali was the rightful successor of Muhammad, while the Sunnis favor Abu Bakr. To support their sectarian claim, a devoted Sunni needs a hadith claiming that Abu Bakr—not Ali—is the most important and close companion to Muhammad, while a Shiite enthusiast wants the exact opposite. Both hadiths circulated among Muslims. One Sunni hadith states that Muhammad said, "If I were to take a Khalil [dearest friend, close companion], I would have taken Abu Bakr."[1] Conversely, in a Shiite hadith we are told that Muhammad said, "Anyone who has me as his *mawla* (close and loyal friend), has Ali as his *mawla*. May Allah love those who love him and be the enemy of those who hate him."[2] These two hadiths offer opposite notions and aim to serve sectarian claims.

Competing hadith statements emerged in the second century of Islam and continued to grow in number over time. By attributing statements to Muhammad, the Muslim writers sought to legitimize them, thus creating a specific memory of Muhammad among Muslims. These were the earliest statements to describe aspects of Muhammad's life. Unsurprisingly, these hadiths provide astonishing details about Muhammad, as if they were documented during his lifetime instead of a century or two later.

1. Bukhari, 5.57.8; 1.8.456; see also Sahih Muslim, book 4, hadith 1083 (hereafter Sahih Muslim, 4.1083).
2. Moosa, *Extremist Shiites*, 96. See also Musnad Ahmad, book 5, hadith 77 (hereafter Musnad Ahmad, 5.77); and Jami' at-Tirmidhi, book 49, hadith 4078 (hereafter Jami' at-Tirmidhi, 49.4078).

We know his favorite food, his habits in his home with his wives, his words to his slaves in private, his height, his skin color, and many other details. Of course there are many contradictions in these hadiths, but the details are astonishing. While Muslims generally trust these hadiths as truthful historical accounts by or about Muhammad, many scholars doubt their reliability. Critical thinkers are hesitant to accept them as descriptions of what actually occurred in Muhammad's time. Scholars view these hadiths as descriptive of the time of their writing, not Muhammad's time. For them, the hadith statements represent the desires of the writers and what they sought to communicate about Muhammad rather than true history. However, to most Muslims the hadiths are second in authority after the Quran. When Muslims seek to follow Muhammad's example, they often refer to a hadith, usually from a collection of "sound hadiths" that is taught and revered by Muslim clerics. Most Muslims view the hadith statements as true historical narratives about Muhammad and his time.

The emergence and growth of hadith writing among Muslims opened a wide gate for other writings that described Muhammad's life. One of these was labeled "maghazi," which refers to accounts about Muhammad's raids and expeditions. The word *maghazi* means "campaigns" or "incursions." It is a famous genre among Muslims, particularly as historical literature. Many short works about Muhammad's maghazi sought to paint a picture of his successful military activities. Over time, these books became voluminous and more sophisticated. These maghazi works rely heavily on hadiths attributed to Muhammad's time. A maghazi work would consist of consecutive hadiths, allegedly describing situations or statements that occurred in various battles and incursions led by Muhammad or commissioned against his enemies. None of the maghazi works originate in Muhammad's time; all were compiled by hadith scholars who lived at least a century after Muhammad. Surprisingly, these maghazi books describe Muhammad's life as a series of successful raids and expeditions. For Muslims, the maghazi was Muhammad's life in its entirety, not only his military campaigns. Early Muslims wanted to represent Muhammad as a true leader and commander in battle for the sake of Islam. The term *maghazi* was not offensive in reference to Muhammad's life and career, as early Muslims did not believe it described their prophet unfavorably. Rather, it was used as a true description of Muhammad's mission. Thus, in addition to hadiths, Muslims use maghazi works to obtain knowledge of the life and deeds of Muhammad, especially his raids and expeditions.

The maghazi works soon developed into a larger literature called the sira.[3] The Arabic word *sira*, which literally means "behavior, life, and conduct," later came to mean "biography"—in particular, that of Muhammad. Muslims refer to Muhammad's biography as his sira. Therefore, what began as merely works with an emphasis on his maghazi developed over time to describe in more detail his sira—that is, words, practices, actions, and all his major life events. Still, the authors of the sira relied heavily on hadiths attributed to Muhammad and his companions, who lived centuries earlier. The early Muslim writers served as hadith scholars who generated numerous traditions. The sira works became the earliest Muslim literature to provide detailed narratives of Muhammad's life. The earliest sira of Muhammad was written under the instruction of the powerful Caliph Mansur, who died in 775 (Muhammad died in 632). We know that Mansur wanted Muhammad's biography to be written in such a way as to legitimize Mansur's claim to power by portraying Mansur's ancestors as great supporters of Muhammad. Scholars often point to the obvious bias in the accounts of the sira, which aimed at supporting the political power—the Abbasid Caliphate—and their religious causes over their rivals.

If the emergence of hadith accounts triggered the writings of Muhammad's maghazi and his sira, the growth of documenting historical accounts did not stop there. Relying on the foundational texts of Muhammad's maghazi and sira, Muslims began to focus on producing more writings that detailed and described the history of Muhammad. Two more collections or literatures emerged: the futuh and the tarikh. The term *futuh* means "conquests," while *tarikh* refers to "history." The futuh literature examines Muhammad's military activities—and his successors' conquests—in more detail, expanding what the maghazi works began, while the tarikh works aim at providing Islam's history as a part of major world events. Many futuh and tarikh collections emerged in the third and fourth centuries of Islam. Though they were written by Muslims who lived well after Muhammad's death, these works allege to

---

3. On this development, see Duri, *Rise of Historical Writing*, 12–75; and Horovitz, *Earliest Biographies*.

document Muhammad's life meticulously. While scholars doubt various claims in these works, Muslims in general trust the material as truthful and accurate.

Based on the discussion above, we can learn details about Muhammad's life—according to the Muslim standpoint—from the hadith, maghazi, sira, futuh, and tarikh works. Though they were written late and include tendentious material, these are the documents that claim to tell about Islam's prophet and his teachings and deeds. The question remains: How can one access these works? They are mainly available in Arabic, which creates difficulty for Western readers who want to learn about Islam and Muhammad from original and Muslim primary sources. The good news is that English translations of these works are growing in number, and the internet offers access to many of them, at least in part. Concerning the hadith collections, the vast majority of Muslims believe that the most trusted hadiths are those by Imam Bukhari (d. 870) and Imam Muslim (d. 875). Both collections, and many others, are available in English on the valuable website sunnah.com, where each Arabic hadith is given next to its English translation. The translations are accurate for the most part. An excellent feature of this website is the option to search the various hadith collections using English words.

Concerning the maghazi collections, while there is no website that exclusively provides maghazi texts in English, a wonderful translation of the earliest available maghazi work, titled *The Expeditions*, was recently accomplished by Sean Anthony from Ohio State University (New York University Press, 2014). Anthony provides both the original Arabic text and a readable English translation; however, the original text's nonchronological ordering of Muhammad's raids may prove unhelpful to some researchers. Anthony is aware of this potential problem and offers a chronological outline of major events in Muhammad's life and a map of the Arabian Peninsula during Muhammad's time—these can prove helpful for beginners in Islamic history. The translator also provides a glossary and an appendix. These explain the historical importance of some of the names mentioned in the maghazi and assist the reader with explanations of key names, locations, and information related to Muhammad's life and raids. The Library of Arabic Literature's website provides a free pdf copy of the original Arabic text. In his English translation, Anthony calls Muhammad's maghazi a description of "how his faith community imagined him centuries after his death."[4] This indicates the hesitancy of scholars to consider the accounts written centuries after Muhammad's death to be a true documentation of his life.

Concerning the sira literature, we have access to an English translation of the earliest—and thus most important—biography of Muhammad. The sira was originally written by Ibn Ishaq (d. 767), a famous scholar of hadiths, about 120 years after Muhammad's death. Ibn Ishaq was instructed to write the biography by the powerful Abbasid caliph Mansur. This biography was lost, but a disciple of Ibn Ishaq named Ibn Hisham (d. 833) allegedly found a copy, arranged and edited its contents, and removed some of its accounts in what many consider a deliberate act of censorship. This text, which became known as the official sira of Muhammad, was translated by British scholar Alfred Guillaume (1888–1965) and originally published by Oxford University Press in 1955. In the translation, Guillaume refers to Ibn Hisham's troubling admission regarding editing Ibn Ishaq's copy: Ibn Hisham stated that he omitted from the biography "things which it is disgraceful to discuss; matters which would distress certain people."[5] While no one knows what Ibn Hisham actually omitted from the original sira, Muslims, past and present, value his edition and celebrate it as the official account of Muhammad's life. Guillaume's translation is a great success, as it allows many in the English-speaking world to access what Muslims consider to be a true account of Muhammad's biography.

Concerning the futuh literature, the English-speaking world is quite fortunate to have an accessible translation of one of the most important works in this genre, *Futuh al-buldan* (The conquests of the lands). The work is written by the renowned ninth-century Muslim Persian historian Ahmad al-Baladhuri (d. 892), who was well connected with several caliphs in his day and wrote most of his works with their approval. The *Futuh al-buldan* includes a well-arranged set of consecutive traditions on the various conquests launched by Muhammad and his successors, classified by lands, including Arabia, Syria, Mesopotamia, Africa, and Persia. Francis Clark Murgotten and Philip Khuri Hitti translated this work as *The Origins of the Islamic State* (Columbia University, 1916–24).

4. Ibn Rashid and al-Sanani, *Expeditions*, xv.
5. Ibn Hisham and Ibn Ishaq, *Life of Muhammad*, 691.

As for the tarikh works, we have access to the English translation of one of the most comprehensive historical Muslim works from the tenth century. It is the *Tarikh* of Tabari (d. 923). Tabari was a renowned Persian scholar of hadiths who received special fame for his thoroughness. Muslims believe that he traveled throughout the Muslim lands to collect his traditions. The work is massive because Tabari included various versions of the same narrative, thus establishing various perspectives on specific historical events, usually without offering his opinion. This work serves as a chronological history of Islam up until a few years before Tabari's death. Tabari also placed the history of Islam within world history, as the first few volumes of the work include general history, such as accounts of the creation, the flood, the prophets, and Israel. The *Tarikh* of Tabari was translated into English as *The History of al-Ṭabarī* and published by the State University of New York Press (1985–1999) in forty volumes with an index added in 2007.

When today's Muslims want to study Muhammad's life, career, and teachings, they consult major Muslim primary sources, including the hadith, maghazi, sira, futuh, and tarikh works. For them, these provide the true outline and content of Muhammad's biography. While these sources were originally all in Arabic, today's English-speaking reader can access good translations of many of them. There is nothing like studying original material. While it is usually easier to absorb information about Muhammad from secondary sources—books discussing him or interpreting aspects of his life—the value of examining Muslim primary sources is unmatched. This provides a deeper understanding of Muhammad's life—an understanding not colored by ideas advanced by other writers, whether popular or scholarly. So here is how to begin learning about Muhammad: read the early Muslim sources written about him. Though they were produced centuries after his death, they still represent what Muslims believe about him and his life. But can we trust the material in these sources as reliable and accurate? We will answer this question next.

3

What Do Scholars Say about the Reliability and Accuracy of Early Muslim Sources?

The Muslim primary sources explored in the previous question—hadith, maghazi, sira, futuh, and tarikh collections—provide the core accounts that help religious followers of Islam emulate Muhammad. When Muslims seek to follow the example of Muhammad's life, they want to imitate his Sunna. The term *Sunna* refers to the thousands of traditions associated with Muhammad, documenting the behavior, conduct, and way of life that characterized him as the master precedent of conduct in Islam. While there is no book or set of books titled *Sunna*, Muslims seek the Sunna in the classical writings mentioned above. Thus, hadiths are part of the Sunna. Muhammad's biographical deeds as found in the maghazi, sira, futuh, and tarikh collections are also part of his Sunna. This is one reason why Muslims honor and value the accounts found in these sources, believing them to be true reports about the life of their prophet.

Non-Muslim scholars, on the other hand, do not share this religious sensitivity toward Muslim sources. These scholars evaluate the Muslim sources critically, and most of them argue that these traditions are late

15

and cannot be supported by independent evidence. Scholars view the vast majority of these traditions as forgeries and observe that the sources were probably written to address questions raised by Muslims at the time of their writing or to support political or religious claims—especially those of the caliphal power. This skepticism toward the reliability of the Muslim sources grew rapidly at the beginning of the twentieth century. Arguably, modern scholarship is indebted to the work of Hungarian scholar Ignaz Goldziher (1850–1921), who is considered a father of modern Islamic studies. He is known as an early skeptic of the reliability of Arabic Muslim sources. Goldziher's studies on Muhammad's hadiths served as a turning point in Islamic studies, providing a foundation for the skeptical approach. He examined the most trusted hadith collections and demonstrated convincingly that many traditions that Muslims treat as sound and authentic are simply invented statements aimed at supporting political or religious agendas. Goldziher wrote, "It is not surprising that, among the hotly debated controversial issues of Islam, whether political or doctrinal, there is not one in which the champions of the various views are unable to cite a number of traditions."[1] Goldziher noticed that all competing hadiths were supported by a strong chain of informants linking them to Muhammad and his companions for legitimization and authentication: "Anything which appears desirable to pious men was given by them a corroborating support reaching back to the Prophet. This could easily be done in a generation in which the Companions, who were represented as the intermediaries of the Prophet's words, were no longer alive."[2] Goldziher's remarks suggest that, centuries after Muhammad, Muslims took the liberty of inventing religious statements whenever it was deemed necessary and created a halo of authentication around the statements by attributing them to Muhammad.

While Goldziher's studies focus primarily on Muhammad's hadiths, his arguments and skepticism toward the Arabic Muslim sources opened the gate wide for other non-Muslim scholars to focus on other Islamic texts, including maghazi, sira, and tarikh. By the last quarter of the twentieth century, a breakthrough occurred, as many built on Goldziher's arguments and skepticism. This became evident through the publica-

1. Goldziher, *Muslim Studies*, 2:44.
2. Goldziher, *Muslim Studies*, 2:42.

tion of two studies by John Wansbrough (1928–2002), who taught at the University of London. Wansbrough argued that Muhammad's sira does not represent a true historical account of Muhammad's life and career but rather a fabricated narrative aimed at explaining various ambiguous Quranic passages. Wansbrough also argued that the Quran underwent two to three centuries of development to become a closed book.[3] For Wansbrough, the Quran has pre-Islamic biblical material, and the sira is forged to explain it. Wansbrough's arguments on the sira and the Quran were influential and foundational among scholars and remain largely useful today. Following in his footsteps, many scholars remained skeptical of the reliability of the Muslim historical accounts, especially those related to the life of Muhammad. Wansbrough's disciple Patricia Crone (1945–2015) argued that whether "one approaches Islamic historiography from the angle of the religious or the tribal tradition, its overall character thus remains the same: the bulk of it is debris of an obliterated past."[4] For Crone, the actual "history" of Islam is utterly destroyed, and the Muslim historical accounts, which we have at hand, do not describe what really happened but instead what the authors claimed or desired to convey. Like Crone, Andrew Rippin (1950–2016), who was also a student of Wansbrough, argued that "the actual 'history' in the sense of 'what really happened' has become totally subsumed within later interpretation and is virtually, if not totally, inextricable from it." For Rippin, "The records we have are the existential records of the thought and faith of later generations."[5] The arguments of Wansbrough, Crone, and Rippin—though shocking to Muslim conservatives—are reasonable because of the various problems in the Arabic Muslim sources, including the later dates and tendentiousness. This is evident in a statement by Chase Robinson (1963–) in which he explains that Muslim historians "were not simply taking liberties with texts: they were generating the texts themselves."[6]

3. Wansbrough, *Qur'ānic Studies*, 12, 58; and Wansbrough, *Sectarian Milieu*, ix, 27, 188–19, 147.

4. Crone, *Slaves on Horses*, 10. See also Crone, *Meccan Trade and the Rise of Islam*, where she argues, "The entire tradition is tendentious, its aim being the elaboration of an Arabian *Heilsgeschichte*, and this tendentiousness has shaped the facts as we have them, not merely added some partisan statements we can deduct" (230).

5. Rippin, "Literary Analysis of Qur'ān, Tafsīr, and Sīra," 156.

6. Robinson, *Islamic Historiography*, 38.

Not all non-Muslim scholars adopt the skeptical approach to Muslim sources. Some are nonskeptics and are identified as sanguine or positivist scholars. They argue that Islamic sources, despite all their apparent problems, have a genuine kernel of truth in them. The nonskeptic scholars claim that this kernel can be identified through various source-critical methods. For these sanguine scholars, "despite the fact that there is virtually no extant written material from the first two centuries of Islam, the later collections of the third and fourth centuries contain an accurate record of the past."[7] This sanguine approach does not mean that these scholars are less critical of the sources but rather indicates that they are hopeful of locating such a kernel of truth through their analysis. In questioning the validity of the sanguine approach, Rippin skeptically asks, "But the real problem here is that even if one admits the existence of such a 'kernel' of history, is it ever possible to identify and extract that information?"[8] In fact, even Fred Donner (1945–), who is considered a nonskeptic and among the sanguine scholars, admits, "There is evidence to support the contention that some reports in the sīra literature are of dubious validity and may, in fact, have originated in the need to invent a supported historical context for exegetical readings of particular [Quranic] verses."[9]

Therefore, while Muslims tend to accept the picture of Muhammad that is painted in the Muslim sources, non-Muslims do not share this same confidence. Whether skeptical or sanguine, non-Muslim scholars find the sources problematic due to internal contradictions and their late compilation. While most Muslims believe that the historical Muslim accounts—including hadiths, maghazi, sira, futuh, and tarikh—preserve the true history of Muhammad, non-Muslim scholars hesitate to accept such claims. While sanguine scholars might hope to find a kernel of truthful material in the Muslim sources, skeptic scholars approach them as documents with descriptions of the time of their writing, not the time of Muhammad. But the question arises: If the Arabic Muslim sources are that unreliable, why should anyone study them in the first place? Why should we read a book on Muhammad's life if the accounts are unreliable?

7. See Berg, "Competing Paradigms in Islamic Origins," 259.
8. Rippin, "Literary Analysis of Qur'ān, Tafsīr, and Sīra," 156.
9. Donner, "Historical Context," 34.

The answer is simple: we study the Muslim portrayal of Muhammad because this is how the Muslim community presents and perceives their prophet. The only Muhammad who exists in the minds of Muslims is connected to their religious texts. There is no other Muhammad with whom Muslims want to associate. If one pursues a discussion with Muslims about religious matters, one must examine what Muslims claim about their past and the days of Muhammad, as written by later Muslim authors. Here, we are not concerned with reconstructing the actual history of Muhammad in the seventh century. We are not concerned with distinguishing truth from fabrication in the Muslim sources. We aim to study what the Muslim community believes about Muhammad's life and career and to engage with this picture critically. While the reliability of the Muslim sources is questionable, the Muslim historical texts can provide a great window into the political, social, and religious debates at the time of their writing. They can also offer a great opportunity for non-Muslim readers to engage the Muslim story based on Muslims' own texts.

4

What Is So Unique about Muhammad's Birth Year?

Muslims believe that Muhammad was born in 570 CE. The year became known in Muslim tradition as the Year of the Elephant. The reason for such a title is the traditional claim that a divine miracle happened in this year. The miracle involved an elephant, and Muhammad was born a couple months after it. For Muslims, this indicates that Allah was working to prepare the way for the advent of Muhammad as the Arabian prophet. Arabs were not familiar with elephants the way people in Africa were—this added to the uniqueness of the miracle. The reasoning here is that just as other prophets were born amid divine interventions and wonders, so was Muhammad. The story of the elephant served as the annunciation of the coming of an Arabian prophet whose divine mission was to establish justice and virtue among his people.

The story begins with Abraha, the Christian king of Yemen, a South Arabian kingdom founded and run by the Abyssinians (Ethiopians). Abraha was jealous of the Arabs, especially of how many people traveled throughout the lands to visit Mecca and, in particular, the Ka'ba—the sacred shrine in its midst. Abraha envied the Ka'ba for the high esteem in which it was held in the hearts of the Arabs. Abraha was a devoted Christian who loathed the notion that the Ka'ba shrine could receive such fame. Consequently, he built a marvelous Christian cathedral in San'aa in Yemen, about 650 miles from the Ka'ba, with the sole aim of drawing all Arab pilgrims away from the Ka'ba to San'aa. According to Muhammad's sira, the cathedral's beauty was unmatched throughout the world. Abraha wrote to the Ethiopian king that the church was dedicated to him and that Abraha would not cease his efforts until all Arab pilgrims abandoned the Ka'ba for it.

To achieve his goal, Abraha decreed that Arabs must perform a pilgrimage to his church in San'aa rather than to the Meccan Ka'ba. According to Muslim traditions, his instructions were not heeded, and people continued to go to the Ka'ba. Then a major conflict occurred: an Arab man from Mecca—who used to work and serve in the Ka'ba—traveled all the way to the cathedral in San'aa and defiled it, apparently to insult Abraha. Muhammad's sira reports that the Arab man believed that Abraha's actions made the Ka'ba unworthy of reverence. After defiling the cathedral, the Arab man returned to Mecca. Abraha soon learned that the offensive act was done by an Arab who had come from the shrine in Mecca and that it was motivated by anger at Abraha's desire to divert the Arab pilgrims to the cathedral. Abraha was furious, and he decided to exact revenge against the Arabs by defiling and demolishing the Ka'ba itself.

Abraha prepared a large army to march toward Mecca. Reinforced with many elephants from the Ethiopian king—one of them bearing Abraha himself—the army marched toward Mecca. Muhammad's sira states that the Arabs were terrified, having never seen elephants. Some Arab tribes, hearing of the army's approach, united to defend the Ka'ba—their holy house, shrine, and source of livelihood. Abraha defeated them, took some of their notables as prisoners, and seized two hundred camels owned by Abd al-Muttalib, who, shortly after, became the grandfather of Muhammad. This brought Muhammad's grandfather to the center of the narrative.

Abd al-Muttalib was, at the time, the leading Arabian chief of the Quraysh, Muhammad's tribe. Along with some chiefs of other tribes, Abd al-Muttalib hoped to fight Abraha, but they knew they were unprepared. In a surprising turn, Abraha sent his personal messenger to Mecca, instructing him to find the chief of the tribe controlling the Ka'ba and to tell him that Abraha did not come to fight the Quraysh or any other tribe but instead to destroy the Ka'ba. Abraha assured the Arabs, through his messenger, that if they did not resist his army, there would be no harm or bloodshed. The messenger reached Mecca, learned that the chief notable was Abd al-Muttalib, and delivered the message. Abd al-Muttalib replied that Allah knew that Abd al-Muttalib and the other Arab chiefs did not want to fight Abraha, as they did not have the power for that; however, said Abd al-Muttalib, the Ka'ba was Allah's holy house and the shrine that was established by Allah's friend Abraham, and Allah would take care of his house. In a statement of devotion, Abd al-Muttalib also declared that if Allah defended the Ka'ba against Abraha, it would be known to be Allah's sanctuary, and if not, no one else would be able to defend it. While the statement shows devotion to Allah, questions remain as to whether Abd al-Muttalib was a true believer in Allah even before Muhammad was born.

Abraha's messenger then asked Abd al-Muttalib to return with him to meet Abraha, and Abd al-Muttalib agreed. When the two met, Abd al-Muttalib asked Abraha to return the two hundred camels he had seized. Although Abraha initially respected Abd al-Muttalib to the extent of sitting next to him on the carpet, Abraha's opinion changed once Abd al-Muttalib seemed more concerned with his own camels than with the religious house that was about to be destroyed. However, Abd al-Muttalib assured the king that although he owned the camels, the Ka'ba was Allah's sanctuary, and he was able to protect it. Abraha returned the camels to Abd al-Muttalib and let him leave. Abd al-Muttalib returned to Mecca and told the people of the Quraysh to leave Mecca and hide in the mountains, because Abraha was coming. Abd al-Muttalib himself decided to pray. Joined by some of his tribe, he took hold of the door of the Ka'ba and declared that the sacred house has a god to defend and protect it.

On the next day, Abraha launched his expedition against Mecca. His army was magnificent and the elephants were enormous. Having learned that Abd al-Muttalib and some men had remained in the Ka'ba instead of fleeing to the mountains, Abraha sent a messenger to warn them to leave the shrine. Abd al-Muttalib stood firm and kept praying for protection. Abraha was approaching, and when he saw the Ka'ba, he instructed his army to utterly destroy it. To his surprise, the elephant he was riding knelt and refused to go forward. The soldiers tried their best to move the elephant, but they failed. The soldiers beat the elephant several times, but it never responded, except when they turned to face Yemen as if they were returning home. All attempts to ride the elephant to the Ka'ba—even beating its head with iron bars and sticking hooks into its underbelly—failed.

While they were trying to move the elephant to attack the Ka'ba, an army appeared in the sky. It was the army of Allah. It emerged as a multitude of small birds forming a dark cloud. The Arabs called the birds "Ababil," and there were enough of them to dominate Abraha's entire army. The Muslim tradition describes the birds meticulously: each bird had three pebbles, one in its beak and two in its claws. The pebbles were small like lentils but tough and destructive in their effect. Allah ordered the birds to pour the pebbles on Abraha's army and his elephants. Anyone hit by a pebble died. Some men from Abraha's army ran away and tried to return to Yemen. Within a few minutes, Abraha's army was defeated and most of his soldiers perished. As for Abraha himself, he was seriously wounded, and he attempted to flee back to Yemen but died on the journey. The Muslim tradition credits this huge victory to Allah's intervention and highlights that it was a precursor of Muhammad's birth soon afterward.

This is the traditional Muslim narrative about the year of Muhammad's birth. The narrative is significant for Muslims not only because the tradition presents it as a divine miracle, preparing the way for the advent of Muhammad as prophet, but also because the narrative explains an obscure chapter in the Quran (Q 105). The chapter, though short and concise, is quite difficult to understand without a story explaining it. Consider it here: "In the name of Allah, the most gracious, the most merciful. Have you not considered how your Lord dealt with the companions of the elephant? Did he not make their plot go astray? He sent against them swarms of birds, throwing at them hard stones, leaving them like devoured green leaves" (Q 105:1–5). Reading this chapter for the first time, without any prior knowledge of Muslim traditions, one finds it impossible to discern the speaker in the passage, its recipient, or the nature of these companions and their elephant. One cannot fathom why an elephant is mentioned in a passage presumably proclaimed in an Arabian setting where elephants are not present. It is difficult to specify a geographical or historical context for the passage. Nor can one identify

reasons for little birds carrying stones and dropping them on the soldiers to destroy them. To all these questions, the Muslim tradition offers
answers. The solution is a story that serves several purposes: to explain
the obscure Quranic passage, create a miracle and link it to Muhammad's life, and establish Allah's intervention in the Arabian history in
an acknowledgment of Muhammad's birth. The story was documented
centuries after Muhammad's birth and after the conventional revelation
of the Quran. While this tradition may appeal to Muslims, scholars are
often skeptical and unconvinced. Many scholars conclude that this tradition was written to explain the obscure passage rather than to record
a true event—especially because the story of polytheistic armies using
war elephants against pious communities exists in famous pre-Islamic
traditions.

Scholar Daniel Beck, who studies the traditional Muslim claims about
this story, argues that Q 105 is better understood as a reflection of a
Syriac Christian tradition that was known during Muhammad's time.[1]
The Christian tradition explains the apocryphal biblical narratives of
2 and 3 Maccabees and highlights an unbelieving royal army attempting
to destroy a Jewish community using war elephants. The similarities
between the Muslim claims and the Christian traditions are obvious. It
appears that Muslim traditions relied on a famous Christian sermon,
added literary features unique to Islam, and advanced a narrative in order
to serve specific Muslim purposes. Beck raises an important observation
as he argues that African elephants were not used for war in Arabia. For
Beck, the Muslim tradition—that Q 105 refers to an expedition by Ethiopian Christians and their elephants against Mecca—is not convincing.[2]

But Muslim traditions seem to have sought miraculous events
associated with Muhammad's birth in order to confirm his prophethood
and affirm the divine support of his advent. Muslims needed miracles
centered on Muhammad similar to those reported about Moses and
Jesus known among the conquered people of the Middle East. The
narrative of the elephant and its Christian army is not the only one

1. Beck, *Evolution of the Early Qur'ān*, 1–41.
2. Beck, *Evolution of the Early Qur'ān*, 4–8. He makes the following conclusion:
"No contemporary record in South Arabia, or any other literate region from Ethiopia
through Persia, shows the slightest awareness of Abraha's alleged expedition or its
demise" (7).

advanced by Muslim traditions to describe miracles associated with Muhammad's advent; there are many others. One narrative claims that on the night of Muhammad's birth in Mecca, the mansion of the Persian king—about a thousand miles away—was shaken, and fourteen of its pinnacles collapsed. We are also told that on that very night the sacred fire of Fars—which had burned continuously for a thousand years—was extinguished. Even the waters of the lake of Sawah sank inexplicably into the earth and destroyed many churches. We are told that Muhammad's mother had no labor pains when she delivered him and that upon her delivery the entire house was filled with divine light. While these traditions aim at establishing convenient religious claims, we should note that not just non-Muslim scholars question the authenticity of these claims—some Muslims reject them and consider them later fanciful fabrications. Nonetheless, the vast majority of Muslims believe Muhammad was born in Mecca around 570, that he came as guidance and light to humankind, and that his advent was divinely supported by Allah. For them, without a doubt, Muhammad's birth was accompanied by great miracles, including the defeat of the Christian army of Abraha and his mammoth elephant.

5

What Is Significant about Muhammad's Genealogy?

Muhammad's biography, the sira, traces his lineage back to Abraham through Ishmael. In this way, Muhammad, like Moses and Jesus, is connected to the great patriarch Abraham. Since Ishmael became known as the father of many Arab tribes, Muslims believe that he was definitely the ancestor of the Arabian prophet Muhammad. Ishmael is revered in the Quran as a prophet of Allah (Q 19:54) and is mentioned explicitly twelve times, even more than Muhammad. The Muslim traditions relate that Muhammad's father was Abdullah, who died three months before Muhammad's birth. Abdullah was the son of Abd al-Muttalib, the son of Hashim, the son of Abd Manaf, the son of Qusayy, the son of Kilab, the son of Murra, the son of Ka'b, the son of Lu'ayy, the son of Ghalib, the son of Fihr, the son of Malik, the son of al-Nadr, the son of Kinana, the son of Khayzama, the son of Mudrika, the son of Ilyas, the son of Mudar, the son of Nizar, the son of Ma'add, the son of Adnan, the son of Udd, the son of Muqawwim, the son of Nahur, the son of Tayrah, the son of Ya'rub, the son of Yashjub, the son of Nabit, the son of Ishmael, the son of Abraham. This lineage connects Muhammad with Abraham, who is well known in Islamic tradition as the friend of Allah.

Tracing Muhammad's lineage to Abraham is very important to Muslims. They not only insist on it but also provide additional traditions to strengthen its plausibility. We are told that Abraham and Ishmael traveled all the way to Mecca to build the Ka'ba. This tradition is found in the most trusted collection of hadiths in Sunni Islam and claims that Abraham told Ishmael that Allah instructed him to build a house of worship in Mecca. In this tradition, Ishmael brought the stones and Abraham built high walls for the sacred place in Mecca. At some point, as the building continued, Abraham stood over its high walls while Ishmael handed him stones, and both praised Allah and asked him to accept this service from them. This tradition requires a belief that Abraham and Ishmael lived and worshiped Allah in Mecca. However, some Muslim traditions contradict that, instead claiming that Allah's angels built the Ka'ba to serve as a place where they could escape the wrath of Allah. Other traditions state that Adam was the true builder, or his son Seth. Some Muslims attempt to reconcile these traditions by claiming that Adam built it and Abraham renovated it. Of course, the tradition necessitated a thread of connection between Muhammad and the Ka'ba: we are told that his great-great-great-grandfather, Qusayy, put its roof in place and that Muhammad himself decided where they should place the sacred black stone within the Ka'ba and placed it with his own hands. But why is it significant for Muslims to insist that Muhammad's lineage traces back to Abraham and that Abraham and his son Ishmael were present at Mecca at some point in history?

The question is important, and its answer arguably points us to the context of the writing of Muslim traditions. Through his raids and expeditions, Muhammad controlled most of Arabia during his lifetime—but no traditions were written during that period. After his death, the Muslim caliphs commissioned commanders to lead conquests that subdued the entire area of today's Middle East and North Africa. This meant that Muslims ruled over non-Muslim lands. The population was mainly Christian and Jewish—though other religions were represented—so the Muslims needed to offer them a compelling religious narrative. They seem to have formed their religious identity in response to the various social and religious communities of the day. During this time, Muslim traditions were written and compiled—particularly under the Abbasid Caliphate. Many of these traditions aimed to present Islam as a religion in conversation with previously existing faiths. As was explained in the previous question, the Muslim tradition necessitated the creation of miraculous narratives concerning Muhammad's birth, just as Christians and Jews spoke of miracles during the births of Jesus and Moses, respectively. In the same vein, a case for Muhammad's genealogy had to be made. We are told that he is a descendant of Ishmael and Abraham. However, can we be certain that Abraham and Ishmael really visited or lived in Mecca? To what extent can one support the notion that Ishmael is the father of the Arabs, let alone the ancestor of Muhammad?

The answer is simple: we cannot be certain that Abraham and Ishmael visited Mecca. Nor can we even establish a connection between Ishmael and the Arabs and, consequently, between Ishmael and Muhammad. In fact, some classical Muslim authorities do not support Muhammad's lineage to Ishmael. Ibn Sa'd (d. 785), a scholar and Arabian biographer, is well known for his multivolume reference *The Book of the Major Classes*, a compendium of biographical information about major Muslim individuals. In describing Muhammad's genealogy, Ibn Sa'd asserts that when Muhammad detailed his lineage, he stopped many generations before reaching Ishmael. The renowned Arab historian and geographer al-Mas'udi (d. 956) writes in two works that Muhammad forbade Muslims from tracing his lineage after Ma'add, who was at least nine generations distanced from Ishmael. While al-Mas'udi acknowledges that some Muslims link Muhammad to Ishmael, he emphasizes that Muhammad commanded Muslims to trace his lineage only to Ma'add, as genealogists are liars. These classical Muslim historians do not support Muhammad's connection to Ishmael. Moreover, classical Sunni hadith expert and jurist al-Bayhaqi (d. 1066) agrees with Ibn Sa'd and al-Mas'udi and writes that although some report that Muhammad was a descendant of Ishmael, this is false, as the lineage goes only to Adnan, the father of Ma'add. Thus, major classical Muslim authorities dispute Muhammad's genealogy.

In addition to classical Muslim writers, critical modern Muslim thinkers disagree with the traditional story of Ishmael and Abraham going to Mecca and question the veracity of any link between them and Muhammad. Muslim scholar Taha Husayn (1889–1973), known as the dean of Arabic literature and nominated for a Nobel Prize in literature more than ten times, does not believe that Ishmael and Abraham ever went to Mecca, let alone that they built the Ka'ba.[1] For Husayn, there is no historical evidence to support such a claim, and it appears that the story is a later fiction forged by Muslim authors for religious reasons. Husayn

1. Husayn, *Fī al-shi'r al-jāhilī*, 38–41, 92–93.

concludes that the story is an obvious attempt to establish a connection between the Jews and the Arabs, on the one hand, and between Islam and Judaism, and the Quran and the Torah, on the other. For Husayn, the emergence of Islam necessitated a link between the religions of Christians and Jews and the one brought forth by Muhammad. Of course, Husayn, in these assertions, contradicts many conservative Muslims.

Non-Muslim thinkers also question the Muslim claims regarding Ishmael, the Arabs, the Ka'ba, and Muhammad's lineage. The well-known Arabist and Islamic scholar Alfred Guillaume (1888–1965) argues that there is no historical evidence for the Islamic claim that Ishmael and Abraham ever visited Mecca.[2] Contemporary scholar René Dagorn contends that the Islamic claim that Ishmael is the progenitor of the Arabs is not supported by evidence—that this is merely a religious claim and a later construction and that in pre-Islamic history there is no evidence of any established connection between Ishmael and the Arabs.[3] Camilla Adang (1960–) argues that after Muhammad's death, particularly in the first century of Islam, Muslims sought to establish Ishmael as a symbol for the Muslim community by utilizing biblical passages about Ishmael to refer to Arabs and Muhammad.[4] Scottish historian William Montgomery Watt (1909–2006) emphatically states that, contrary to Muslim tradition, Abraham never reached Mecca.[5] Like Watt, Maxime Rodinson (1915–2004) argues that for a critical historian there is no evidence to support that Arabs are descendants of Ishmael, the son of Abraham.[6]

This discussion helps the reader understand a major point: even though Muhammad was allegedly born and raised in Mecca, a compelling connection to significant patriarchs was needed. Since no patriarch is more important to Christians and Jews than Abraham, Muhammad's lineage had to be connected to him. If Jesus and Moses are connected to Abraham through Isaac, Muhammad is linked to Abraham through Ishmael. Is this a myth or truth? While the vast majority of Muslims argue that Muhammad is a descendant of Ishmael, who built the Ka'ba with Abraham, many are not convinced of the claim and argue that it is either incorrect or an outright fabrication.

2. Guillaume, *Islam*, 61ff.
3. Dagorn, *La geste d'Ismael d'après l'onomastique*, 33–104.
4. Adang, *Muslim Writers on Judaism and the Hebrew Bible*, 147n37.
5. Watt, *Muslim-Christian Encounters*, 136.
6. Rodinson, *The Arabs*, 44.

6

What Do Muslims Believe about Muhammad's Attributes?

Muhammad is immensely important to all aspects of Islam. For Muslims, he is Allah's chief and final messenger, who came to guide humankind to the truth of the oneness of Allah after many other messengers failed (Q 3:144; 33:40). His book, the Quran, is the supreme and greatest revelation. Muhammad, Muslims say, is the best example of humankind, as he lived a life of piety and complete devotion. He is a man of unmatched conduct, unparalleled wisdom, and unequaled godliness—the perfect exemplar who fulfilled Allah's laws. Muslims describe themselves as Muhammad's followers and believe he led his early followers from the darkness of pre-Islamic ignorance to the guidance and light of Islam and its monotheistic belief. Muslims take pride in following Muhammad's sunna, which is his conduct and teachings. In seeking to please Allah, they ultimately hope to imitate Muhammad. Whatever he said or did, they seek to follow. Understandably, Muslims seek to provide the most compelling portrayal of their prophet. Anything honorable, pleasant, or praiseworthy is emphasized, while any claim that depicts him unfavorably—even if it is from the Muslim sources themselves—is dismissed. A reader in the West today, even before examining any Muslim claims, can easily predict what depiction of Muhammad they will find.

In general terms, however, one should observe that what Muslims often believe about Muhammad does not always match what the Islamic sources say about him. Their portrayal is built on a collective memory advanced by religious scholars of their day. These clerics often emphasize particular reports about him while ignoring others in order to portray Muhammad in a certain way. Consider the fact that the earliest Muslims—those who first wrote about Muhammad—labeled his life in its entirety "maghazi" (raids and expeditions), portraying it as a series of military campaigns and incursions against non-Muslims, whereas today's Muslims—especially since Islam came to the forefront of world events in 2001—emphasize Muhammad as a prophet of peace who sought only reconciliation and tolerance. Today's Muslims do not describe Muhammad as initiating raids against anyone. In a sense, we have many Muhammads, including the one of tradition and that of the Muslim memory of the day. So what do Muslims generally believe about Muhammad's attributes?

Centuries after Muhammad's death, many Muslim traditions emerged about his attributes, describing him before and after he received Allah's revelations. Some of these traditions offer astonishing details. Muslims claim that Muhammad was truthful before he became a prophet and that his character was as marvelous before he received the revelation as it was afterward. Among his tribesmen, Muhammad was known for his honesty and integrity in all he said and did. This made him the most trustworthy among his people, to the extent that the Meccan Arabs used to entrust him with their valuables for safekeeping. He was known as al-Sadiq ("the honest") and al-Amin ("the faithful"). This was one reason why Khadija loved him and proposed to him. Although his Meccan relatives worshiped idols, he never did (Q 6:14). He was pure, and Allah protected him even before the initial revelation.

After he received Allah's calling, Muslims claim, Muhammad was characterized by many exceptional qualities. He uttered kind words and never spoke ill of anyone. Muhammad was patient in the numerous tribulations he faced from his pagan foes. He was just and sought equality for all people. He was known, Muslims say, for his unmatched humility in providing for his own needs and never depended on others, nor did he take what was not his rightful portion. He helped others—both his followers and his enemies. He was generous with the poor of Mecca. He was friendly, charitable, and cheerful. Muhammad smiled at anyone he saw. He was particularly kind to children and always greeted them. He used humor with the slaves in his household, treating them as free people. Muslims insist that, contrary to the customs of his day, he freed slaves and was generous with them. He was always considerate and merciful to those around him. He knew that his followers included weak and aged people as well as vulnerable and young people, so he did not prolong the time of the ritual prayer. He never ate or drank in excess, nor did he acquire fancy clothes. If anyone gave him a gift, he would kindly accept it but would soon return the gesture with a better gift. Muslims believe Muhammad never abused his wives or concubines—he always treated them equally and justly. Even when he took his son's wife, it was not out of lust but due to a revelation of Allah. According to traditions, Muhammad paid attention to his personal hygiene, used toothpicks to clean his teeth frequently, and always showed modesty in his appearance. Finally, Muhammad was tolerant and courageous. He was gracious and forgave those who offended him, calling out wrong-doings bravely but also kindly. He not only commissioned his soldiers to go on raids and expeditions but also participated with them. He was their example of courage and was identified as "the best and the bravest amongst the people."[1]

Furthermore, some traditions portray Muhammad's appearance and physical features, claiming his skin color was the best in humankind. He was white, not black, and had thick hair that was neither curly nor straight. His face was round and his head was large, showing strength and dignity. He had thin lips, quite suitable to his facial features, as well as a wide mouth, white teeth, and thick beard hair. His eyes were wide and black, to the extent that people used to admire how deep and awe-inspiring they looked. His eyebrows were thin and long, beautifully matching his facial features. He was of moderate height, and his cheeks were reddish. We are told that Muslims were able to identify "the Seal of Prophethood between his shoulders."[2] Moreover, we are told, Muhammad's palms were soft, and he had big hands and feet, to the extent that Muslims marveled that they had not seen anybody like him. When he spoke, light seemed to emerge from his forehead. He was neither fat nor skinny. His height was consistent with his width in the best way. In an interesting hadith, identified by Muslims as among the most reliable, we are told that the mother of one of Muhammad's companions brought a bottle in which

1. Bukhari, 4.52.156.
2. Sahih Muslim, 30.5793.

to collect Muhammad's sweat while declaring, "That is your sweat which we mix in our perfume and it becomes the most fragrant perfume."[3]

To revere and respect Muhammad, Muslims never mention his name without following it with a phrase of honor and admiration: *salla allahu alayhi wa sallam*, which translates as "May Allah send prayers and peace upon him." The phrase is usually translated in English as "peace be upon him," but this is inaccurate—the Arabic phrase is lengthier and more descriptive of respect and esteem. When Muslims mention the name of another prophet, they usually use a shorter honoring phrase, *alayhi al-salam*, which means "peace be upon him." This phrase is used after mentioning Moses, Jesus, or any other prophet recognized in Islam. However, when one is mentioning Muhammad, the longer version of the honorary phrase is preferred. Shiite Muslims, on the other hand, use a variation of the longer phrase. They add a piece to recognize their first major imam, Ali, and his household, who represent an important component of spiritual and political guidance in Shiism. After mentioning Muhammad's name, Shiites say *salla allahu alayhi wa aalihi wa sallam* ("May Allah send prayers and peace upon him and his household").

Muslims also have special titles used for Muhammad alone. These titles are quite complimentary, and to Western ears, they might come across as hyperbolic. He is not only the final prophet to humankind but also the beloved of Allah and the seal of all prophets and messengers (Q 33:40). Muhammad is known as the genuine, the faithful, the chosen, and the appointed one (Q 22:75; 69:40). He is also the perfect man and the best of humankind. He is called the virtuous and the model of excellent conduct, the warner and the bearer of good news to humans. He is known as the compassionate and merciful to the universe, the caller unto Allah, the reminder of the truth, and the personified light. He is the illuminated lamp, the bringer of light, and the divine's favor to humanity. He is the destroyer of unbelief and the prophet of penitence. He is the strengthened one, the dignified one (by Allah). He is the opener and the seal. These titles are merely a sample of the various honorifics given to Muhammad by Muslims. Some of them rely on vague assertions in the Quran (e.g., Q 2:119; 33:45–46; 73:1; 74:1; 88:21), while others come from hadiths. Although Muslims use them exclusively for Muhammad, an observer may find similarities between these titles and those used by

3. Sahih Muslim, 30.5761.

Jews and Christians for Moses and Jesus. It appears that Muslim traditions sought to offer a portrayal of Muhammad that fit the sectarian milieu of their day. The logic goes as follows: Muhammad is the final and chief among all prophets because he possesses every honorable quality and exceptional characteristic they had.

This detailed and flattering portrayal of Muhammad is believed and wholeheartedly cherished by the vast majority of Muslims. They hear about it constantly in the mosques and repeat it passionately on every possible occasion. It is a part of their daily devotion and an essential component of the popular Muslim piety. However, apart from religious enthusiasts and devout apologists, this depiction is hardly trusted because of the numerous Arabic Muslim accounts that contradict it. These Islamic accounts themselves—some of which are so-called trusted hadiths—provide a completely opposite picture of Muhammad. The portrayal depends on which traditions one chooses and which one dismisses. This is evident in the assessment of Muhammad's biography by renowned scholar Patricia Crone (1945–2015). She argues that there is a lack of continuous transmission of historical facts in the first Muslim generations. Crone doubts Islamic traditions, labeling them unreliable and pure fabrications, as they conflict to the extent that one could rewrite Muhammad's biography in reverse. Crone comes to the conclusion that "the entire tradition is tendentious," and "this tendentiousness has shaped the facts as we have them, not merely added some partisan statements we can deduct."[4] In the same vein, Fred Donner (1945–), a well-known historian of Islam, voices some doubts about the traditions concerning Muhammad's life. He states, "Some reports in the *sīra* literature are of dubious validity and may, in fact, have originated in the need to invent a supposed historical context."[5] Thus, it appears that there are rival portrayals of Muhammad. In a sense, it is impossible to talk about one Muhammad, because there are several Muhammads, including the Muhammad who is cherished in the Muslim popular memory and the one who is buried within ample competing traditions. These two are joined by the supposedly true historical Muhammad, about whom we have very few pieces of independent evidence. This begs the question: Was Muhammad a real historical figure? We answer this next.

4. Crone, *Meccan Trade and the Rise of Islam*, 230.
5. Donner, "Historical Context," 34.

7

Was Muhammad a Real Historical Figure?

The answer to the question "Was Muhammad a real historical figure?" depends on which Muhammad we are discussing. There seem to be different Muhammads—though overlapping in some sense—based on the rival depictions we have of him. Identifying which Muhammad we are examining determines the answer concerning his possible historicity. By and large, we can identify at least three Muhammads: the one in popular and cultural Islam, that of the Muslim traditions, and finally the Muhammad of history. We can label these three Muhammads the legendary, the traditional, and the historical. One way or another, all three refer to the person whom Muslims view as their prophet. Muslims do not necessarily attempt to distinguish between the three. Rather, they cherish a collective memory of their prophet that is a product of their cultural, social, and religious contexts. Whether it is the legendary or the traditional, or to a lesser extent the historical one, Muslims have a portrayal of Muhammad that they trust to represent the man who lived in seventh-century Arabia and received Allah's proclamations from Gabriel. So what do we actually know about each of these Muhammads?

The legendary Muhammad is the one revered by most cultural and nominal Muslims. This is the Muhammad of popular Islam, which is the

version of Islam followed by over two-thirds of Muslims worldwide—
often labeled "folk Islam." Among the vast majority of the socially
underprivileged and less religiously educated Muslims, this legendary
Muhammad is believed to be true. His portrayal consists roughly of
three layers: a few ideas from the Quran, some hadiths or traditions
in general, and plenty of mythical, mystical, and metaphysical stories
embedded in superstitious notions. This legendary Muhammad is often
less connected to the statements from Islamic texts and more associated
with supernatural tales and legends from the culture. For instance, while
the Quran presents Muhammad as an ordinary man who needed Allah's
mercy and forgiveness, the legendary Muhammad—in the minds of
Muslims—is venerated to the point of worship. This veneration of the
legendary Muhammad is unique to popular Islam. Muslims sometimes
believe that he possesses divine qualities and attributes and that he has
access to and influence on their daily lives. They believe he can know the
future, raise the dead, and heal the sick, and they seek him to perform
signs and wonders. He is understood to be able to grant children to
barren women through the use of amulets. Through magical formulas
and religious pronouncements, this Muhammad is sought by parents to
find a husband for their less-fortunate and less-desired daughters. He is
believed to visit sick people in dreams, especially after they enter places
deemed sacred or drink water after reciting some Quranic verses. Since
this legendary Muhammad has metaphysical abilities, these Muslims
seek to visit holy places, including shrines and graves, associated with
him or his immediate family. These visitations are not supported by
mainstream Sunni Islam, but cultural Muslims seek them to receive
power, blessing, and protection from evil. This legendary Muhammad serves as a living intercessor between humans and Allah. While
such notions are condemned by mainstream Muslim theologians as
idolatry, this legendary Muhammad is cherished by many Muslims,
especially in tribal and animistic communities. Through stories about
divine visitations, interpretations of dreams, and fortune-telling, this
legendary Muhammad receives divine attributes and flourishes among
the masses of nominal Muslims. While this is not the Muhammad of
the Quran or the Muslim traditions, or the Muhammad of history, he
is revered and venerated in popular Islam. So is this legendary Muhammad, then, a real historical figure who flourished in seventh-century

Arabia? The answer is negative, at least insofar as the historical evidence is concerned.

The traditional Muhammad is the one of the Quran and the Muslim traditions. This is the Muhammad who is revered, honored, and believed among religiously informed Muslims, whether conservative or progressive. He is the one preached by Muslim clerics and imams in mosques daily. His portrayal relies mainly on Muslim traditions because the Quran does not speak much about Muhammad—it refers to him explicitly only four times, with no precise information about his life, time, or location. Unlike the Quran, Muslim traditions—including accounts of hadiths, sira, maghazi, and other historical books—provide thousands of reports allegedly describing Muhammad's life, character, and deeds in detail. While the vast majority of religiously informed Muslims cherish these accounts and view them as historically reliable, many non-Muslims have difficulties trusting them. Many self-identified Muslims do not believe these traditions to be sound or authentic. These Muslims, consequently, do not trust the historicity of the traditional Muhammad. It is important to note that the reliability of these traditions is questionable because they were created centuries after Muhammad and are full of contradictory details. Moreover, some of these traditions—like those about Muhammad's birthplace, the location of his prophetic career, his death date and place, and the number of his wives—cannot be supported by independent evidence or any eyewitness accounts. If one relies on these traditions alone, it is difficult to portray a clear picture of one Muhammad who lived in seventh-century Arabia.

Many scholars believe that most of these traditions are forgeries, as they describe a particular Muhammad who is better viewed as fiction.[1] Even though many Muslims believe the details about him in Islamic texts, scholars treat these traditions as descriptive instead of an accurate record of the historical Muhammad. For these scholars, the Muslim

1. See Goldziher, *Muslim Studies*; Goldziher, *Mohammed and Islam*; Crone, *Meccan Trade and the Rise of Islam*, 230; and Crone, *Slaves on Horses*, 10, 230. Chase Robinson explains that Muslim writers "were not simply taking liberties with texts: they were generating the texts themselves." Robinson, *Islamic Historiography*, 38; see also chap. 1 in Robinson's book. Regarding scholarly discussions on hadith reliability, see Berg, "Competing Paradigms in Islamic Origins," 259ff.; and Berg, *Development of Exegesis in Early Islam*, chap. 1. See also Donner, *Narratives of Islamic Origins*, 5ff.; and Ibrahim, *Conversion to Islam*, 20ff.

traditions represent a picture of Islam's prophet that appealed to the writers' audience at the time of their writing rather than addressing an audience at the precise time of Islam's prophet. In a sense, this traditional Muhammad reveals more about what later Muslims believed than about who he really was. It is plausible that the Muhammad of tradition is simply a figure whom the Muslim historians chose to present to their audience for religious and political reasons.[2] Religiously, Muslim historians needed a specific portrayal of Muhammad to astonish Christians and Jews who rejected his prophethood. Thus, this Muhammad had to be circumcised. This Muhammad reportedly used to seclude himself in prayer and fasting, met angels, performed wonders, was mentioned in the Bible, did not practice idol worship or polytheism, and so forth. This portrayal had little to do with the Muhammad of seventh-century Arabia. It mainly responded to the religious questions posed by non-Muslims to Islam in later times. In this portrayal, Muhammad was created as an exemplar among other prophets. Politically, this traditional portrayal of Muhammad, scholars believe, aimed to elevate and legitimize the claims of the caliphal power or to advance sectarian claims at the time of the traditions' writing.[3] For instance, during the Abbasid era, when these traditions were generated, it was important for the writers to provide a description approved by the caliphal power. Thus, they described Muhammad as highly connected with the Abbasid family instead of their rivals. To help the Abbasids gain legitimacy in ruling the Muslims, the authors of Muhammad's biographies sought to depict the Abbasid ancestors favorably, highlighting them as good Muslims who supported Muhammad from the start.[4] Thus, these authors chose to depict the traditional Muhammad instead of the one who presumably lived in past generations.

One should distinguish between Muhammad's existence and Muhammad's historicity. While this traditional Muhammad is generally accepted and revered in mosques and Islamic circles based on the trust

2. See Ibrahim, *Stated Motivations*, 11–12, 30–33, where a discussion of source problems is offered; and Ibrahim, *Conversion to Islam*, 20–25.

3. See Sellheim, "Prophet, Chalif und Geschichte," 33–91, where Sellheim identifies three kinds of reports in Muhammad's sira, including myths and legends as well as political propaganda by the Abbasid against their Umayyad rivals.

4. For the religious and political inclinations of the Muslim historians, see Ibrahim, *Conversion to Islam*, chaps. 2–3.

Muslims invest in their sacred sources, his historicity is doubted. This is evident in the numerous scholarly attempts to deny that Muhammad existed. But, one may ask, which Muhammad are these scholars talking about? Is he the Muhammad of tradition or that of history? While many scholars are skeptical of the historicity of the traditional Muhammad, some have even argued that the supposedly historical Muhammad is a later invention since there is no independent evidence or archaeological indication to point to his existence. However, we have pieces of evidence that demonstrate the existence of a seventh-century Arabian prophet who led armies and conquered lands. Some documents name him clearly as Muhammad.

The historical Muhammad concludes our discussion of the various Muhammads. He stands in contrast to both the legendary and the traditional Muhammads. We know about the historical Muhammad from contemporary or near-contemporary documents written about him by non-Muslims who were flourishing in Syria, Armenia, Egypt, Persia, and many other lands around Arabia. These non-Muslims were aware of what was taking place in Arabia in the seventh century. Their sources present a vivid picture of a statesman in Arabia who led armies and had some sort of a religious message. Muhammad appears in these sources as a shepherd, trader, monotheist proclaimer, false prophet, lawgiver, conquest initiator, and king. One unique feature of the non-Muslim sources is that, unlike the Muslim sources, they are contemporary to the events they describe. One disadvantage of these sources is that they are few in number and do not provide adequate details, such as we usually find in the later Muslim traditions.

In 1997, Robert G. Hoyland, professor of late antique and early Islamic Middle Eastern history at New York University, gathered an extensive collection of non-Muslim primary sources written between 620 and 780 in the Middle East. This time period is crucial to Islam's formation, and these sources are significant to our understanding of Islam's origins. Hoyland translated these texts into English from their original languages, which include Greek, Armenian, Latin, Coptic, and others. These sources provide a collection of eyewitness reports of momentous historical events during the earliest period of Islam. The book is unique in its content, massive in its length, and helpful in its scope. According to Hoyland, the first explicit reference to Muhammad in a non-Muslim source dates precisely to Friday, February 7, 634. This reference is attributed to Thomas the Presbyter, a seventh-century Middle Eastern Christian: "There was a battle between the Romans and the Arabs of Muḥammad. . . . The Romans fled, leaving behind the patrician *bryrdn*, whom the Arabs killed. Some four thousand poor villagers of Palestine were killed there, Christians, Jews and Samaritans. The Arabs ravaged the whole region."[5] This quotation suggests that in 634—only two years after Muhammad's death—a Syriac Orthodox priest from Mesopotamia was aware of the Arabs of Muhammad and their military conquests. This is a very compelling reference in support of the existence of a conqueror named Muhammad whose armies attacked Roman lands during the period given in the Muslim tradition for his career in Arabia. In fact, there are numerous non-Muslim (Jewish, Christian, Samaritan) and even Muslim sources indicating that Muhammad's death could have occurred two to five years after 632. These sources suggest he was still alive after 634 and led the conquest of Palestine in 634–35.[6] If this is true, then the words of Thomas the Presbyter are of utmost importance and serve as eyewitness testimony to the existence of a historical Muhammad. Moreover, around the same time in 634, a Greek source tells of "the prophet who has appeared with the [Arabs]" and identifies him negatively: "He is false, for the prophets do not come armed with a sword."[7] While this reference does not explicitly mention Muhammad's name, it is difficult to imagine a more famous religious preacher among the Arabs during that period. It appears that non-Muslims were aware of an Arabian prophet who was launching raids during the first half of the seventh century. This is evident in an important sermon preached by the patriarch of Jerusalem, Sophronius, in 636 or 637 (four or five years after Muhammad's supposed death). In his sermon, Sophronius describes "the Arabs' atrocities and victories" as they "overrun the places which are not allowed to them, plunder cities, devastate fields, burn down villages, set on fire the holy churches, overturn the sacred monasteries." He goes on to speak of them as "vengeful and God-hating" Arabs, "who insult the cross, Jesus and the name of God, and whose leader is the devil."[8]

5. Hoyland, *Seeing Islam as Others Saw It*, 120.
6. See Shoemaker, *Death of a Prophet*, 1–17.
7. Hoyland, *Seeing Islam as Others Saw It*, 55.
8. Hoyland, *Seeing Islam as Others Saw It*, 72–73.

The testimony of Sophronius suggests that Christians contemporaneous with Muhammad's time were aware of his existence and identified him as a God-hating Arab and a devil leading warriors who insulted Jesus, the cross, and the name of the true God. Though the words of Sophronius do not explicitly mention Muhammad's name, there is a similar description in another source. A Middle Eastern Syriac testimony from 637 mentions Muhammad's name explicitly and refers to the fact that the "Arab troops decisively defeated Byzantine forces" and that "many villages were destroyed through the killing by [the Arabs of] Muhammad."[9] In this source, Muhammad is explicitly mentioned as the leader of Arab soldiers who attacked Christian Byzantine forces. Thus, it is plausible to conclude that in the seventh century there existed an Arabian commander named Muhammad who led troops and adopted a religious message that opposed Christian claims.

So was Muhammad a real historical figure? The answer depends on which Muhammad we consider. Muhammad's existence is separate from his historicity. While the legendary and traditional Muhammads hardly reflect a true historical figure, the historical Muhammad likely existed. We have a vague portrayal of him in non-Muslim sources, contemporary or near-contemporary to his life and career in seventh-century Arabia. These sources suggest his existence and describe some of his activities as a military commander and a religious preacher.

9. Penn, *When Christians First Met Muslims*, 22, 24. See also Hoyland, *Seeing Islam as Others Saw It*, 116–17.

What Do We Know about Mecca, Muhammad's Birthplace?

Mecca is the heartland of Islam. If Islam has a holy of holies, it is definitely Mecca, because it is both the birthplace of Muhammad and the location of the most sacred Islamic place of worship, the Ka'ba, where millions of Muslims perform the ritual pilgrimage every year. All Muslims face toward Mecca—particularly the Ka'ba's position—during their ritual prayer five times per day. It is their qibla (direction of prayer). If Mecca is the heart of Islam, the Ka'ba is the heart of Mecca. The Ka'ba is now inside the Great Mosque, which is known as al-Masjid al-Haram—literally, "The Sacred Mosque." Muslims believe that fighting is forbidden in the Ka'ba; this has been the case ever since Muhammad returned victorious in 630 after overcoming his Meccan enemies (although Muslim histories detail several fights between Muslims in the Ka'ba after Muhammad's death, which resulted in the destruction of the Ka'ba at least twice). Based on traditions attributed to Muhammad, Muslims believe that one prayer in the Meccan Ka'ba is equal to a hundred thousand prayers elsewhere.[1] Even the most trusted Sunni hadith collection, that

---

1. See Sunan Ibn Majah, vol. 1, book 5, hadith 1413 (hereafter Sunan Ibn Majah, 1.5.1413), which states, "A man's prayer in his house is equal (in reward) to one prayer;

of Bukhari, contains a chapter with many traditions that is titled "The Superiority of Offering Prayer in the Mosque of Mecca and Medina."[2]

For Muslims, Mecca is the first of three most sacred cities in Islam, followed by Medina and Jerusalem. Today Mecca is known as an exclusively Muslim sacred place, as it has no other religion besides Islam. No Jewish synagogue or Christian church exists in Muhammad's birth-land. Non-Muslims are not allowed to visit the city. Geographically, Mecca is located in a dry valley surrounded by a few mountains, including Mount Hira, where Muhammad allegedly received the first divine revelation in an encounter with the archangel Gabriel. Due to the high temperature, agriculture is rare, except for herbs and plants that can grow in such a climate. However, the Quran claims that its original Meccan recipients were agriculturalists who grew fruits, olives, palm trees, and grapevines (Q 16:11). Muslims call the Meccan valley Wadi Ibrahim, which means "Abraham's Valley," as they believe Mecca was built and sanctified as a holy city by Patriarch Abraham himself. Muhammad is reported to have said, "The Prophet Abraham made Mecca a sanctuary, and asked for Allah's blessing in it. I made Medina a sanctuary as Abraham made Mecca a sanctuary."[3] Thus, for Muslims, just as Abraham dedicated Mecca as sacred, Muhammad dedicated Medina. According to tradition, Muhammad praised Mecca as the best place on earth: "By Allah, you are the best land of Allah, and the dearest of the land of Allah to me. By Allah, had I not been expelled from you I would never have left."[4]

Although the Quran explicitly mentions Mecca only once (Q 48:24), Muslims believe that there are indirect or implicit references to it in many verses. They claim that Mecca is implied in what the Quran calls the "mother of the cities" (Q 42:7; 6:92) and "Bakka" (Q 3:96). Due to its superior status in the hearts of Muslims and their reverence for it, some insist that Mecca is the center of the universe. In fact, some

---

his prayer in the mosque of the tribes is equal to twenty-five prayers; his prayer in the mosque in which Friday prayer is offered is equal to five-hundred prayers; his prayer in Aqsa Mosque is equal to fifty thousand prayers; his prayer in my mosque [in Medina] is equal to fifty thousand prayers; and his prayer in the Sacred Mosque [in Mecca] is equal to one hundred thousand prayers." See also Sahih Muslim, 7.3209, 3210, and especially 3212; and Bukhari, 2.21.282.

2. See https://sunnah.com/bukhari/20.

3. Bukhari, 3.34.339; 2.23.432; 4.52.139.

4. Sunan Ibn Majah, 4.25.3108. See also Jami' at-Tirmidhi, 1.46.3925.

classical Muslims made substantial claims about Mecca and its Ka'ba
that are hard to believe. For instance, Abu al-Walid al-Azraqi, a native
of Mecca who died in 865 (about 230 years after Muhammad), wrote
a history of Mecca titled *The Chronicles of Mecca*. In his reports, al-
Azraqi claims that the Meccan Ka'ba existed forty years before Allah
created the earth and that when Adam was created, he descended to
earth, established the specific place of the Ka'ba in Mecca, and performed the hajj (ritual pilgrimage) in it. Moreover, al-Azraqi claims that
Mecca and the Ka'ba were completely destroyed by the flood of Noah's
time and that Allah later took Abraham up to heaven and allowed
him to choose the location of the Ka'ba at the heart of Mecca—then
Abraham descended to earth and built the Ka'ba using stones from the
mountains. The angels assisted him by handing him the stones. Once it
was completed, Abraham performed the hajj and the circumambulation
around the Ka'ba. After his death, Ishmael succeeded him in managing
the Ka'ba's affairs, although his descendants began to worship stones
instead of Allah, until Muhammad came as the final prophet to bring
them back to the right worship.[5] While many reports about the historicity of the Ka'ba and Mecca are hardly convincing, these accounts
convey the superior status that this edifice and city occupy in the hearts
of Muslims.

But there is a problematic question: Are we certain of the historicity
of Mecca in the first place? Can we trust the Muslim traditions about
Mecca? Some scholars have voiced strong doubts about the historical
Mecca. On the one hand, the Muslim traditions insist that Mecca was a
place of pagan worship—presumably to establish that Muhammad could
not have borrowed anything from, for instance, Christianity or Judaism.
Muslims insist there were neither Jews nor Christians in Mecca, as it was
entirely pagan. On the other hand, the Quran itself is full of statements
addressed to Christians and Jews as well as numerous biblical materials.
How was the Quran proclaimed in a pagan city when many parts of it
are addressed to religious people with biblical knowledge? This led some
scholars to doubt that Muhammad's career ever took place in Mecca.
They suggested that his career most likely took place in a religious milieu

5. Azraqi, *Akhbār Makka*, 31–32 (on the Ka'ba's creation before the earth), 36–44
(on Adam and the Ka'ba), 52–73 (on Abraham and the Ka'ba).

where Christianity and Judaism were flourishing—a place like Greater Syria. In her skepticism of the Muslim reports about Mecca, Patricia Crone states, "It is difficult not to suspect that the tradition places the prophet's career in Mecca for the same reason that it insists that he was illiterate: the only way he could have acquired his knowledge of all the things that God had previously told the Jews and the Christians was by revelation from God himself."[6] It appears that the historiographical accounts about Mecca as a city of great religious stature and political importance are dubious.

But there is a deeper problem with Mecca. Major world maps from the sixth and seventh centuries do not include it. If the city was as famous as Muslim traditions claim, how was it overlooked on maps while other, less important cities in Arabia often appeared? No map shows Mecca until the late ninth century. The Byzantines and Persians were aware of Northern and Southern Arabia and wrote about them. There are also ample inscriptions referring to these two parts of Arabia; however, the middle part, which includes Mecca, is entirely unknown, although traditions describe this as an important place in Muhammad's career. Some scholars conclude that the location of the city was "doctrinally inspired" and invented later for religious and political reasons.[7] Crone casts more doubt as she questions the Muslim claims that Mecca was a flourishing city in trade routes between Southern and Northern Arabia. In her examination of Greek trading documents, Crone observes that Mecca was simply unknown. Although the documents refer to places in Arabia, such as Yathrib and Khaybar, Mecca is never mentioned in the first two centuries of Islam. Crone argues, "Despite the considerable attention paid to Arabian affairs there is no mention at all of Quraysh (the tribe of Muhammed) and their trading center Mecca, be it in the Greek, Latin, Syriac, Aramaic, Coptic, or other literature composed outside Arabia."[8] In continuing her skeptical line of argument, Crone questions why a camel trade caravan would journey off road for hundreds of miles inland to pass by Mecca when they could have used the road adjacent to the Red Sea. Given that there is a lack of continuous transmission of historical facts in the earliest Muslim generations, Crone concludes

6. Crone, "What Do We Actually Know about Mohammed?"
7. Crone, "What Do We Actually Know about Mohammed?"
8. Crone, *Meccan Trade and the Rise of Islam*, 134.

that the historical accounts about Mecca and its status as a major city on trade routes are "pure fabrications," and the "Meccans did not trade outside of Mecca on the eve of Islam."[9] It appears that what we know about Mecca from the Muslim sources aims to serve religious claims rather than provide historical records.

Other scholars voice skepticism about Mecca, its location, and its history. While Crone focuses on the history of Mecca, archaeologist and historian Dan Gibson (1956–) has concentrated his research for over three decades on Mecca as the qibla (direction of prayer) in Islam. Gibson begins with the Islamic claim that each mosque should have a point that specifies the qibla so that Muslims can face Mecca and the Ka'ba as they pray. In his study of the geography of the Quran, Gibson examined over sixty important locations in the Quran.[10] Nine of them are explicitly named, but none are near the traditional location of Mecca; some are more than five hundred miles away. For Gibson, the descriptions of Mecca found in the Quran and in Muslim traditions do not match what we know about today's Mecca. Moreover, Gibson studied the qibla pointers of many of the earliest mosques of Islam.[11] Surprisingly, he found none of them facing Mecca, although Arabs—nomads and shepherds—are supposedly known to be outstanding with directions. He asserts that dozens of qiblas in early mosques actually faced Petra, in today's Jordan, with extraordinary accuracy. Thus, he argues that the original qibla was more likely Petra, not Mecca. Gibson is therefore convinced that Islam began in Petra, not Mecca. For him, Mecca as a central sacred location emerged later in history. While Gibson's arguments reflect genuine research, some of his claims require more work. Some scholars critique his thesis and voice skepticism regarding the claim of the remarkable ability of Arabs to determine directions. To these critics, the accuracy of the qiblas is not an indication of a different sacred city; consequently, they reject Gibson's findings. However, Walter Schumm, a Kansas State University professor, seems to support some of Gibson's arguments when he writes, "While some architects were more accurate than others, early Muslim architects seemed, in general, quite capable of placing qiblas with reasonable accuracy, even though their accuracy may have improved

9. Crone, *Meccan Trade and the Rise of Islam*, 114, 432.
10. Gibson, *Qur'ānic Geography*.
11. Gibson, *Early Islamic Qiblas*.

slightly over the first two centuries of Islam."[12] Furthermore, Crone, in focusing on the Quran's descriptions of the Meccan environment and wondering how a city full of rocks and desert could be suitable for planting fruits, olives, and trees, seems also to align herself with Gibson. She writes, "The Qur'an describes the polytheist opponents [of Muhammad] as agriculturalists who cultivated wheat, grapes, olives, and date palms. Wheat, grapes and olives are the three staples of the Mediterranean; date palms take us southwards, but Mecca was not suitable for any kind of agriculture, and one could not possibly have produced olives there."[13] Thus, it appears that many scholars believe a more plausible place for Muhammad's career is near the Mediterranean, not in a traditionally prescribed pagan Mecca. While the Mecca of the Muslim traditions is the holiest city of Islam, what we read about Mecca in the traditions is unsupported by contemporary independent evidence. As for Mecca's location as given by Muslim traditions, it is at best a mistaken place or, at worst, a doctrinally driven myth.

12. Schumm, "How Accurately Could Early Muslims (622–900 CE) Determine the Direction of Prayers?"

13. Crone, "What Do We Actually Know about Mohammed?"

9

What Is the Black Stone in the Ka'ba?

Today's Ka'ba is a majestic cubic structure with exterior walls covered by a black silk cloth of highest quality that costs over $4 million and is replaced once each year. Due to the sacredness of the Ka'ba, the cloth cannot be thrown away. After the completion of the hajj, the Islamic ritual pilgrimage, the sacred cloth is cut into pieces and distributed among many Muslims. These pieces, for some Muslims, serve as a blessing of supernatural power from the holiest place on earth. In pre-Islamic times, the Ka'ba was an abandoned structure with no significant form, roofless and full of rocks in the middle of a desert. Today's Ka'ba is vastly different, due to the investment of the Saudi government, which supervises the ritual pilgrimage of millions of Muslims annually. In today's Ka'ba, however, there is nothing of major importance except a black stone. It is located in the eastern wall of the Ka'ba. This stone is of utmost value to Muslims, as there are traditions attributed to Muhammad and his companions regarding the stone's origin, importance, and power. It is an object of veneration. For any Muslim performing the pilgrimage to Mecca, it is a crucial part of the religious ritual to touch or kiss the black stone, and some believe a mere touch abolishes one's sins.

Most Muslims believe that this is the most sacred stone on earth and that it came down from heaven to become the cornerstone of the Ka'ba. According to tradition, Muhammad said, "The Black Stone descended from the [sic] Paradise, and it was more white than milk, then it was blackened by the sins of the children of Adam."[1] This drives the common belief that the stone came from paradise in heaven and that it changed color from white to black due to the sins of the people who touched it. This propels many Muslims to revere it and ascribe to it metaphysical power. We are told that Muhammad spoke highly of the stone's value: "Whoever faces it is facing the Hand of the Most Merciful."[2] This is one reason why most Muslim pilgrims want to touch or kiss the black stone. By kissing the stone, these Muslims believe they are following in the footsteps of Muhammad, who also kissed it. In fact, some believe that the black stone will intercede for Muslims in the last day, as Muhammad reportedly said, "By Allah! Allah will raise [the black stone] on the Day of Resurrection with two eyes by which it sees and a tongue that it speaks with, testifying to whoever touched it in truth."[3] This tradition makes millions of Muslims eager to touch the stone so that they will receive its support in the last day.

While the Quran never mentions the black stone, the Muslim traditions establish a strong connection between Muhammad and the stone, even before he allegedly received his first divine revelation. Muhammad's sira reports that five years before he encountered Gabriel, he worked with the Meccans to rebuild the Ka'ba and acted as umpire among them. When the Quraysh sought to place the black stone inside the Ka'ba, they quarreled because they realized it was a huge honor to place the heavenly stone. They decided that the first comer to the Ka'ba at that time would be given the honor. The first comer was Muhammad. He took the black stone and set it in its position, where it has remained for fourteen centuries.[4] Because of this tradition, in Muhammad's famous biography, Muslims believe this stone is unlike any other. They do not question its validity, nor do they question whether heaven has rocks in

1. Jami' at-Tirmidhi, 2.4.877; see also Sunan an-Nasa'i, vol. 3, book 24, hadith 2938 (hereafter Sunan an-Nasa'i, 3.24.2938).
2. Sunan Ibn Majah, 4.25.2957.
3. Jami' at-Tirmidhi, 2.4.961; see also Sunan Ibn Majah, 4.25.2944.
4. Ibn Hisham and Ibn Ishaq, *Life of Muhammad*, 86.

the first place. Very few would think to doubt that the stone turned black after sinners touched it because strong traditions confirm its sacredness. Many cultural Muslims venerate the rock and hesitate to question any of the Muslim traditions that create a halo around it.

But there are some troubling Muslim traditions about the black stone. In the most trusted Sunni hadith collection, that of Bukhari, it is reported that the second Muslim caliph, Umar, "came near the Black Stone and kissed it and said 'No doubt, I know that you are a stone and can neither benefit anyone nor harm anyone. Had I not seen Allah's Messenger kissing you I would not have kissed you.'"[5] Umar's statement indicates his skepticism of the value of a mere stone—but seeing Muhammad kiss it propelled Umar, and later Muslims, to do the same. In another tradition, also attributed to Umar, he again appears to question the importance of the stone, calling it mere dust and claiming that there was no reason for Muslims to respect it, "except that [they] wanted to show off before the pagans, and now Allah has destroyed them."[6] Based on this tradition, it appears that the sacredness of the black stone was merely a claim advanced by Muhammad's followers who desired to boast before the unbelievers of Mecca. To Umar, the unbelievers of Mecca were doomed, so it was unnecessary to revere a stone or show off.

Still, the vast majority of Muslims venerate the black stone and assume it possesses divine power. The stone is central to the proper fulfillment of the Islamic ritual pilgrimage, or hajj. The hajj is one of the Five Pillars of Sunni Islam—which are the obligatory religious practices divinely prescribed for every Muslim—in addition to the Shahada (profession of faith), fasting, prayer, and almsgiving. During the hajj, every Muslim is required to perform a series of rituals for five to six days. On the first day, a pilgrim begins the hajj by performing the circumambulation around the Ka'ba seven times, beginning and ending at the black stone, always moving counterclockwise. Circumambulation means walking or running around the Ka'ba in circles. One of the first obligatory ceremonies during the circumambulation is touching or kissing the stone, which can be seen through a very small portal in the corner of the Ka'ba. It is difficult for thousands of pilgrims to enter and touch

5. Bukhari, 2.26.667, 675; see also Musnad Ahmad, 2.18.
6. Bukhari, 2.26.675.

or kiss the stone, and even more so for those who are sick or those with special needs. Because of this, Muslim jurists and clerics issued religious rulings that provided alternative ways to connect with the stone. For example, a pilgrim can use something else to touch the stone, then kiss that thing. Those who are entirely unable to touch or kiss it are encouraged to point to the stone and say the Islamic phrase "Allahu Akbar," meaning "Allah is greater," which suffices in these cases. The bottom line is that Muslims want to touch or kiss the stone due to the strong belief that it will intercede on the day of judgment for those who touched it. Without a doubt, these religious claims reflect the significant position of this stone in the hearts of the believers.

While Muslims tend to view today's Ka'ba as the same structure from the time of Muhammad or even—according to other traditions— from the time of Adam, non-Muslim scholars are hesitant to share these views. Ample historical reports indicate that the Ka'ba was frequently destroyed—even by Muslim warriors themselves—and rebuilt and that the black stone was stolen and restored many times. In a sense, today's Ka'ba is the new look of a frequently demolished structure, and certainty about the location of the real black stone is elusive, as Muslim histories indicate that Shiites removed it and hid it for over two decades in the 900s. Moreover, while Muslims tend to view the rituals of the hajj—including the circumambulation around the Ka'ba and kissing the stone—as a purely Muslim ceremony, scholars trace in them pre-Islamic pagan worship. For scholars, the pre-Islamic Ka'ba and its pagan pilgrimage continued into the Islamic era and were adopted by the believers with only minor adjustments. Non-Muslims may view the black stone and the claims about it as fanciful or even idolatrous, but its veneration among millions of Muslims is unmatched.

10

What Do We Know about Muhammad's Wives and Their Roles in Islam?

According to Muslim tradition, Muhammad had eleven wives, although in some reports there were twelve if Maria the Copt—who was sent to Muhammad as a gift from the Byzantine patriarch of Alexandria—is included. The list of his wives arranged chronologically is as follows: Khadija, Sawda, Aisha, Hafsa, Zaynab bint Khuzayma, Umm Salma, Zaynab bint Jahsh, Juwayriyya, Umm Habiba, Safiyya, Maymuna, and Maria.[1] The list does not include Muhammad's concubines, or the women whom he married without consummating the marriage. Two of his wives, Khadija and Zaynab bint Khuzayma, died during his lifetime. The rest were present when he died. Khadija was his first wife, and while she lived he did not marry another woman. Six of his wives were Arabs from his tribe, the Quraysh, and four were Arabs from other tribes. In addition, he married a Jew, Safiyya, and a Christian, Maria. As mentioned, some Muslims consider Maria a slave concubine and do not include her as one of Muhammad's wives. Nevertheless, each of his

1. For a Muslim perspective on Muhammad's wives, see Haykal, *Life of Muhammad*, 307–21.

wives is known among Muslims as "A Mother of the Believers," which is a title of respect and esteem.

Muslims believe that all of Muhammad's marriages were noble, honorable, and, more importantly, due to Allah's revelations; none were motivated by lust, gain, or benefits. In this way, Muhammad was the example of conduct to humankind. The noble causes included protecting and taking care of widows after their husbands died in battle, as in the case of Juwayriyya, or marrying the daughters of his supportive companions, as in the case of Aisha and Hafsa. To affirm that Muhammad did not marry without a clear revelation from Allah, Muslims often highlight Allah's revelation to Muhammad concerning Zaynab bint Jahsh (Q 33:37). She was initially the wife of Muhammad's adopted son, Zayd, but Allah, we are told, revoked the adoption and instructed Muhammad to marry her. Some Muslims claim that it was a divine ordinance that Muhammad, unlike other prophets, married many wives so that they could support the responsibility he assumed as a prophet and serve as credible voices of knowledge of his life and deeds. This necessitated the creation of embellished traditions claiming that Muhammad had the unmatched ability to perform sexually frequently enough to fulfill his responsibilities with all of his wives: "The Prophet used to visit all his wives in a round, during the day and night and they were eleven in number. . . . We used to say that the Prophet was given the strength of thirty men."[2] From his wives, Muhammad had three sons and four daughters. His sons were al-Qasim, Abdullah, and Ibrahim. None of them survived childhood. His daughters were Zaynab, Ruqayya, Umm Kulthum, and Fatima. All his daughters were from his first wife, Khadija, and all of them died before his own death except Fatima, who died six months after him.

Among Muhammad's wives, some appear more important to his life and career than others. Khadija was not only his first wife but also the one who supported him from the start, both financially, because she was wealthy, and emotionally and psychologically once he received the revelation in his reported encounter with Gabriel. She was fifteen years older than Muhammad, and he was her employee until she proposed and married him when he was twenty-five. Her Christian cousin, Waraqa, was the first man to confirm Muhammad's prophethood, though he did

2. Bukhari, 1.5.268.

not convert to Islam himself. Khadija had children from two previous marriages and died only three years before Muhammad emigrated from Mecca to Medina. A few days after Khadija's death, to overcome his sadness, a marriage was arranged for Muhammad. He married Sawda, who was his relative from the Quraysh on her father's side. On her mother's side, she was from the supporters of Medina. This was significant, as these Medinan supporters would later welcome Muhammad and his followers when he needed to escape Mecca. On the personal side, Sawda seems to have been concerned about her age and afraid that Muhammad would divorce her for a younger wife. When she knew that Muhammad favored the young Aisha, Sawda was willing to give away her day of marital time with Muhammad to Aisha. Sawda declared that "she was old, and cared not for men; her only desire was to rise on the Day of Judgment as one of his wives."[3] Sawda lived for some fifteen years after Muhammad's death.

Muhammad's third wife, Aisha, is arguably one of the most important wives of Islam's prophet. She was traditionally known as his favorite and is thus considered among Sunni Muslims to be one of the trusted hadith narrators, as she always accompanied Muhammad. According to numerous traditions, "he married Aisha when she was a girl of six years of age, and he consummated that marriage when she was nine years old."[4] Aisha's age when she married is controversial for obvious reasons. Muhammad was older than her father. While Aisha's age is stated in many of the so-called authentic hadiths as well as in Muhammad's trusted sira, some contemporary Muslims attempt to dismiss these traditions and claim that Aisha was seventeen or eighteen when Muhammad consummated the marriage.[5] However, other Muslim traditions emphasize that Aisha took her toys to her new home with Muhammad: "Aisha reported that Allah's Apostle married her when she was seven years old, and she was taken to his house as a bride when she was nine, and her dolls were with her; and when he died she was eighteen years old."[6] There are numerous hadiths regarding Aisha's dolls and toys,

3. Vacca, "Sawda bt. Zam'a," 9:89–90.
4. Bukhari, 5.58.236.
5. Muhammad's biography states, "He married Aisha in Mecca when she was a child of seven and lived with her in Medina when she was nine or ten. She was the only virgin that he married." Ibn Hisham and Ibn Ishaq, *Life of Muhammad*, 792.
6. Sahih Muslim, 8.3311.

and in some hadiths we are told that Muhammad joined in her games. Aisha reportedly stated, "I used to play with the dolls in the presence of the Prophet, and my girl friends also used to play with me. When Allah's Messenger used to enter (my dwelling place) they used to hide themselves, but the Prophet would call them to join and play with me."[7]

The tradition emphasizes Aisha's physical beauty and insists that she remained Muhammad's favorite wife until he died, although he married other beautiful women. She was the daughter of his chief follower and main companion, Abu Bakr. While Muslims claim that Muhammad's marriages aimed to help his friends, scholars argue that other reasons took precedence. In analyzing Aisha's marriage to Muhammad, Scottish scholar William Montgomery Watt (1909–2006) writes, "Since Muḥammad had a political aim in nearly all his marriages, he must have seen in this one a means of strengthening the ties between himself and Abū Bakr, his chief follower."[8]

Aisha was accused of adultery, specifically for cheating on Muhammad about five years before his death.[9] Sunnis unanimously claim that she was innocent, and some Shiites agree—although a number of Shiites believe she never loved Muhammad but used him and was actually instrumental in his death. The story of her alleged affair is as follows: Muhammad took Aisha on one of his military expeditions when she was about fourteen. On the journey back to Medina, Aisha left the caravan to relieve herself. She dropped her necklace and began searching for it, while the caravan left without noticing her absence. It was night, and she was troubled, so she sat down and waited in hopes that they would return for her. A good-looking man, Safwan, found Aisha and recognized her, even though it was dark. He was a soldier in Muhammad's army and had also been left behind. Unwilling to leave Aisha unprotected, Safwan escorted her back to Medina—they were alone the entire way. When people saw them together, it caused a crisis that exploded through

7. Bukhari, 8.73.151. According to other traditions, Aisha reported, "The Messenger of Allah married me when I was six and consummated the marriage with me when I was nine, and I used to play with dolls." Sunan an-Nasa'i, 4.26.3380. In a different hadith, Aisha also said, "I used to play with dolls. Sometimes the Messenger of Allah entered upon me when the girls were with me. When he came in, they went out, and when he went out, they came in." Sunan Abi Dawud, 42.4913, 4914.

8. Watt, "'Ā'isha Bint Abī Bakr," 1:307.

9. For the entire account of the accusation, see Bukhari, 3.48.829; 5.59.462; and Sahih Muslim, 37.6673.

significant rumors, as they were not married. The situation was unacceptable according to the norms of the day. Many believed Safwan and
Aisha planned to be alone. The Muslim tradition states that the enemies
of Muhammad and Abu Bakr (Aisha's father) declared her adulterous,
whereas Muhammad's supporters believed her to be innocent. Muhammad abandoned her for a month, and Ali advised him to divorce her.
After Muhammad himself investigated the matter, she was found innocent, and Allah gave Muhammad a revelation rebuking those who
attacked Aisha (Q 24:11–20) and commanding that four witnesses are
needed to prove adultery—a requirement that became the mandatory
default in Islamic law.

Sunni scholars believe that through these verses in Q 24 Allah acquitted Aisha and spoke highly of her virtues. Most Shiite scholars view these
verses not as confirming her virtues but only as honoring Muhammad for
denying that his wife cheated on him. For Shiites, a primary reason for
disbelieving this story is that it portrays Muhammad negatively. Shiites
mock the fact that most hadiths quoted by Sunnis to prove Aisha's innocence and virtue are attributed to her own narration. Shiites do not trust
hadiths narrated by Aisha, as they do not see her as virtuous. In many
Shiite traditions, she is portrayed as ungodly, a conspirator, immature,
envious, jealous, and disrespectful of Muhammad. Shiites dislike that
Aisha opposed Imam Ali, initiated war against him, and served as one
of the three leaders fighting him in the Battle of the Camel, two decades
after Muhammad's death. In fact, a Shiite theological practice, *tabarru'*,
involves making a cursing statement when the name of any evil Muslim
is mentioned. The practice is used after the mention of Aisha and the
first three caliphs: Abu Bakr, Umar, and Uthman. This is contrasted with
a favorable view of Aisha among the Sunnis, to the extent that a hadith
attributed to Muhammad reports her to be superior to other women:
"The superiority of Aisha to other ladies is like the superiority of Tharid
to other kinds of food."[10] Tharid was Muhammad's favorite food, and
this hadith is repeated many times in many trusted collections.[11] Thus,
Aisha was reportedly Muhammad's favorite, youngest, and most beautiful wife, yet many aspects of her life remain controversial.

10. Bukhari, 7.65.339.
11. Bukhari, 4.55.643, 623; 5.57.113, 114; 7.65.330, 339. It is also found in Sahih
Muslim, 31.5992, 5966.

The remaining wives of Muhammad are somewhat less influential when compared to Khadija and Aisha and the roles they played in Muhammad's career. However, two of them stand out with some importance. His seventh wife, Zaynab bint Jahsh, married him based on a divine revelation (Q 33:37–38). We are told that she "used to boast to the other wives of the Prophet and say: 'Allah married me to him from above the Heavens.'"[12] She was married to Muhammad's adopted son, Zayd, who, in some traditions, was the first believer in Muhammad's message. He is also the only Muslim apart from Muhammad mentioned in the Quran. However, it seems that after Zayd married Zaynab, things did not go well. Muslims believe that Allah spoke to Muhammad, saying, "You concealed in your soul what Allah brings to light" (Q 33:37), which indicated a desire for Zaynab. Allah then required Zaynab's divorce from Zayd and prescribed the abolishment of the institution of adoption so that Muhammad could marry her. Muhammad repudiated Zayd as his son and married Zaynab. Because of this, adoption is not permitted in Islam. In some hadiths, we are told that Aisha was jealous of Zaynab and questioned both Muhammad's actions and Allah's decree. Aisha complained to Muhammad, "It seems to me that your Lord hastens to satisfy your desire."[13]

The final example of Muhammad's wives is Safiyya. She was his tenth wife and a Jew. She was married to Kinana, who was the chief of Khaybar, a Jewish settlement near Medina. After Muhammad led the raid against Khaybar and defeated the Jews, he saw her. The reports tell that Muhammad took Kinana's entire family—including Safiyya—captive at Khaybar. Afterward, Muhammad chose her for himself. In some traditions, Safiyya is described as a war captive: Muhammad "manumitted Safiyya and then married her."[14] Early accounts do not explicitly mention that Safiyya converted to Islam, but later historians redesigned the story to indicate her conversion. She was seventeen years old, and Muhammad was sixty. This marriage, according to Muslims, allows Muslim men to marry women of Jewish background.

While conservative Muslims view Muhammad's marriages as motivated by godly and humane—indeed, divine—reasons, many scholars

12. Bukhari, 9.93.517; and Sunan an-Nasa'i, 4.26.3254.
13. Sahih Muslim, 8.3453, 3454; see also Sunan an-Nasa'i, 4.26.3201; and Sunan Ibn Majah, 3.9.2000.
14. Bukhari, 7.62.98.

view the marriages as a method of creating alliances and establishing tribal ties with powerful people. Conservative Muslims usually view Muhammad's wives as the most pious among women. Some critical Muslim thinkers, however, disagree with such a claim. They refer to the Quran itself as rebuking Muhammad's wives: "It may happen that his Lord—if [Muhammad] divorced you all—would substitute for him wives better than you; submissive, believing, contently obedient, repentant, worshiping, and striving in fasting, whether previously married or virgins" (Q 66:5). This verse suggests that there were better women and that Allah could have chosen better wives for Muhammad than those he did. Still, conservative Muslims highly esteem Muhammad's wives and view them as the Mothers of the Believers.

11

Was Muhammad Always
a Monotheist?

The consensus among Muslims is that Muhammad never worshiped any deity but Allah, even before his encounter with Gabriel, when he became the prophet of Allah at age forty. Muslims emphatically believe that although the Meccan people were idolaters, Muhammad never participated in idol worship. Some conservative Muslims even claim that Muhammad was born a believing Muslim and never associated with any belief except Islam; in this case, *islam* means "devoted submission to Allah." Or, as some Shiite scholars observe, Muhammad was guided by Allah and his angels from a young age to protect him from evil and error. These religious scholars believe that before Islam even emerged, Muhammad was following its precepts and laws. In fact, a story in Muhammad's biography illustrates this thesis.

At age twelve, Muhammad traveled with his uncle Abu Talib to Syria, where they met a monk named Bahira. In conversation with Muhammad, the monk said, "Boy, I ask you by al-Lat and al-Uzza [two pagan goddesses] to answer my question," to which Muhammad quickly responded, "Do not ask me by al-Lat and al-Uzza, for by Allah nothing is more hateful to me than these two."[1] The monk looked at Muhammad's back and discovered the seal of prophethood between his shoulders, which confirmed what the monk was waiting for: a divinely inspired prophet. The narrative emphatically depicts Muhammad as a believer in Allah and a rejecter of idols at twelve years old. The story aims to prove that Muhammad was always a monotheist, even before he received the divine revelation.

Some Muslim scholars believe that Muhammad was a hanif. The term *hanif* refers to a believer in Allah—a monotheist who is neither a Jew nor a Christian (Q 3:67). The term is used to describe the belief system of pre-Islamic believers in Allah and his oneness who belonged to the religion of Abraham (Q 3:67; 16:120). Thus, Abraham was a hanif. Linguistically, the word *hanif* describes a devoted inclination to Allah's worship, which propels one to abandon polytheism and all forms of religion to adhere to the true deity. Muslims believe Muhammad, like Abraham, was a hanif (Q 2:135; 3:95; 4:125; 6:161). In fact, some Muslims argue that even Muhammad's family was following the same hanif religion. This argument seeks to distance Muhammad and his family from any association with the pagans of Mecca. According to Muslims, Muhammad never worshiped an idol or bowed before a statue. He was never a mushrik—that is, someone who associates other deities or partners with Allah. According to the Quran, the hanif religion is basically the natural religion. It is part of the natural divine composition of humankind, which means that each human is created to follow such a religion (Q 30:30). In a sense, Muslims view Muhammad as a natural devotee or a born believer who required no help to become a monotheist (Q 6:75–79). For them, Muhammad reached the true belief by himself with no other help.

However, some Muslims reject the claim that Muhammad was a hanif, following Abraham's religion, since this claim portrays Abraham's religion as superior to that of Muhammad. These Muslims do not accept that Muhammad would follow any other religion. The logic is expressed by this question: How could the final and best prophet follow any previous religion, whether of Noah, Abraham, Moses, or Jesus? For these Muslims, Muhammad was born a strict monotheist, always devoted

1. Ibn Hisham and Ibn Ishaq, *Life of Muhammad*, 80.

to Allah and his laws, and he reached this conviction on his own or by divine guidance.

Furthermore, not only do some Muslims reject the notion that Muhammad was a hanif, but the claim that he was a born believer who required no help to become a monotheist also may contradict certain statements in the Quran. In one verse, the Quran seems to instruct Muhammad to become a hanif, which suggests he was not a hanif at some point: "Then we inspired you: Follow the faith of Abraham, a hanif, for he was not of the idolaters" (Q 16:123). If Allah instructed Muhammad to follow Abraham's faith, it is plausible to conclude he was not already a hanif. Here is a similar verse: "Set your face toward the hanif religion and do not be of the idolaters" (Q 10:105). Here, Allah presumably instructs Islam's prophet to follow the hanif path and warns him against worshiping idols; however, some may read this verse as Muhammad himself calling people to the hanif religion. But the Quran contains other verses that call Muhammad to repent: "Ask forgiveness of your sins and the sins of all believing men and women" (Q 47:19). Here, the Quran presumably speaks to Muhammad about his sins. Would the Quran instruct Muhammad to seek forgiveness if he was not a sinner? In another verse, Muhammad is asked, "Why do you forbid that which Allah has made lawful for you, in order to please your wives?" (Q 66:1). In this verse, Muhammad appears to go against Allah's will. In the same vein, Allah seems to address Muhammad, saying, "You hid inside yourself that which Allah desired to proclaim—you feared the people, while you were supposed to fear only Allah" (Q 33:37). These verses, at least at first glance, do not demonstrate Muhammad's complete obedience and total innocence. It appears that the Quran does not view Muhammad as infallible or immune from sins.

But why is it so crucial for Muslims that Muhammad was a monotheist even before he received the divine revelation? The answer lies in the Islamic doctrine of *isma*, which means infallibility and immunity from sin, fault, and error. All Muslims—both Sunnis and Shiites—believe that the term *isma* applies to all prophets; they are impeccable, infallible, and not liable to sin. In addition to prophets, Shiites add the twelve imams (descendants of Ali) to the list of the infallibles. For Shiites, an imam is a divinely designated religious guide and political leader of the community.[2] As such, he must be infallible and immune from errors and transgressions. While the notion of isma does not appear in the Quran, this doctrine is crucial to the Muslim understanding of prophets and prophethood: a prophet cannot err. While some Muslims say that the isma relates only to matters of inspiration and divine proclamations, the vast majority of Muslims claim that prophets can never err. This is one reason why Muslims believe that Muhammad must have been a monotheist for his entire life, even before he encountered Allah. Muhammad had to have possessed every virtue and made no mistake. While this is a common understanding among Muslims, scholars do not find enough support for such a claim in the early historical accounts about Muhammad: "In early Islam moral failures and errors of Muḥammad were freely mentioned, although there was an inconsistent tendency to minimize the shortcomings of the Prophet and in particular to deny that he had ever participated in the worship of idols."[3] It appears that early Muslims did not find value in depicting prophets as immune from error, but in later generations attempts were made to ensure that the prophets were depicted as infallible. This is evident in the incident of the so-called satanic verses, which reportedly involved Muhammad and occurred after he received Allah's divine revelation.

The incident of the satanic verses is well known in the Muslim tradition. According to various trusted accounts, Muhammad was once deceived by Satan and thus spoke satanic words as divine proclamations—that is, as Quranic verses. The incident reportedly occurred about ten years after Muhammad received the first revelation from Allah. It is mentioned in the Quran in chapter 53. The satanic words, according to Muslim traditions, were placed on Muhammad's tongue and made their way into Islam's scripture. These words clearly praised three pagan goddesses—idols, not Allah—and affirmed them as intercessors whose intercessions should be sought: "Verily their intercession is accepted with approval."[4] The proclamation of satanic words suggests that Mu-

2. For a good study on the infallible imams, see Pierce, "Remembering the Infallible Imams."

3. Madelung and Tyan, "'Iṣma," 4:182.

4. Tabari, History, 6:109. For a detailed account and analysis of the satanic verses incident, see Ibrahim, Concise Guide to the Quran, chap. 19; also Nagel, Muhammad's Mission, 53–62. For a Muslim perspective, see Haykal, Life of Muḥammad, 115–26.

hammad—at some point in his life—was a believer in pagan goddesses. In fact, the incident itself suggests that he could not discern the voice of Satan from that of Gabriel. Muslim traditions reveal that when the pagans of Mecca heard Muhammad's approval of their idols, they rejoiced, as Muhammad praised their goddesses "in the most favorable way possible, stating in his recitation that they are the high-flying cranes and that their intercession is received with approval."[5] If true, this incident refutes the claims of Muhammad's infallibility and immunity from sin, or, worse, it presents him as a nonmonotheist—at least in a temporary concession—even after he encountered Allah and received the Quran. According to tradition, these satanic words circulated widely, even reaching Muslims in Ethiopia. The words remained in the Quran for a time, until Gabriel came and rebuked Muhammad. Allah had to abrogate these words from the Quran. Undoubtedly, this incident causes significant embarrassment for Muslim apologists, who seek to defend Islam's prophet against any possible error or fallibility. So do Muslims accept what the Muslim traditions claim about Muhammad's deception by Satan?

In the first three centuries of Islam, Muslims treated the story as fact and reported it in numerous writings: hadith, sira, maghazi, and tarikh accounts. Three or four centuries after Muhammad's death, however, Muslim writers—especially advocates of Muhammad's traditions— began to dismiss the incident and claim it never happened, especially because it was evidence used by Islam's critics against Muhammad. Later Muslim generations became adamant that the incident never occurred. One can understand why religious enthusiasts would emphatically reject a story that depicts Muhammad as fallible, a polytheist, and unable to distinguish Satan from Allah—which, more importantly, questions the reliability of what Muhammad proclaimed, the Quran. Although the incident is reported as fact in the earliest trusted Muslim accounts, its recent rejection appears to be based on religious devotion rather than historical accuracy. In response to this rejection, non-Muslim scholars make a good argument: the satanic verses incident cannot be dismissed as fabrication because no Muslim would seek to fabricate a negative account about Muhammad and place it in Muslim trusted sources. Scottish scholar William Montgomery Watt (1909–2006) argues, "It is

5. Tabari, *History*, 6:109.

unthinkable that anyone should have invented such a story and persuaded the vast body of Muslims to accept it."[6] He concludes, "Muhammad must have publicly recited the satanic verses as part of the Quran; it is unthinkable that the story could have been invented by Muslims, or foisted upon them by non-Muslims."[7] In recent scholarship, Pakistani-American scholar Shahab Ahmed (1966–2015) analyzes in painstaking detail fifty Muslim reports from early sources, all of which narrate the satanic verses incident. He concludes, "It has now been categorically established that the Satanic verses incident constituted a standard, widely circulated, and generally accepted element in the historical memory of the Muslim community on the life of Muhammad in the first two centuries of Islam."[8] For Ahmed, "Given the centrality of the *authoritative* persona of the Prophet to the logic of the Ḥadīth movement, it is obvious that the idea of an *infallible* or *impeccable* Prophet whose words and deeds might reliably be taken to establish a model for detailed pious mimesis must have possessed a particular appeal for the [traditionists]."[9] Thus, according to Ahmed, later Muslims—who revered the hadith traditions of Muhammad—had to deny the historicity of the satanic verses incident in order to support Muhammad's infallibility. This was necessary to ensure he was portrayed as a monotheist both before and after he received the divine revelation. Thus, was Muhammad always a monotheist? Muslims insist he was, although their traditional sources tell a different story.

6. Watt, *Muhammad at Mecca*, 103.
7. Watt, *Muhammad: Prophet and Statesman*, 61.
8. Ahmed, *Before Orthodoxy*, 265.
9. Ahmed, *Before Orthodoxy*, 268–69.

12

What Is Muhammad's Night Journey to Jerusalem and Heaven?

One of the most popular stories about Muhammad is known as the night journey. Muslims view it as a divine miracle. It includes two parts; in the first, Muhammad rides a winged horse-like creature from Mecca to Jerusalem, and in the second, he ascends from Jerusalem to heaven on this mystical creature to meet previous prophets, leads them in a Muslim ritual prayer, then meets Allah in person before descending back to earth. The Muslim tradition gives the winged animal a name, Buraq. In many historical accounts, we read that the night journey occurred immediately after the saga of the satanic verses to boost the morale of Muhammad and the Muslims. Some traditions specify the date as six months prior to Muhammad's hijra (emigration from Mecca to Medina). The story is known among Muslims as the Isra and the Mi'raj, where the Isra refers to the first part of the night journey and the Mi'raj to the second. While both parts form Muhammad's night journey, sometimes Muslims give each event its own name: the night journey and the ascension to heaven. Today's Muslims celebrate it annually as it exemplifies for them a major miracle by Muhammad. While the vast majority of cultural and religious Muslims believe the story narrates an actual physical event, many progressive Muslims argue that it was merely a dream given to encourage Muhammad.[1]

The night journey and the ascent to heaven appear in Muslim traditions as a fascinating event. The narrative begins by describing Muhammad as being sad because his message calling the Meccans to worship Allah and forsake idols was not well received. One night, Muhammad was asleep near the Ka'ba in Mecca. Gabriel came to him, nudged his side three times, and woke him up. Gabriel showed Muhammad a unique creature, Buraq, an animal the traditions describe as winged but also as something between a mule and a donkey. Gabriel and Muhammad mounted Buraq and flew to Jerusalem, and on the way they passed Bethlehem. In Jerusalem, they stopped at the temple and met earlier prophets: Abraham, Moses, and Jesus, among others. Muhammad led them all in ritual prayer, acting as their imam (leader). In what appeared as a test, Gabriel offered three vessels to Muhammad containing milk, wine, and water, respectively. Muhammad rejected the vessel containing wine and took the one of milk and drank from it. Gabriel said to Muhammad, "You have been rightly guided and so will your people be, Muhammad."[2] This portrays Muhammad as being naturally divinely guided. It also concludes the night journey to Jerusalem, the Isra. For Muslims, Muhammad's prayer in Jerusalem and his leadership over the other prophets established Jerusalem as an exclusively Muslim land.

Next, Gabriel and Muhammad ascended to the seven heavens. In each heaven, Gabriel sought permission for Muhammad to enter. In the first heaven, Muhammad met Adam, and they greeted each other. Prophets recognize each other. In the second heaven, Muhammad met Jesus and John the Baptizer, and they exchanged charitable and commending greetings. In the following heavens, Muhammad met with other prophets: Joseph, Idris, Aaron, Moses, and finally Abraham. After Muhammad spoke with Abraham in the seventh heaven, traditions claim, he was taken to an unmatched and unique place beyond a divine veil above the seventh heaven. At this point, Gabriel could not continue to accompany Muhammad, as no one had ever gone there. Beyond the veil, Muhammad

---

1. See Gruber, "Prophet Muḥammad's Ascension," where she provides a thematic study of narratives of Muhammad's reported ascension to heaven. For a Muslim perspective on Muhammad's night journey, see Haykal, *Life of Muḥammad*, 144ff.
    2. Ibn Hisham and Ibn Ishaq, *Life of Muhammad*, 182.

heard a voice shouting, "Allahu Akbar," meaning "Allah is greater." At this point, Muhammad met with Allah and spoke with him. In this meeting, Allah prescribed the duty of ritual prayer for Muslims, instructing Muhammad that Muslims must pray fifty times a day.[3] However, during his descent Muhammad met Moses again, and Moses told him that this number was too much and that he should ascend back to ask Allah for a reduction. Muhammad kept going back and forth between Allah and Moses until the number of prescribed prayers went down to five. Muhammad descended to earth and was then taken back to Mecca.

Since the earliest days of Islam, Muslims have debated whether this journey was an actual physical event or a mere dream or vision. Most traditional Muslims adopt a conventional conservative interpretation. For them, Muhammad journeyed in both soul and body; he was completely awake as he traveled with Gabriel. These traditionalists offer several reasons for their interpretation.[4] Because the miracle impressed every unbeliever, and the Meccan pagans denied its existence, these Muslims claim that it had to be an actual physical event. Traditionalists also assert that the Quran refers to the miracle: "Praise be to him, who took his servant by night, from the sacred mosque to the Aqsa mosque" (Q 17:1). This verse, for them, speaks of a night journey between two mosques—from the one in Mecca to the one in Jerusalem. However, there are problems with their argument. The verse is ambiguous and is linked to Muhammad's supposed journey based only on later exegetical tradition. There is no reference to a location, either Mecca or Jerusalem. Nor does the verse indicate that there was a mosque in Mecca during Muhammad's time—after all, he and his people were reportedly under persecution from the Meccans, unless one assumes that the idol-filled Ka'ba was a sacred place of Muslim worship at that time. Similarly, there was no mosque in Jerusalem at the time, and, historically, the Aqsa Mosque itself was built some sixty years after Muhammad's death. Even the "servant" in the verse is not identified as Muhammad. It might refer to any other person, since the immediate context refers to Moses, Noah, and the Children of Israel (Q 17:2–4).

3. See the entire account of the story in Sahih Muslim, 1.313.
4. Note that a traditionalist refers to a thinker who adopts traditional—usually conservative—views in interpreting the Islamic texts, while a traditionist is a scholar or an expert of the Muslim traditions (i.e., scholar of the hadith).

While some critical thinkers claim that the word *Aqsa* in the verse is anachronistic and that it was later interpolated into the Quran after the building of the Aqsa itself to provide legitimacy, Muslims believe this is the same Aqsa Mosque of today. It is the major reason for the high esteem given to the mosque: Muhammad visited the location. Some read the Arabic word *Aqsa* to mean the farthest mosque, but this does not solve the dilemma of the nonexistent mosques at that time, unless one considers a Jewish temple in Jerusalem to be a Muslim mosque. Furthermore, while the Quran is vague, Muhammad's sira is absolutely clear: it never mentions that Muhammad was taken to a mosque in Jerusalem. Rather, the sira emphasizes twice that Muhammad traveled from Mecca "until he came to Jerusalem's temple" and states that "the apostle and Gabriel went their way until they arrived at the temple at Jerusalem."[5] This is significant, as the earliest accounts we have for Muhammad's life do not indicate a mosque visited by Muhammad in Jerusalem. Finally, if this verse relates to the night journey, why does it not include the supposed ascension to heaven? Was the ascension not important in establishing the five daily prayers for Muslims? In fact, the story about Muhammad receiving the prescription of the ritual prayer in heaven is contradicted by Muhammad's own sira: in the first year of Muhammad's prophetic career, he and his wife Khadija learned the ritual prayer directly from Gabriel. This was about ten years before his supposed ascension to heaven. The sira reveals that Gabriel taught Muhammad the ritual ablution and the right way to pray five times each day, and all the times are listed in the account.[6] Thus, in a sense, the entire story of Muhammad meeting Allah and receiving the fifty prayers, then reducing them to five, appears unneeded and misplaced. Overall, this traditional argument—about a physical miracle, traveling to Jerusalem, and ascending to heaven—does not find traction among Muslim critical thinkers, especially in modern and contemporary circles.

Many modernist and progressive Muslims view the story as a dream or vision, not an actual event. They refer to Muhammad's biography itself, which portrays the event as part of a long dream. Muhammad reportedly said, "I prayed with you the last evening prayer in this valley as you saw. Then I went to Jerusalem and prayed there. Then I have just

5. Ibn Hisham and Ibn Ishaq, *Life of Muhammad*, 182.
6. Ibn Hisham and Ibn Ishaq, *Life of Muhammad*, 112–13.

prayed the morning prayer with you as you see."[7] The entire journey, for these Muslim thinkers, was part of a prophetic dream. To support their argument, they refer to two important reports in the same sira. According to Muhammad's wife Aisha, "The apostle's body remained where it was but God removed his spirit by night."[8] This suggests that the journey was spiritual, not physical. The second report is attributed to Mu'awiya, a major Muslim leader and later caliph: "It was a true vision from God."[9] These reports suggest that the journey was a dream, a vision, or a mere soul activity, not a physical experience. Nonetheless, traditionalist Muslims emphatically dismiss these reports—although they are present in Muhammad's trusted sira—by affirming that at the time of the journey Aisha was very young and Mu'awiya was a pagan idolater. Neither Aisha nor Mu'awiya, according to traditionalists, can be trusted as an authority for denying the physical miracle. This traditionalist claim does not seem to consider that Aisha lived with Muhammad for over ten years afterward and that Mu'awiya met Muhammad and believed in his message years before Muhammad's death. Arguably, Aisha and Mu'awiya could have acquired firsthand knowledge of the journey from Muhammad later. But why is it important to traditionalists that the miracle was physical and not only a dream? The answer is simple: legitimacy.

The journey establishes legitimacy for Jerusalem as a Muslim land and Muhammad as a divinely supported prophet. Consider the time of writing of these Muslim traditions. If the accounts were written in a religious environment full of Christians and Jews, it is plausible that Muslims needed an Islamic claim for Jerusalem to be made in order to compete with earlier claims of legitimacy. If Jews and Christians consider Jerusalem a significant holy city due to their respective histories, Muslims can—the rationale goes—claim the same based on Muhammad's night visit. Moreover, in a religiously mixed context, Muslims needed to portray Muhammad as a performer of supernatural miracles, just as Moses and Jesus were. The story of the night journey to Jerusalem and the ascension to the seven heavens most likely impressed non-Muslims living under Islamic rule. In fact, some scholars believe that the accounts

---

7. Ibn Hisham and Ibn Ishaq, *Life of Muhammad*, 184.
8. Ibn Hisham and Ibn Ishaq, *Life of Muhammad*, 183. See also Haykal, *Life of Muhammad*, 144ff.
9. Ibn Hisham and Ibn Ishaq, *Life of Muhammad*, 183.

in Muhammad's sira were developed both to make sense of the Quran and to address the non-Muslim communities at the time of their writing. In other words, the story of Muhammad's journey was created to explain an ambiguous verse in the Quran and to establish Muhammad's prophetic legitimacy against non-Muslim religious claims. Most Muslims consider the journey to Jerusalem and the ascension to heaven to be Muhammad's most important supernatural miracle. However, there is a major problem: the Quran insists that Muhammad's only miracle was the Quran itself.

Muhammad's lack of miracles is unambiguous in the Quran. It is actually a sign for polytheists and unbelievers who do not believe without miracles. The Quran questions the unbelievers: "Is it not enough of a miracle that we sent down to you this book [the Quran]?" (Q 29:51). The verse responds to Muhammad's enemies skeptically questioning his prophetic talents: "If only miracles could come down to him from his Lord" (Q 29:50). People were unconvinced of Muhammad's prophethood, which we see in various verses. They compared him to Moses: "Why has he not been given the like of that which Moses was given?" (Q 28:48). They said, "Why has no sign been sent down upon him from his Lord?" (Q 6:37). For these skeptical people, other prophets could perform wonders and miracles—why not Muhammad? The Quran emphasizes that Allah did not send Muhammad with miracles because Muhammad was merely "a warner" without a sign (Q 29:50). This verse was in response to unbelievers who rejected Muhammad's message and said, "If only a miracle could come down to him from his Lord (we will then believe)" (Q 13:7; 11:12). Therefore, the Quran is clear about Muhammad's lack of miracles. Surprisingly, the same chapter in the Quran that Muslims use to claim that Muhammad's night journey from Mecca to Jerusalem occurred instead denies that he performed miracles: "What stopped us [Allah] from sending the miracles is that the previous generations have rejected them" (Q 17:59). According to this verse, Allah did not give Muhammad any signs or wonders because they are not effective in convincing unbelievers. Thus, while the Quran clearly and explicitly denies that Muhammad performed miracles, many Muslims, past and present, insist that he did. For Muslims, these miracles include a journey on a winged creature from Mecca to Jerusalem, where he led earlier prophets in prayer before ascending to meet Allah and receive instructions regarding the ritual prayer—instructions given to him by Gabriel ten years earlier.

13

Why Did Muhammad Strike a Peace Treaty with the Jews?

The Muslim traditions divide Muhammad's prophetic career into two parts: the Meccan period (thirteen years) and the Medinan period (ten years). His mission began when he was forty, in Mecca, and ended when he died at age sixty-three, in Medina. After he encountered Gabriel and received the first Quranic revelation in 610, he did not leave his hometown of Mecca for about thirteen years. During these years, traditions reveal, he and his followers were constantly persecuted and mocked by the Meccan pagans. In 613, under severe pressure, the Muslims attempted to emigrate from Mecca to an Arabian city named Ta'if, but they were rejected by its hostile people. In 615, another attempt to escape Mecca was successful, when the Christian kingdom of Abyssinia (today's Ethiopia and its neighboring lands) welcomed the Muslims. A group of about fifteen Muslims emigrated to Abyssinia, but Muhammad remained in Mecca. Around 619, when the satanic verses incident occurred, these emigrants received news of the harmony between the Muslims and the Meccans and thought that the Meccans had converted to Islam and a peace had been reached. Because of this, some of them returned to Mecca, only to find unrest. Despite the reports about Muhammad's night journey in 620, no new followers joined the vulnerable Muslim community. In 621,

Muhammad began to travel to a nearby city named Yathrib, where he had relatives. Muslims later renamed this city Medina, which means "the city"—that is, the city of Muhammad. Between 621 and 622, Muhammad traveled to Yathrib several times to form tribal alliances and ensure that its people would receive him and his followers. These alliances, as described in Muslim accounts, meant that the people of Yathrib would accept Islam. The tradition reveals that Muhammad indeed called them to Islam, and some converted and gave him the oath of support, should he emigrate to Yathrib. In 622, Muhammad took his followers and emigrated to Yathrib, which became known as Medina. This was a very important event in Islamic history, which later became the starting point of the Muslim calendar. In Arabic, the emigration to Medina is called the hijra, and it marks the beginning of the Hijri lunar calendar.

Once Muhammad arrived in Medina, according to traditions, he began to act as a peacemaker. Arab Bedouin tribes tended to fight constantly, and Muhammad sought to form a unified city. He first worked to reconcile rival Arab clans who had lived in Medina for a long time. Many of them accepted Islam, but not all. He also worked diligently to create peace between two groups of Muslims: those who had emigrated with him from Mecca (known as the muhajirun, "emigrants") and those from Medina who had supported him upon his arrival (known as the ansar, "supporters or helpers"). Reconciling the two groups was a strategic move by Muhammad that was necessary in order to create harmony within the Muslim community. Moreover, Muhammad realized there were many Jews in Medina. They had their own religious conviction, which was distinct from that of Muhammad. According to traditions, he called them to Islam, but most of them rejected his call. In his attempt to create a fruitful cooperation between his people and the Jews of Medina, says the tradition, Muhammad struck a treaty known as "The Charter of Medina." Some call it "The Constitution of Medina." In Arabic, it is known as the Sahifa, which simply means "scroll" or "book." Muslims celebrate the Sahifa as the first peace treaty struck by any founder of a world religion and view it as evidence that Muhammad was a prophet of peace.

The Sahifa organizes, defines, and outlines the relationship between the three main groups in Medina: the emigrants, the supporters, and the Jews. The emigrants were Muslims from Mecca who had emigrated to Medina. All were from the Quraysh, the tribe of Muhammad, and were mainly from two families. The supporters were Arabs from Medina who had converted to Islam, and they were from eight clans. The few Jews who signed the Sahifa were from various small clans that had existed in Medina for a long time. These Jews, due to their historical presence in Medina, were a unified group and were the actual dominant power, politically and militarily. It was a strategic move by Muhammad to cooperate with them to ensure receiving their support and loyalty.

The major goal of the Sahifa was to create an alliance between its signers so that they could confront any external aggression against Medina. In a sense, it unified the Muslims and regulated their relationship with their Jewish neighbors. According to the Sahifa, the Jews were not required to convert to Islam as long as they kept the political alliance with the Muslims intact. Dutch historian Arent Jan Wensinck (1882–1939) argues that the Sahifa "is the first evidence of Muhammad's authority in Medina. It becomes immediately apparent that it served purely political ends and that its aims, too, were merely political in nature."[1] This suggests that the Sahifa was not necessarily about religious liberty and mutual coexistence but rather about political stability and consolidation. This is echoed by renowned Israeli historian Mose Gil (1921–2014), who states that the Sahifa "contains little that can be ascribed to the religious sphere."[2] Indeed, one should note that in this early stage of Islam, conversion to Islam did not necessarily require full acceptance of a detailed religious system. It merely meant the show of political loyalty and tribal allegiance to Muhammad. Islam as a religion—like we know it today—was far from being formed. This early "islam" simply meant an agreement of submission to a growing tribal power, not necessarily a sincere belief in religious codes or doctrines.

The Sahifa is celebrated by Muslims as a document of peace and coexistence surviving from the time of Muhammad. Muslims claim that the Sahifa, unlike later Muslim sources, is a direct witness from Muhammad's time. Even some non-Muslim scholars subscribe to this claim. However, they seem to miss an important fact: we know about the Sahifa from two main sources, one by Ibn Ishaq (d. 768), which was later edited by Ibn Hisham (d. 833), and the other by Abu Ubayd (d. 838). This is to say

1. Wensinck, *Muhammad and the Jews of Medina*, 68.
2. Gil, *Jews in Islamic Countries*, 21.

that the report of the Sahifa has reached us by way of Muhammad's sira, which was written by Ibn Ishaq and edited by Ibn Hisham, and a book on Islamic finances, written by Abu Ubayd. Both are products of the ninth century. The Sahifa is not mentioned in any other surviving document from Muhammad's time. Thus, its reliability and authenticity mirror that of the later Muslim sources, written centuries after Muhammad.

The Sahifa defines the people of Muhammad as the "Believers" and the "Muslims," which led some scholars to speculate that the distinction is between those who converted to Islam in Mecca (Believers) and those who did so in Medina (Muslims). However, it is difficult to draw these lines, especially because the text is not clear. What is certain in the text is that the Believers and the Muslims are the people of Muhammad, and together they form one unified umma (community). Scholar Michael Lecker (1951–) argues that the Believers included the Meccan emigrants and some of the Medinan supporters, while "Muslims" refers to some from Medina who converted to Islam.[3]

As for its function, the Sahifa regulates the relationship between the people of Muhammad (Believers and Muslims) and the few Jewish clans who signed it. The Jews who agreed with the Sahifa acted as a nonbelligerent group. According to Muslim interpretations, these Jews enjoyed benefits and rights and also had responsibilities and duties toward the people of Muhammad. The Sahifa also indicates that any group following these Jews—even if the groups were not among the signers—became part of the treaty and thus benefited from the rights and was required to assume the duties. Finally, it is important to note that many people in Medina—including Arab idolators and major Jewish tribes—did not sign the Sahifa. This sheds doubt on the scope of the Sahifa and its implementation, as many pagans and Jews from Medina were excluded.

Muslims celebrate the Sahifa and advance it as a declaration that Islam is a religion of peace. It inspires Islamic pride among the nations because it serves as a landmark of Islam's political and social achievement. They claim that the Sahifa replaced Arab tribalism with the notion of a unified Muslim umma, as it states, "They are one community [umma] to the exclusion of all men."[4] The Sahifa, for Muslims, declared Medina a

3. Lecker, "*Constitution of Medina*," 43–45.
4. The quotations in this paragraph are from Ibn Hisham and Ibn Ishaq, *Life of Muhammad*, 231–33.

state, established Muhammad as its leader, and proved that his people were the best nation brought out for humankind. This is indicated, Muslims argue, in the way the Sahifa elevates religious ties above social and tribal solidarity, unifying new converts who came from different factions. Muslims view the document as a confirmation of safety for Muslims, because it states, "A believer shall not slay a believer for the sake of an unbeliever." This, for Muslims, strengthens their community against any outside attack. They also claim that the Sahifa provided protection for the non-Muslim Jews because it affirms, "To the Jew who follows us belong help and equality." It also guaranteed the Jews' freedom of belief: "The Jews have their religion and the Muslims have theirs." Muslims celebrate these statements as indicating Islam's tolerance and peaceful intent. For them, the Sahifa is a milestone in human history, supporting financial independence for each sect involved: "The Jews shall contribute to the cost of war so long as they are fighting alongside the believers." In every aspect, Muslims highly esteem and cherish the Sahifa, declaring it a political, social, and economic achievement of Islam.

The question of the Sahifa's historicity is vital. If Muhammad actually initiated and signed a peace treaty upon his arrival in Medina in 622, this would have been both a strategic move and an extraordinary initiative—there is no doubt about that. However, such a claim requires evidence of the hijra as well as confidence in the reliability of the documentation of such a treaty. From a scholarly standpoint, there are doubts about both the historicity and the content of the Sahifa. As for its historicity, we know about it only from later Muslim writings—none were contemporary, near-contemporary, or eyewitness accounts. There is no independent witness of the supposed treaty. No one seems to have heard of the Sahifa, let alone seen its fruits of mutual coexistence. The Jews did not appear to have enjoyed harmony or mutual coexistence in Medina. In fact, the documentation of this so-called treaty occurred at a time when there were no Jews at all in Medina. Within five years after Muhammad's alleged signing of the Sahifa, according to Muslim historical accounts, there were no Jews remaining: some were expelled and others were beheaded after Muslims raided their homes. Although the Jewish tribes had dwelled in Medina for centuries and accumulated wealth and power, they were considered disloyal by their Muslim neighbors and thus exiled or eliminated. It appears that the growing power of the Muslim

community was threatened by the Jewish presence in Medina and necessitated their expulsion or extinction. Since they rejected "islam"—that
is, submission—they were no longer welcome in Medina. In a sense, the
Sahifa was a theoretical framework that was never applied.

But there are other problems, problems with the Sahifa's scope and
statements. In addition to skepticism about its application, scholars
voice doubts about the Sahifa's scope, as it excluded the vast majority
of people in Medina, including the three most significant Jewish tribes
and a large number of Arab idol worshipers. If it ever existed, the Sahifa
seems not to have had any substantial goals. Some scholars are skeptical that the Sahifa actually included the Jews.[5] While the scope seems
limited, the content appears problematic and confusing, particularly
because it seems to contradict explicit statements in the Quran and the
hadiths. If the Quran was proclaimed during the same time as the Sahifa,
one would expect them to match each other regarding the treatment of
the Jews. This does not appear to be the case. The Quran instructs the
Muslims, "O you who believe, do not take the Jews and the Christians
as friends. They are but friends to each other. He among you who takes
them for friends is one of them. Allah does not guide the unjust people"
(Q 5:51; see also 2:41; 48:13). It also declares, "You will find the most
hostile of men to the believers are the Jews and the associaters" (Q 5:82;
see also 5:41). These two verses, according to Muslim exegetes, were
proclaimed in Medina. They do not reflect a friendly attitude toward
the Jews, nor do they describe a context of mutual respect and peaceful
coexistence.

As for the hadiths attributed to Muhammad, the matter is similar.
While they too do not match what we find in the Sahifa, there is one important observation about the hadith traditions: they come to us from the
same time as the documentation of the sira, which tells us about the Sahifa.
In other words, the hadith traditions and the sira accounts come from
the same time period, roughly the ninth century onward. They emerged
from the same historical context. One may expect them to paint a similar
picture about coexistence with the Jews, but they do not. The trusted Muslim compiler of Muhammad's hadiths, Imam Muslim (d. 875), reports
that Muhammad declared, "I will expel the Jews and Christians from the

5. See the important discussion in Gil, *Jews in Islamic Countries*, 35–41.

Arabian Peninsula and will not leave any but Muslim."[6] This contradicts the Sahifa. We are also told that Muhammad prophesied, "You will fight against the Jews and you will kill them until even a stone would say: Come here, Muslim, there is a Jew (hiding himself behind me); kill him."[7] This too does not reflect a peaceful treaty aiming to advance mutual coexistence. Similarly, Muhammad is reported to have linked the coming of the last hour with killing the Jews: "The last hour would not come unless the Muslims will fight against the Jews and the Muslims would kill them until the Jews would hide themselves behind a stone or a tree."[8] While most Muslims wholeheartedly believe that Muhammad made these statements, from a critical standpoint, whether he did is not the issue. The point is that they come from the same pool of traditions that produced the Sahifa, and they do not paint the same picture. Thus, the Sahifa and its presumed call for mutual coexistence and religious freedom appear to be in dissonance with explicit statements from the Quran and the hadiths.

If it were ever issued, the Sahifa should be viewed as a remarkable achievement and a strategic initiative. The truth is that its historicity is shrouded in uncertainty. It appears that—even if the treaty were established immediately after the hijra—the Sahifa did not aim for or achieve any major goals. It excluded major Arab tribes as well as Jewish communities. A treaty as such appears to have been largely irrelevant. Muslim histories never state that the Sahifa was applied, not even in a single situation. How could this major treaty have no effect on the relations with the Jews in Medina? In fact, Muslim sources reveal that the vast majority of Jews in Medina were forced from their homes within a few years of the alleged signing of the Sahifa. Was there even a treaty? Was it ever applied? The Muslim sources also explain that Muhammad's community began to grow in power and gain control over the western parts of Arabia by launching raids and expeditions against other Arab tribes. In particular, Muhammad commissioned or led numerous raids against the Meccan pagans of the Quraysh (his own tribe), which forced him and his followers to emigrate to Medina. The study of these raids and their motivations can help the reader understand the context of the early Muslim community and its growing power.

6. Sahih Muslim, 19.4366.
7. Sahih Muslim, 41.6981.
8. Sahih Muslim, 41.6985. The same is mentioned in Bukhari, 4.52.177.

14

Why Did Muhammad Raid the Pagans of Mecca?

Early Muslims defined Muhammad's life as maghazi, which described it as a series of successful military campaigns and incursions. They wrote many works detailing these raids and advancing them as proof of Allah's support for his prophet against the enemies, who were essentially identified as unbelievers. Thus, Muhammad's life is portrayed as a testimony of how the believers overcame the unbelievers in military campaigns. While this description might sound odd today, this is how the classical Muslims depicted the life of their prophet.

According to Muslim histories, Muhammad launched at least twenty-seven military expeditions, all of which occurred after his hijra to Medina. Muhammad personally participated in about ten of them. Muslim authors distinguish between the campaigns he led in person and those he only commissioned, as the former were often larger and achieved more significant results. Yet all these raids are described by Muslim historians as both holy incursions for Allah's cause and legitimate campaigns in Allah's path. After all, Muhammad, in these sources, is Allah's final prophet, who fought infidels, pagans, and non-Muslims in fulfillment of divine prescriptions.

From a critical standpoint, however, it appears that Muhammad continued the pre-Islamic tribal custom of incursions and raids—only this time they were defined as battles for Allah and not for one's own tribe. A warrior in Muhammad's army still sought the spoils of war he used to seek in pre-Islamic times; however, if he died, he would be a martyr for Allah and be rewarded with paradise instead of with a mere memory in some tribal chronicles. As I note elsewhere, "In that early period, Islam unified scattered tribal Bedouins under one banner. Becoming a 'Muslim' probably meant declaring loyalty and adherence to ruling elites, mostly Meccan aristocrats."[1] Although classical Muslim sources describe these military activities as Allah at work, they are better understood as incursions primarily for the purpose of gaining spoils and solidifying tribal power rather than as holy raids for religious causes.

These raids, according to Muslim sources, targeted several non-Muslim communities, including Arab pagan tribes, Jewish communities, and some Christian groups in Northern Arabia. None targeted Muslims. In the end, all Muslims are considered one umma (community); one Muslim cannot wage war against another. The Muslim sources reveal that the majority of Muhammad's campaigns were against his own Meccan tribe, the Quraysh, as they reportedly forced him to leave his hometown and emigrate to Medina. While non-Muslims may describe Muhammad's raids against the Meccans as revenge and retaliation, Muslims avoid such terms. They generally claim them as nonoffensive, religiously driven raids for the purpose of proclaiming Islam. For Muslims, Muhammad never initiated the raids; all were defensive. This is an ideological claim, repeatedly advanced by Muslims throughout history. However, a thorough reading of the Muslim histories does not support this claim. The raids were initiated by the Muslims, and there was no religious proclamation. This is one reason why non-Muslim scholars—and even some Muslim historians—rightly view these battles as tribal raids to gain political dominion and to secure wealth. In a previous publication, I examined Muhammad's major raids as described by the earliest Muslim historians and studied the Muslim conventional claims about them. I concluded, "Contrary to traditional Muslim interpretations, the early Believers did not seem to have marched to war to proclaim Islam, but rather to secure

1. Ibrahim, *Stated Motivations*, 236.

financial resources in the form of booty, ransoms, and possessions," as they "initiated the campaigns to gain hegemony through the subjugation of the Meccan pagans."[2]

While the study of Muhammad's twenty-seven expeditions extends beyond the scope of this short entry, a sample will suffice to highlight some of what the Muslim histories reveal about these military incursions. Without a doubt, one of the earliest major raids led by Muhammad against the pagans of Mecca was the Battle of Badr. Muslims celebrate it as the great victory given by Allah to his prophet, and it took place in Ramadan of the second year after the hijra, 624 CE. The details of how and why the battle took place can be traced in major Muslim sources, such as Muhammad's sira by Ibn Hisham (d. 833) and the historical work of Tabari (d. 923).[3] Ibn Hisham writes of how the battle started: Muhammad heard that the Meccan leader Abu Sufyan "was coming from Syria with a large caravan of Quraysh, containing their merchandise, accompanied by some thirty or forty men."[4] As he realized this was a great opportunity, Muhammad "summoned the Muslims and said, 'This is the Quraysh caravan containing their property. Go out to attack it, perhaps God will give it as a prey.'" Apparently, some of the Muslims were shocked because they realized they would be fighting their own tribe and families. These Muslims were reluctant to participate in the attack because they thought an "apostle would [not] go to war." However, Muhammad encouraged them, emphasizing the Meccans' great amount of merchandise and their scarce number of escorts. While Muhammad exhorted the Muslims to fight the Meccans, the situation was different among the Meccans who were returning with their caravan. The Meccan leader Abu Sufyan realized he could not face Muhammad's army and be victorious. He wanted to avoid war, so he chose a different return route to Mecca and sent a messenger to his Meccan relatives seeking reinforcements. Unlike Abu Sufyan, Muhammad was not ready to abandon such a great chance to accomplish a victory over his Meccan rivals. He told his

2. Ibrahim, *Stated Motivations*, 238; see the detailed discussion of Muhammad's major raids in 66–119. For a Muslim perspective on Muhammad's raids, see Haykal, *Life of Muhammad*, 216–306.

3. See Ibn Hisham and Ibn Ishaq, *Life of Muhammad*, 289ff.; and Tabari, *History*, 7:26ff.

4. Details of the battle that follow are as quoted in Ibn Hisham and Ibn Ishaq, *Life of Muhammad*, 295.

soldiers, "This Mecca has thrown to you the pieces of its liver," meaning, the very best of its people. Muhammad also again reminded them of the ample merchandise and possessions waiting in the Meccan caravan.

Once the Muslims raided the Meccans, it was clear that Muhammad's camp had the advantage. In describing the battle as an act of Allah's divine work against the Meccans, Muslim traditions claim that angels wearing colorful turbans and riding horses appeared in the sky. These angels, Muslim authors claim, emerged from between the mountains and beheaded the Meccan infidels. The angels were so bright that one solider lost his sight. Moreover, Muslim historians describe miracles of Muhammad during the battle. He took dust in his hand and threw it against the Meccans, damaging their eyes, noses, and mouths as they fled. This is one reason why Muslim writers—and Muslims in general—tend to believe that the real actor in this battle was Allah himself. It was he who killed the Meccan pagans: "It appears that the early Muslim narrators found it necessary to add various religious elements, sometimes with exaggeration, in order to portray the victory as a religiously and divinely supported phenomenon."[5] Once the battle was over, disputes erupted among the Muslims, as they disagreed concerning the distribution of the spoils. When Muhammad handed each warrior his share of the booty, an even bigger quarrel occurred as each one sought more. Nonetheless, the reported Muslim victory was phenomenal, and many Meccans were killed. There was so much blood, according to Muslim accounts, that it reached as high as the armpit of Ali, Muhammad's cousin. While we cannot be certain of the accuracy of these reports, this is the account of the Battle of Badr provided by Muslim sources. Although here we examined only one battle reportedly led by Muhammad, this narrative is largely representative of the various raids he led in Medina. However, a few questions remain: Was this battle launched for the purpose of proclaiming Islam? Was it for self-defense? Based on the Muslim histories, the answers to both of these questions appear to be negative. The battle seems to have been a strategic initiative by the Muslims for revenge against the Meccans who had expelled them two years earlier.

While it can be problematic for today's thinkers to consider military campaigns as religious acts, this is the picture early Muslims sought to

5. Ibrahim, *Stated Motivations*, 76.

advance about the raids of Muhammad. Although we cannot be certain of the details of these reports, the vast majority of today's Muslims believe these accounts to be a true description of Muhammad's expeditions. Muslim writers were religious narrators who sought to describe Allah at work for the umma. Describing Muhammad as a warrior leading an army of soldiers did not cause these writers any concern. While the Muslim historical accounts describe raids for tribal dominion and looting, many Muslims, past and present, argue that Muhammad's campaigns were all defensive and motivated by the desire to proclaim the message of Islam. They interpret these raids as proselytism campaigns, which is erroneous and unsupported by the evidence. In my estimation, this argument—that the raids were for the purpose of proclaiming Islam—hurts the cause of Islam greatly, as it rests religious proclamation upon the shedding of the blood of non-Muslims. Some modern and contemporary Muslim thinkers reject the conventional claims about raids under the banner of Islam and instead use nonreligious motives to explain them. Indeed, it is more helpful to view Muhammad's raids as part of the overall tribal incursions of his day rather than linking them with his presumed prophetic career.

15

Was There Ever a Truce between Muslims and Meccans?

Six years after Muhammad arrived in Medina, he already had a strong Muslim tribal base. Muslims were ready to fight for Allah instead of keeping their past tribal commitments. Muhammad was able to defeat his major enemies—the Meccan pagans—in more than one raid, and, to a large extent, he succeeded in controlling the people of Medina under his leadership. In 628, it was a strategic time for a truce between Muhammad and the Meccans. He needed this truce in order to focus on building the Muslim community at Medina, since the Meccans had openly challenged him in various raids. According to Muslim sources, he desired to begin sending Muslim messengers outside Arabia to call non-Muslims to Islam. A truce with the Meccans was tactical: it secured enough time and energy for the Muslims to build up their community and spread their message among non-Muslims, which advanced their influence and expanded their alliances. The truce between the Muslims and the Meccans is known as the Treaty of Hudaybiyya. While it is sometimes called a pact, truce, or treaty, some Muslim sources treat it as an expedition, calling it the Raid of Hudaybiyya and claiming it was a great victory for Muslims.

Hudaybiyya was a place near Mecca where the treaty was signed. The two parties involved in the treaty were Muhammad and the Quraysh. According to Muslim sources, the Meccans were hostile toward Muhammad and his followers and forbade them from performing the hajj (pilgrimage) to Mecca. Through this treaty, Muslims were permitted to access Mecca in the following year to perform the hajj. The treaty also guaranteed there would be no raids between the Muslims and the Meccans for ten years. This was a success for the Muslims. Yet many understand the treaty as a compromise that Muslims had to accept at that time. Specifically, they accepted two major concessions. First, the treaty did not recognize Muhammad as Allah's messenger but merely as a political leader. When Muhammad sought to indicate Allah's name and his role as the messenger of Allah in the treaty, the Quraysh refused. Muhammad yielded to their pressure and signed his name only, without recognition of his prophethood and without affirmation of the Islamic statement, "In the name of Allah, the most gracious, the most merciful." Second, Muhammad conceded that the Meccans who sought to accept Islam must first request and obtain their family's approval and that those Muslims who abandoned Islam would not be forced to remain in Medina—they would be sent unharmed and unopposed to their families in Mecca. Thus, the treaty stipulated a privilege for the Meccans: a Meccan fleeing to Medina must receive consent from his family, while a Muslim abandoning Islam would not be opposed. It appears that the treaty gave the Quraysh freedom and the upper hand. Muslims, according to tradition, were disappointed that Muhammad gave in to such a compromise.

Nonetheless, Muslims generally argue that the treaty was a huge victory for Islam, as the Quraysh treated Muhammad and the Muslims as an equal political opponent. Indeed, the treaty provided Muhammad the chance to focus on other opponents. According to tradition, six months after the treaty, he led a raid against two Jewish settlements outside Medina, defeated them, and secured their wealth. The treaty also gave Muhammad freedom, time, and energy to begin sending messengers to non-Muslims outside Arabia to call them to Islam. The renowned Muslim historian Tabari (d. 923), in a section titled "The Missions to Foreign Rulers," explains how Muhammad sent about fifteen Muslim envoys to various non-Muslim kings and governors, calling them to Islam.[1] The act of calling people to Islam is known as da'wa. The term *da'wa*, which literally means "inviting people in," receives its importance from the example of Muhammad and his attempts to convince foreign leaders of Islam. One of the letters was sent to the Byzantine emperor Heraclius: "In the name of Allah, the most gracious and most merciful. This is from Muhammad, Allah's messenger, to Heraclius, the esteemed of the Romans. Peace to those who follow the right guidance. Convert to Islam, and you shall be spared. Convert to Islam, and Allah will grant you two-fold of your reward. But if you turn away, the transgression of the [past generations] will come upon you. Here."[2]

In response to Muhammad's letter, Muslim traditions claim, Heraclius was convinced of Muhammad's prophethood and Islam and told the Muslim envoy, "I know that your master is a prophet sent (by God) and that it is he whom we expect and find in our book, but I go in fear of my life from the Romans; but for that I would follow him."[3] While there is no independent evidence to prove that Muhammad actually sent the letter, or that Heraclius responded in the above way, the Muslim tradition—written centuries after Muhammad—presents this example as a case for Islam's hegemony and success in persuading Christian emperors. We are told that Heraclius recognized Muhammad's prophethood because he was expecting Muhammad to come in fulfillment of what Heraclius found in his Bible. This narrative is repeated in many Muslim traditions. It aims, at best, to persuade Christians and Jews who lived centuries after Muhammad of his message and, at worst, to establish the corruption of the Bible, since it includes no mention of Muhammad. Muhammad's letter to Heraclius is an example of many he reportedly sent to non-Muslim rulers, including the Persian emperor, the king of Ethiopia, and the ruler of Egypt. Some rulers accepted Islam, and others rejected it.

The Treaty of Hudaybiyya was a strategic truce that opened the door for Muhammad to focus on other matters after six years of continuous fighting with the Meccans. It reduced the hostility between the Meccans

1. Tabari, *History*, 8:98ff.
2. The translation is mine based on the original Arabic. See Tabari, *History*, 8:104; and Ibn Hisham and Ibn Ishaq, *Life of Muhammad*, 655. For a discussion and resources on da'wa, see chap. 20.
3. Ibn Hisham and Ibn Ishaq, *Life of Muhammad*, 656.

and the Muslims and provided Muhammad and his followers "enough
time, power, and resources to strengthen their Medinan community."[4] It
was a few months after the treaty, Muslim sources reveal, that Muhammad executed his successful campaign against two Jewish settlements
outside Medina. Two years later, Muslims accused the Meccans of break-
ing the treaty, and Muhammad victoriously launched his conquest of
Mecca, which made him the sole ruler of West Arabia.

4. Ibrahim, *Stated Motivations*, 86.

16

Did Muhammad Really Fight the Jews?

Muhammad's biography emphasizes that his raids had two major targets: the pagans of Mecca and the Jews of Medina and its neighboring Jewish settlements. All of his raids began after he emigrated from Mecca to Medina. His raids against the pagans of Mecca included three of significance: (1) the Battle of Badr, in which the Muslims defeated the Meccans in the second year after the hijra; (2) the Battle of Uhud—only one year after Badr—in which the pagans of Mecca defeated the Muslims and Muhammad was injured and almost died; and (3) the conquest of Mecca—five years after Uhud—in which Muhammad returned victoriously from Medina to Mecca, leading a marvelous campaign and declaring himself the sole leader of Western Arabia.[1] As for the Jews, the Muslim sources reveal that there were three major tribes in Medina—the Qaynuqa, Nadir, and Qurayza—in addition to two Jewish settlements on the outskirts of Medina: Khaybar and Fadak. Within a seven-year period after the emigration to Medina, Muhammad effectively eliminated the Jewish presence in these lands. According to Muslim sources, the Jews

1. For a detailed discussion of these three raids, see Ibrahim, *Stated Motivations*, 69–97. For a Muslim perspective, see Ahmad, *Muhammad and the Jews*; and Haykal, *Life of Muḥammad*, 322ff.

in the area were evil and hypocrites. They did not deserve peace, as they never accepted Muhammad's religious message. He could not trust them to be neighbors in Medina or around it, as he knew their wicked schemes and how they sought to kill him.

Two years after his arrival in Medina (AH 2, meaning the second year after the hijra), Muhammad dealt with the first Jewish tribe, the Qaynuqa. According to Muslim tradition, the Jews of this tribe were wicked and violators of the peace in Medina. Muhammad marched with his companions to raid the tribe. Muslims refer to this as a raid against the sons of Qaynuqa. Muhammad met their chiefs in the market, threatened them with his vengeance, and called them to accept Islam. They declared they were Jews, refused his message, and said they did not fear fighting. The Muslim sources reveal a random yet consequential incident that occurred immediately after this meeting: an unnamed Jew assaulted an Arab woman by lifting up her dress; consequently, a Muslim man murdered that Jew in revenge. In response, the Jews of the tribe killed the Muslim man. This incident led the Muslims to raid the tribe of Qaynuqa. Although the first person killed in the dispute was a Jew, the Muslims declared the Jews to be violators of the political peace treaty. It appears that for the Muslims, lifting up a woman's dress was considered a violation of a political arrangement. Muhammad commanded his companions to lay siege against the tribe. Fifteen days later, the Jews lost all hope of resistance. They surrendered, and Muhammad ordered their expulsion from their properties and businesses.[2] As is usually true in the Muslim sources, the Jews are depicted as evil and as unfaithful to covenants and treaties. It seems a random story was created in order to allow the Muslims to expel the Jews.

One year after the expulsion of the Jews of the Qaynuqa, the Muslims addressed the second Jewish clan, the Nadir. Muslim sources report that in the year AH 3—after the Meccan pagans defeated the Muslims in the Battle of Uhud—the Muslims were concerned about the loyalty of their Jewish neighbors. They needed to ensure that the Jews would not take advantage of the Muslim defeat at Uhud and rebel against them. In what appears to have been an attempt to regain power and secure his com-

2. The raid of the Qaynuqa took place in (AH 2/624 CE), after Badr and before Uhud.

munity, Muhammad issued a decree expelling the Jews of the Nadir clan from their homes. The decree came after Muhammad received a message from heaven warning him that the Jews were plotting to kill him—while he was surrounded by his companions—by throwing a huge rock from the roof on his head. Because of the Jews' treachery and disloyalty, according to Muslim traditions, Muhammad instructed his followers to raid the tribe of Nadir. Consequently, the Muslims marched against the tribe, plundered their possessions, and burned their homes and their palm trees. The Jewish tribe surrendered and evacuated their homes, leaving not only their land but also their gold, silver, and weapons.

According to Muslim histories, Muhammad's decree expelling the Nadir from Medina came after he called for the assassination of two of their chiefs, Ka'b and Abu Rafi'. According to Muslim traditions, these two Jews were haters of Muhammad who deserved death because they insulted him and exhorted his enemies to fight the Muslims.[3] Their actions and Muhammad's response reflect the enmity between the Muslims and the Jews in Medina. In the end, Muhammad and the Muslims successfully eliminated the second Jewish tribe from Medina. While the Muslim sources justify the expulsion of the Jews from Medina by depicting them as hypocrites and initiators of offense, scholars view the Muslim-Jewish tension in Medina differently. It is plausible to argue that expelling the second Jewish tribe was a strategic move by Muhammad after his defeat at Uhud. It was important for the Muslims to regroup and consolidate power. The Jews were a threat to the growing power of the Muslim community from within Medina, as the Jews did not want to accept Muhammad's message or leadership. Moreover, their presence, with their holy book and their wealth—which they accumulated over the years in Medina—made it difficult for the two camps to coexist. The Muslims needed to secure the religiopolitical exclusivity of their community, and the presence of the Jews was not helpful. They had to be expelled. While this is evident in the cases of the first two tribes, the Qaynuqa and the Nadir, it is even clearer in the case of the third major Jewish tribe, the Qurayza.

Two years after the expulsion of the Nadir clan, the Muslims targeted the Qurayza in AH 5. Muslim tradition highlights the raid against the

3. For the story of Ka'b, see Bukhari, 5.59.369. As for that of Abu Rafi', see Bukhari, 5.59.371. See also Ibn Hisham and Ibn Ishaq, *Life of Muhammad*, 364ff.

Qurayza as subsequent to another battle named the Battle of the Trench (or of the Confederates), in which the Muslims defeated a coalition of non-Muslims. The sources describe Allah granting the Muslims victory over the confederates and, immediately after, giving Muhammad a revelation instructing him to march against the Jews of the Qurayza. In accordance with Allah's command, the Muslims besieged the Qurayza for about a month while Allah cast terror in the Jews' hearts. The Jews surrendered and promised to leave their town. However, Muhammad identified them as deceptive, disloyal, and unreliable. According to traditions, Muhammad refused to let them go unpunished for their hypocrisy and wickedness. He asked them to accept the judgment of one of their own named Sa'd. They agreed, thinking Sa'd would be merciful because he was one of them, not knowing that Sa'd had already accepted Islam and was a loyal member of Muhammad's community. Sa'd judged that "the men should be killed, the property divided, and the women and children taken as captives."[4] The Muslim traditions reveal that to execute this judgment, Muhammad ordered the digging of trenches and the beheading of the Jewish men in those trenches. In addition to all the men, Muhammad instructed the killing of "all those [males] with pubic hair."[5] This resulted in the beheading of "600 or 700 in all, though some put the figure as high as 800 or 900."[6] After killing the men, Muhammad divided the property, women, and children of the Qurayza clan among the Muslims. Muslim tradition reveals that he also sold some of the captive women in exchange for horses and weapons. Finally, Muhammad selected one of the Jewish women, Rayhana, as his wife, "although she refused to quit Judaism to convert to Islam."[7]

The raid against the Qurayza clan received attention in secondary studies by Muslims and non-Muslims alike. Some self-identified Muslims call it massacre and butchery yet argue that despite the aggressiveness of the raid, it was in harmony with the customs of seventh-century Arabia. Other Muslims claim the incident never occurred but was later fabricated

---

4. Ibn Hisham and Ibn Ishaq, *Life of Muhammad*, 464. See also Kister, "Massacre of the Banū Qurayẓa," 96.

5. Baladhuri, *Origins of the Islamic State*, 41.

6. Ibn Hisham and Ibn Ishaq, *Life of Muhammad*, 464.

7. Ibrahim, *Stated Motivations*, 93. Rayhana was a concubine, but some Muslims still identify her as one of his wives.

and inserted into the Muslim sources by wicked Jews to portray Muhammad unfavorably. Some non-Muslims, on the other hand, consider it genocide and study it as "a tribal incursion to gain hegemony and secure resources like any other pre-Islamic raid."[8] Many non-Muslims view the Qurayza raid not only as a tribal conflict that led to a military campaign but also as the natural result of Jewish-Muslim religious tension. Tor Andræ (1885–1947) argues that for the Muslims, "the Jews were the sworn enemies of Allah and His revelation."[9] It appears that a variety of political and religious reasons motivated the raid. However, some scholars doubt these reports entirely. Because of the late date of documentation for these sources and the contradictions within, we cannot be certain that these events actually occurred. Some scholars assume that these stories were forged for religious and political reasons relevant to the time of their writing and do not record actual events. While we cannot be certain whether the raids actually occurred, we can be sure that these Muslim accounts have for centuries affected the mutual relations between Muslims and Jews because they were taken to be prescriptive, not descriptive.

With the elimination of the third major Jewish clan, the Muslim community seems to have had no major rivals left within Medina. Scholars observe that Muslims "were growing in power and wanted to keep the Hijaz free from the Jews, after having vanquished and expelled the three leading tribes."[10] According to Muslim traditions, only two more Jewish settlements—Khaybar and Fadak—remained in the neighboring region outside Medina. Consequently, Muhammad led two campaigns against them after defeating the Qurayza. The raid on Khaybar is described by a major Muslim historian as a military invasion: "The Prophet invaded Khaybar in the year 7."[11] As Muhammad marched to Khaybar, he "seized the property piece by piece and conquered the forts one by one as he came to them."[12] When Muhammad arrived at Khaybar, he shouted a victorious declaration, "Allahu Akbar. Khaybar is ruined."[13]

8. Ibrahim, *Stated Motivations*, 93.
9. Andræ, *Mohammed*, 155.
10. Ibrahim, *Stated Motivations*, 95.
11. Baladhuri, *Origins of the Islamic State*, 42; see also Ibn Hisham and Ibn Ishaq, *Life of Muhammad*, 510ff.
12. Ibn Hisham and Ibn Ishaq, *Life of Muhammad*, 511.
13. Sahih Muslim, 8.3325.

The religious phrase "Allahu Akbar" frightened the Jews. Muhammad summoned their chief, Kinana, and demanded the treasure that the Nadir clan had hidden at Khaybar. When Kinana said he knew nothing about such a treasure, Muhammad ordered a search of the lands until the Muslims found it. He also accused Kinana of treachery and disloyalty and ordered his death. The death sentence was accomplished by two Muslim men. According to Ibn Hisham, "[The first man] kindled a fire with flint and steel on [Kinana's] chest until he was nearly dead. Then the apostle delivered him to [the second] and he struck off his head."[14] Murdering Kinana secured a big victory for the Muslims over the Jews of Khaybar. Additionally, the Muslim sources highlight Kinana's beautiful wife, Safiyya, as having desired to marry Muhammad because he was growing in power as the king of West Arabia. Once Kinana was killed, Safiyya was given to Muhammad as his wife, and she "was brought to him along with another woman."[15]

Various Muslim traditions reveal that after suppressing Khaybar, Muhammad kept all property and possessions for himself.[16] When some of Muhammad's companions acted lawlessly and disgracefully by raping Jewish women, including some who were pregnant, he rebuked these Muslims and condemned their actions. Once Khaybar fell, the other Jewish settlement, Fadak, surrendered without a fight: "When the people of Fadak heard of what had happened they sent to the apostle asking him to let them go and to spare their lives and they would leave him their property, and he did so."[17] In some Muslim traditions, all property from the people of Fadak was given to Muhammad himself.[18]

While cultural and religious Muslims commonly believe these stories about the negative characterization and harsh treatment of the Jews, a number of modernist and progressive Muslims contextualize the accounts, claiming that they had their own historical circumstances and that they cannot be prescriptive for Muslim-Jewish relations in our day. Although Muslims in past centuries repeatedly used these accounts to

14. Ibn Hisham and Ibn Ishaq, *Life of Muhammad*, 515; and Ibn Hisham, 3.1564. See also Ibn Hisham, 3.1547–1548.
15. Ibn Hisham and Ibn Ishaq, *Life of Muhammad*, 514.
16. Ibn Hisham and Ibn Ishaq, *Life of Muhammad*, 515.
17. Ibn Hisham and Ibn Ishaq, *Life of Muhammad*, 515.
18. For more references, see Ibrahim, *Stated Motivations*, 95.

make sweeping decisions about Jewish-Muslim relations, some Muslims today—especially in the West—reject these stories entirely and argue that they never took place. While we cannot determine whether these incidents occurred, it is plausible to argue that their documentation in Muslim historical accounts—several centuries after Muhammad—was driven by the religious and political necessities of the day. So if these are the Muslim accounts about raids against the Jews, what about the Christians? Did Muhammad ever target Christian communities? This is discussed next.

17

Did Muhammad Launch Raids against Christians?

Muhammad's raids had two major targets: the Meccan pagans and the Medinan Jews. According to Muslim sources, Muhammad successfully overcame the Meccans and the Jews by the year AH 8. Thus, he became the sole leader of the region of West Arabia, known as the Hijaz. Muslim traditions place his death in AH 11 and claim that between the years 8 and 11 he launched several raids against the Christian lands controlled by the Byzantine Empire in Northwest Arabia. Three of these raids appear unique in the Muslim sources: the raid against Mu'ta in AH 8, the raid against Tabuk in AH 9, and the raid against Syria in AH 11. Many scholars voice doubts about these raids because the extant accounts of them exaggerate the military power of both the Muslims and the Christian Byzantines and are therefore hard to believe. However, ample Muslim sources describe these raids in some detail.[1]

According to tradition, in AH 8 Muhammad sent a Muslim envoy to the village of Mu'ta, located in North Arabia, east of the Jordan River.

1. See Ibn Hisham and Ibn Ishaq, *Life of Muhammad*, 531ff. (on Mu'ta); 602ff. (on Tabuk); 652 (on Usama's expedition to Greater Syria). See also Buhl, "Mu'ta," 7:756–57. For a Muslim perspective on Mu'ta, see Haykal, *Life of Muḥammad*, 416–23. For a study on Mu'ta and Tabuk, see Gabriel, *Muḥammad*, 152–204.

A Christian man from the Ghassanid tribe at Mu'ta killed the envoy. In response, Muhammad sent three thousand soldiers to fight "the Christian Arabs there."[2] These Arabs were of the Ghassanid tribe, which was supported and controlled by the tremendous Byzantine Empire. The Muslim sources claim that two hundred thousand men were led by their great Byzantine emperor Heraclius. Muhammad did not participate in the raid himself. In the battle, Muslim commanders were portrayed as courageous, and they succeeded—by Allah's intervention—in combating the military power of the Byzantines, who were forced to flee from the fighting. The accounts are ambiguous and do not indicate an outright victory for the Muslims, but nonetheless, they were reportedly not defeated. We are told that 3,350 Christians were killed, but only 12 Muslims died in battle, including Muhammad's former adopted son, Zayd. While Muslims generally claim this raid a victory, some are doubtful and describe it as a defeat. Still, many scholars do not believe this raid actually occurred. They view the account of the raid on Mu'ta with skepticism because the Byzantine Empire was far more powerful than the Arab Bedouins and therefore unlikely to be defeated by them. A raid such as this would have been suicide for Muslims. In evaluating the account, one scholar observes, "The tendency of the [Muslim] stories to describe the dangers of the expedition and the overwhelming nature of the opposing force as very great in order to put the unfortunate result of the battle in a better light is quite evident."[3]

In the year AH 9, one year after Mu'ta, Muhammad prepared a raid against the Arab Christians in Tabuk, a town in Northwest Arabia. Some Muslim sources describe the raid as a defensive, preventive battle because Muhammad "had heard the Byzantines and Arab tribes were assembling."[4] He wanted to defend Medina. Other Muslim sources describe it as a defensive jihad raid to fulfill the Quranic verse, "O believers, the associators are definitely unclean—they shall not be allowed to come near the Sacred Mosque" (Q 9:28). Some Muslim exegetes describe it as a fulfillment of the Quranic call to "fight those who do not believe

2. Buhl, "Mu'ta," 7:756.
3. Buhl, "Mu'ta," 7:756.
4. Bakhit, "Tabūk," 10:50. For a detailed account in a primary source, see Sahih Muslim, 30.5662. For a Muslim perspective on Tabuk, see Haykal, *Life of Muhammad*, 476ff.

from among those who received the scripture" (Q 9:29). Overall, Muslim traditions claim that Muhammad sought to defend his community, although there is no indication that the Byzantines had launched any attack against the Muslims.[5]

Tabuk is considered Muhammad's last military expedition. Muslim sources reflect many Muslims' reluctance to march to Tabuk; consequently, a Quranic verse was revealed to Muhammad that rebuked them: "They have turned men away from [Allah's] Way—evil is that which they do" (Q 9:9). Some believe that in the last days of Muhammad's life, Muslims were far from unified as internal dissent grew among them due to fighting about the wealth accumulated from their raids. Still, Muslim sources claim that Muhammad succeeded in gathering thirty thousand Muslim warriors, and they fought forty thousand Christians (Arabs and Byzantines). The battle did not last long, as Allah confused the Byzantines, who were distracted and scattered. Even the allies of the Byzantines, according to Muslim sources, forsook them and sought to support the Muslims. Overall, it appears that Muhammad did not face any major power at Tabuk and that the raid's goals were limited. Nonetheless, he received a clear statement of submission from some Arab chiefs in Northern Arabia, who agreed to pay the jizya (a special tax imposed on non-Muslims by Muslim rulers).

In the year 11, a few months before Muhammad's death, he reportedly ordered the Muslims "to make an expedition to Syria" and assigned an eighteen-year-old man, Usama, to lead the army. The goal of the expedition was to invade the southeastern regions of the Byzantine Empire. In particular, we are told that Muhammad wanted to avenge the loss of the twelve Muslims who had died in the raid on Mu'ta, including Usama's father, Zayd. This is one reason Muhammad put Usama in command of the army; however, some of the older Muslims, especially from among the emigrants, disapproved of Muhammad's choice because they despised Usama. In fact, two close companions of Muhammad—Abu Bakr and Umar, who later became the first two successors of Muhammad—resisted joining Usama's army because of his young age. In response, Muhammad rebuked them and insisted that the young man would remain the army's leader, affirming, "[Usama] is the

5. Bakhit, "Tabūk," 10:50–51. See also Tabari, *History*, 9:47ff.

most beloved of all people to me."[6] As Usama's army began marching to Syria, news erupted that Muhammad was dying. Usama paused the move, and Muhammad died a few days later. Thus, the expedition did not march to Syria while Muhammad was alive. Once Abu Bakr became the first successor of Muhammad, his first decision was to dispatch Usama's army in fulfillment of Muhammad's wish.[7]

These three incidents describe Muslim attempts to reach the Byzantine Empire during Muhammad's lifetime. However, they do not seem convincing as successful campaigns, although the Muslim sources paint these military activities as defensive, preventive, and—for the most part—successful under Allah's support. They conclude the brief study of Muhammad's life at Medina, during which he reportedly launched raids against Meccan pagans, Medinan Jews, and Arab Christian tribes outside Medina and on the Syrian frontier. When Muhammad died, Muslims were not unified. According to the vast majority of Sunni Muslims, Muhammad did not appoint a successor, although Shiites believe he did. After his death, Muslims began an age of caliphates. While it is important to study Muhammad's successors, we should first ask: How did Muhammad die? Or, as some ask, Who killed Muhammad?

6. Bukhari, 5.59.744.
7. For an account of Usama's expedition, see Ibrahim, *Stated Motivations*, 139ff. For the raids discussed in this section, see Gabriel, *Muhammad*, 152–203.

18

Who Killed Muhammad?

Muslim traditions generally agree that Muhammad did not die a natural death. He was killed—specifically, poisoned.[1] However, Muslims disagree concerning who killed him. Traditions adopted by Sunni Muslims advance a famous account stating that a Jewish woman from Khaybar poisoned a sheep and presented it as a cooked dinner for Muhammad. After he ate, the poison's effects appeared on his body and remained in his blood for about three years, until he died.[2] Shiites, on the other hand, generally believe that two of Muhammad's wives conspired to kill him.[3]

1. A case for poisoning by evil Jews is made in the following article, Islam Question & Answer, "The Jews' Attempts to Kill the Prophet," December 18, 2002, https://islamqa.info/en/answers/32762/the-jews-attempts-to-kill-the-prophet-peace -and-blessings-of-allaah-be-upon-him. This conservative Muslim website discusses several attempts by Jews to kill Muhammad based on Muslim classical sources. For non-Muslim studies, see Watt, *Muhammad at Medina*, 54, 234; Rodinson, *Muhammad*, 254; and Szilágyi, "After the Prophet's Death."

2. See Ibn Hisham and Ibn Ishaq, *Life of Muhammad*, 210, 516; Bukhari, 3.47.786; Sahih Muslim, 26.5430; and Sunan Abi Dawud, 40.4494, 4497. For reports on Muhammad's death, see Nagel, *Muhammad's Mission*, 148–58. See also Faizer, "Ibn Isḥāq and al-Wāqidī Revisited," where the author concludes, "Three years later, however, [Muhammad] dies a martyr from that very poison, which was surely a fine note on which to conclude the life of this 'most heroic of Prophets'" (126).

3. Here I rely on the Shiite classical work of Muhammad ibn Masʿud al-Ayyashi (d. 932), *Tafsīr*, 1:200; and the magnum opus of the Shiite hadith traditions by

In the accepted Sunni tradition, after Muhammad raided Khaybar and ordered the killing of its chief, Kinana, the Jews surrendered. When he sat down to rest after the battle, a wicked Jewess named Zaynab approached him and offered to cook him a meal, and he accepted. She prepared roast lamb. She asked his companions which joint of lamb Muhammad preferred. They relayed it was the shoulder. Zaynab was full of hate toward Muhammad because of what he had done to her people and the murder of Kinana. She poisoned the whole lamb and added more poison in its shoulder. When she brought it, Muhammad ate from it. Muslim reports differ concerning whether he swallowed it or not. Some reports claim that Muhammad "took hold of the shoulder and chewed a morsel of it, but he did not swallow it," as he declared, "This bone tells me that it is poisoned." However, other reports claim that on his deathbed—three years later—he clearly referred to this lamb as the reason for his poisoning and deadly pain: "This is the time in which I feel a deadly pain from what I ate . . . at Khaybar." This is why Sunni Muslims commonly attribute Muhammad's death to a Jewish scheme and believe that Muhammad "died as a martyr."[4]

Shiite Muslims mock these Sunni claims and argue that Muhammad was not so naive as to accept a meal from a Jewess, especially after he defeated and murdered her people. For many Shiite scholars, Muhammad was poisoned by two of his wives, Aisha and Hafsa.[5] Aisha was Abu Bakr's daughter, and Hafsa was Umar's daughter. Abu Bakr and Umar, according to Shiite claims, conspired with their daughters to kill Muhammad, especially after Muhammad assigned the young Usama—whom Abu Bakr and Umar despised—as commander of the military expedition to Syria. Shiites believe Muhammad was killed by his two wives and their fathers, who became Muhammad's first two successors—that is, caliphs. According to the Shiite exegete Qummi (d. 920), Muhammad prophesied to Hafsa that Abu Bakr and Umar would succeed him forcibly. Hafsa

Muhammad Baqir al-Majlisi (d. 1699), *Biḥār al-anwār*, 22:516; 31:641; as well as the modern study Habib, *Obscenity*, 455ff., and compare with Sunni traditions in Bukhari, 5.59.735; 7.71.610; 9.83.25, 35.

4. See the discussion of these conflicting reports in Ibn Hisham and Ibn Ishaq, *Life of Muhammad*, 516.

5. Qummi, *Tafsīr*, 2:376; Ayyashi, *Tafsir*, 1:200; and Majlisi, *Biḥār*, 22:516; 31:641. For the importance of the "poisoning" narratives in Shiite Islam and how they convey grief, martyrdom, and hope, see Pierce, "Remembering the Infallible Imams," 220ff.

told Aisha, and they informed the two men, who came together and joined efforts to poison him.[6] Contemporary Shiite scholar Yasser al-Habib (1979–) provides ample references from Sunni and Shiite sources to support his argument that Aisha was the "head of infidelity" who planned to poison Muhammad. For al-Habib, the ambitious and wicked Aisha conspired with her father, Abu Bakr, to forcefully steal power.[7]

While these views mostly flourish among Shiites, some Sunni authorities admit the existence of such reports yet deny them. The renowned Sunni Muslim traditionist (hadith scholar) Ibn Hazm (995–1064) reports that some Muslims believed that Abu Bakr, Umar, Uthman, and Talha (four major Meccan companions) conspired to kill Muhammad after the Battle of Tabuk.[8] In fact, from a trusted Sunni hadith in Sahih Bukhari, it appears that Umar refused to allow Muhammad to write his will on his final day. On his deathbed, Muhammad was surrounded by some of his people, so he said, "Come, let me write for you a statement after which you will not go astray." In response, Umar refused and told everyone that Muhammad "is seriously ill and you have the Qur'an; so the Book of Allah is enough for us." Unsurprisingly, Umar's statement created confusion, as some people in the house agreed with him while others sought to hear what Muhammad wanted to say. However, Muhammad just sighed and said, "Go away!"[9] These Sunni traditions suggest that Umar was not in harmony with Muhammad and that some of the companions wanted to stop Muhammad from speaking about the future of the Muslim community after his death.

The same can be said about Aisha, as she reportedly acted against Muhammad's wishes, according to some Sunni hadiths. Although Muhammad instructed his companions, "Don't pour medicine into my mouth," Aisha reported, "We poured medicine into the mouth of the Prophet during his ailment," and, "When he improved and felt better he said, 'There is none of you but will be forced to drink medicine.'"[10] Although this hadith is ambiguous, it reflects not only how people around Muhammad ignored his instructions but also Muhammad's own desire

6. Qummi, *Tafsīr*, 2:376.
7. Habib, *Obscenity*, 769–72.
8. Ibn Hazm, *Al-Muḥallā*, 12:160.
9. Bukhari, 7.70.573. See also Sahih Muslim, 13.4016.
10. Bukhari, 9.83.25.

to ensure that those in the room with him would taste the substance that he received against his will. This may support the Shiite claims regarding Muhammad's murder by his own companions. Problematically, there are many Sunni traditions about forcing "medicine" in Muhammad's mouth on his deathbed.[11] Referring to these Sunni traditions, Shiites claim that the "medicine" was actually a poison and that this is why Muhammad rejected it, while Sunnis argue that he rejected it merely because he was ill. Still, there is a Shiite minority who does not completely reject the possibility that Muhammad was poisoned by someone other than Aisha.

While it is impossible to determine whether the Sunni or the Shiite claim is true, the Sunni narrative appears to have some obvious gaps in it. Even if one ignores the tendency of Muslim traditions to blame the Jews for evildoings and mischief, there are still unanswered questions related to the Sunni claims about the Jewess who poisoned Muhammad. The Sunni narrative requires us to believe that poison remained in Muhammad's blood for at least three years (the Khaybar poisoning was in AH 7, and Muhammad died in AH 11). In fact, Ibn Hisham writes in Muhammad's sira that a man who ate from the same lamb died immediately.[12] If Muhammad indeed ate from the lamb but spat it out without swallowing, why was he affected by the poison at the end of three years and not sooner? How can a poison take three years to be effective? Muhammad is reported to have said to his wife Aisha, "I still feel the pain caused by the food I ate at Khaybar, and at this time, I feel as if my aorta is being cut from that poison."[13] Thus, he appears to have been truly affected by the poison in the cooked meal. Why was he unaware of the poison before he ate from the meal, especially as Muslim traditions insist on his prophetic abilities in knowing the unseen? Even the Jewess Zaynab reportedly said to Muhammad after she poisoned him, "You know what you have done to my people. I said to myself, 'If he is a king I shall ease myself of him and if he is a prophet he will be informed (of what I have done).'"[14] While this indicates the intention of revenge on the part of the Jewess, it does not support the traditional Muslim claims about Muhammad's prophetic capabilities. In the end,

11. Bukhari, 5.59.735; 7.71.610; 9.83.25, 35.
12. Ibn Hisham and Ibn Ishaq, *Life of Muhammad*, 516.
13. Bukhari, 5.59.713.
14. Ibn Hisham and Ibn Ishaq, *Life of Muhammad*, 516.

he was affected by the poison he consumed in this meal. Furthermore, if, according to traditions, the lamb shoulder did tell Muhammad it was poisoned, why did it not tell him before he ate from it so that he would not be affected?

But there is a deeper problem with this Sunni version if we consult the Quran. According to the Quran, Muhammad was promised, "Allah will certainly shelter you from the people" (Q 5:67). If Allah promised to protect Muhammad, it is problematic that a Jewish woman was able to evade this divine protection and kill Muhammad. Moreover, the way by which Muhammad died creates a huge problem if we continue examining more Quranic verses. In a Quranic passage, Allah warns, "If [Muhammad] had invented concerning Us any sayings, We would have definitely seized him by the right hand and cut off his aorta (life artery)" (Q 69:44–46). Thus, Muhammad should have expected a painful death—such as the cutting of his main artery—if he forged any false sayings about Allah. Surprisingly, on his deathbed, Muhammad reportedly said to his wife Aisha, "I feel as if my aorta is being cut from that poison."[15] This hadith creates confusion if we contrast it with the Quranic claim about the aorta being cut as a punishment. Did Muhammad falsify statements and receive divine punishment? If not, why was he killed in a way that the Quran describes as the result of forging false statements about Allah?

Due to these critical observations, many scholars tend to agree more with the Shiite version of Muhammad's death. The Shiite claim appears plausible, especially when we consider that Sunni and Shiite sources reveal a struggle for power on the day of Muhammad's death.[16] However, the notion that a divinely sent prophet died in such a way appears to contradict Islamic claims of divine protection and prophetic ability.[17] This is why many modern Muslims began to reject the entire story of Muhammad's death and instead claim he died naturally.[18] In doing so,

15. Bukhari, 5.59.713.
16. Ouardi, *Les derniers jours de Muhammad*, focuses on the last three days of Muhammad's life and studies schemes led by Muhammad's companions to kill him.
17. For an excellent overview of the literature on Muhammad's death and how the topic of poisoning Muhammad was later used by Christians in conversations with Muslims, see Szilágyi, "After the Prophet's Death."
18. See the study by feminist Muslim scholar Kecia Ali, *Lives of Muhammad*, 22, where she dismisses the poisoning traditions and calls those accounts relying on

they had to reject the traditional narrative that was built on the hadiths and the sira accounts. For these Muslims, Muhammad could not have died due to a plot by any human. He was protected and divinely guided. Still, if they discredit the hadiths and the sira, how can they deal with the other accounts found in these trusted sources of Islam? This is a difficult question, and the answer is uncertain.

---

it "hostile accounts," because the "poisoning by a Jewish woman allows critics to view Muhammad as bereft of God's protection and therefore clearly not what he claimed to be."

19

Did Muhammad Appoint a Successor?

On the day of Muhammad's death, in a controversial move, Abu Bakr became his first successor—that is, caliph. The Muslim sources differ greatly in their portrayal of Abu Bakr's appointment. Shiite Muslims believe that Abu Bakr—with the support of Umar (who later became the second caliph)—seized power against Muhammad's wishes. For Shiites, Ali was the legitimate successor of Muhammad not only because he was the first male to convert to Islam, which indicates his piety and devotion, but also because Muhammad had actually appointed him to lead the Muslims religiously and politically. Sunnis, on the other hand, claim that Muhammad never appointed Ali, nor was Ali actually the first convert to Islam—Abu Bakr was the first to believe and trust Muhammad. While the Sunni and Shiite sources dispute the identity of Muhammad's legitimate successor, they agree on one matter: in Muhammad's last days, the Muslim community was in a state of disarray and full of tribal quarrels.

If Muslims consisted of two major groups, the Meccan emigrants and the Medinan helpers, these two groups were far from united, as they sought to secure power while their leader was dying. It appears that disharmony between Muslims was subtle while Muhammad was alive, but once he became ill, the problem of his succession arose. This is significant because it contradicts the traditional Muslim claim, which tends to portray early Muslims as unmatched, exemplary believers who should be imitated in matters of religion and politics. On the day of Muhammad's death, these Muslims, according to primary sources, were fighting and quarreling and killing each other, and many were occupied with seizing power to the extent that they did not go to prepare Muhammad for burial.

The renowned Muslim historian Tabari (d. 923) explains that once Muhammad died, the Medinan Muslims did not wait. Instead of going to Muhammad's place to take care of his burial, they organized a gathering in a Bedouin home, known as the Saqifa, to declare a successor of Muhammad from among them.[1] They were adamant that Muhammad's successor must be from the Medinan Muslims since they supported Muhammad when he emigrated from Mecca and was vulnerable. They believed they deserved to take power because it was only due to their support that Muhammad—during his ten years among them—gained hegemony over the Arabs. Meccan emigrants—including Abu Bakr and Umar—were not informed of the meeting at the Saqifa. Once the two men learned of the gathering, they rushed to it. A quarrel erupted between the Medinans and the Meccans over Muhammad's legitimate successor.

The Medinan Muslims declared their right to choose Muhammad's successor and advanced the name of a man from among them, Sa'd. Abu Bakr and Umar refused and were joined by other Meccans from the Quraysh. Since the Medinans were ready to appoint Sa'd, Umar declared that no one could succeed Muhammad unless he was from the emigrants of Muhammad's tribe, the Quraysh. One rationale was, "We are the [emigrants] and the first companions of the Apostle of God; we are his kinsmen and his friends." In response, the Medinans offered, "Let us have a leader from among ourselves, and you a leader from among yourselves."[2] Umar adamantly rejected this, "Absolutely not." He then offered Abu Bakr as a successor. The Medinan Muslims were not in favor of Abu Bakr. They suggested that they would accept Ali as a successor, declaring, "We will not give the oath of allegiance [to

1. See Tabari, *History*, 9:183–209; 10:1–17. See also Kennedy, *Great Arab Conquests*, 54–55.
2. Tabari, *History*, 10:3.

anyone] except Ali."[3] To this, Umar and other Meccans were opposed. The Muslim traditions appear ambiguous and contradictory in discussing what occurred next. We learn that the Medinan Muslims gave up; their prospective caliph, Sa'd, was murdered; and Abu Bakr was declared a caliph. Some reports indicate that Umar shouted, "Kill Sa'd," while others state, "Allah killed Sa'd."[4] Ultimately, Abu Bakr was appointed. However, not only the Medinan Muslims but also many Meccans refused his appointment. Tabari lists key Meccan Muslims who refused Abu Bakr and claims that "the decision was forced on them by 'Umar."[5] Still, it is reported that Muhammad's daughter Fatima rejected Abu Bakr's appointment. She never gave him the oath of allegiance, and she died, presumably of sadness (or violence against her, according to Shiites), six months later. Her husband, Ali, waited until she died to accept Abu Bakr's appointment.[6]

The matter of the appointment of Abu Bakr indicates a clear tribal dispute between the Muslims on the very day Muhammad died. It appears that the majority among Muslims did not care as much about Muhammad's burial as they did about seizing power after his death. In fact, Tabari states that when Abu Bakr and Umar rushed into the Saqifa, Ali was not there—he was preparing Muhammad's body for burial.[7] While Tabari is not commonly considered a Shiite historian, his report shows Ali as devoted to Muhammad while all other Muslims—Meccans and Medinans—were in disarray. This is evident in another account, where Ali rebuked Abu Bakr in front of many Meccans, saying "We have a right in this authority which you have monopolized."[8] Eventually, Muslims in power decided that any Muslim who refused to give the oath of allegiance to Abu Bakr would be considered an apostate.[9]

The Shiite sources provide a completely different narrative, insisting that Muhammad openly appointed Ali as the imam of the Muslims—their religious teacher and political commander. While the Sunni sources

3. Tabari, *History*, 9:186.

4. Compare Tabari, *History*, 9:194; 10:8.

5. Ibrahim, *Stated Motivations*, 128. See the detailed analysis of Abu Bakr's appointment (127–30).

6. Tabari, *History*, 9:188–89.

7. Tabari, *History*, 10:3.

8. Tabari, *History*, 9:197.

9. See Tabari, *History*, 9:195; and Ibrahim, *Stated Motivations*, 129.

generally suggest that Muhammad died without declaring a successor or providing a method of choosing one, Shiites have always rejected these claims. For Shiites, a few months before Muhammad's death, he appointed Ali in the sight of many Muslims at an event known as "The Pond of Khumm." During that event, Muhammad reportedly declared, "If I am a person's mawla (friend and supporter) then Ali is also his mawla; O Allah, take as friends those who take him as a friend, and take as enemies those who take him as an enemy."[10] Shiites insist that in this hadith, found in Shiite and Sunni collections alike, Muhammad designated Ali as the legitimate successor by using the word *mawla* only with Ali. Sunnis refuse and argue that the word *mawla* does not necessarily mean "caliph" or "ruler." Rather, it refers to Muhammad's admiration and affection for his son-in-law; it merely reflects friendship, love, and support. Shiites also refer to a narration accepted by the Sunnis in which Muhammad is reported to have openly told Muslims at the Pond of Khumm, "I am leaving among you two weighty things: the one being the Book of Allah in which there is right guidance and light. . . . The second are the members of my household I remind you (of your duties) to the members of my family."[11] For Shiites, Muhammad's emphasis in this hadith on the two weights is unprecedented. He clearly elevates the importance of his household, placing it next to the Quran. Muhammad's household, Shiites emphasize, included Ali and his wife, Fatima, which reflects the unique position granted to Ali as Muhammad's successor. Whether this is true is not the issue, as Ali was not appointed after all.

Sunnis emphatically argue that Abu Bakr deserved to succeed Muhammad. They claim that Muhammad called him al-Siddiq, which literally means "the truthful, trusted, and faithful." This title, for Sunnis, indicates his unmatched character. They argue that Abu Bakr was called al-Siddiq not only because he believed that Muhammad physically traveled in the night journey from Mecca to Jerusalem on a winged horse creature, while many doubted him, but also because he was the first to trust Muhammad's message and convert to Islam. However, some Muslim reports question the claim that Abu Bakr was really the first

10. See Musnad Ahmad, 5:386. The hadith is mentioned in Sunni and Shiite collections. This reference is from a famous Sunni collection. See other occurrences in Musnad Ahmad, 5:713; Jami' at-Tirmidhi, 1.46.3713; and Sunan Ibn Majah, 1.1.121.
11. Sahih Muslim, 31.5920.

to convert to Islam. According to Tabari, "More than fifty people accepted Islam before [Abu Bakr]."[12] Still, Sunnis claim that Abu Bakr was designated by Muhammad to succeed him in leading the Muslims, as evidenced in one important incident that occurred before Muhammad's death: while Muhammad was ill and could not lead the Muslims in ritual prayer, he entrusted Abu Bakr with this role. Sunnis commonly reject the claims that Abu Bakr—with Umar's help—seized power. For them, Abu Bakr was loved and respected by all Muslims and was appointed by consultation among Muhammad's major companions. His appointment received open acceptance by trusted Muslims. Nonetheless, this seems to contradict a famous Sunni hadith by Bukhari in which "the pledge of allegiance to Abu Bakr was nothing but a prompt sudden action which got established afterwards."[13] Indeed, while some historical accounts indicate that major companions of Muhammad—including Ali and others—did not support Abu Bakr's appointment, Sunnis still claim that there was a unanimous agreement due to Abu Bakr's integrity and Muhammad's reported designation.

On the day of Muhammad's death, Muslims were in discord. They appeared more concerned about who would succeed him than about how to bury him in honor and dignity. While Ali seems to have been near him, preparing his burial, many so-called trusted companions were fighting for power at the Saqifa. It is difficult to believe the traditional Islamic claims that early Muslims were the exemplary religious generation of Islam and were driven by piety and religious zeal more than by desire for material gain. The incident of the appointment of Muhammad's successor demonstrates how these early Muslims were still managing their affairs using pre-Islamic tribal considerations. Their conversion to Islam does not seem to have changed their worldview or their treatment of each other. Rather, it seems that "lust for power, tribal considerations, and political concerns were the driving force behind the decisions."[14]

---

12. Tabari, *History*, 6:85.

13. Bukhari, 8.82.817. Tabari states, "The oath of allegiance given to Abū Bakr was an event that happened without consideration." *History*, 9:192.

14. Ibrahim, *Stated Motivations*, 130. For the incident of the Saqifa, see the detailed analysis of Abu Bakr's appointment in Ibrahim, *Stated Motivations*, 127–30. See also Madelung, *Succession to Muḥammad*, 27–67.

20

What Are Some of the Early
Non-Muslim Views on Muhammad?

During his lifetime, Muhammad was known for his constant da'wa—that is, Islamic preaching or inviting people to Islam. After his death, his followers continued the da'wa activity. Da'wa is a missional activity in Islam, understood as a duty divinely prescribed for every Muslim to advance the message of Islam. As I have written previously, "In the earliest centuries of Islam, the faith spread among non-Muslims through the da'wa of Arab merchants trading in non-Muslim lands as well as through the da'wa of Muslim settlers following military raids led by Muslim armies. Coercive conversion was only one way of accepting Islam."[1] In their da'wa, Muslims had to present Muhammad to the non-Muslims as an unmatched person: a final prophet and an example of conduct to humankind. For the most part, non-Muslims did not view Muhammad favorably.

Some early sources do not explicitly mention Muhammad but nonetheless describe him with a high probability. In a Greek source titled *Doctrina Jacobi*, probably written in July 634, we read of "the prophet who has appeared with the [Arabs]," and the text identifies him unfavorably:

1. Ibrahim, *Concise Guide to the Quran*, 150–51. On Islamic da'wa, see the important studies by Kuiper titled *Da'wa* and *Da'wa and Other Religions*, chaps. 1–3.

"He is false, for the prophets do not come armed with a sword."[2] The source is anonymous and is attributed to a recently baptized Christian from a Jewish background. While the source does not mention Muhammad by name, it acknowledges a well-known prophet among the Arabs and describes him as armed with a sword. The time period matches that of Muhammad in Arabia, and one may wonder: Was there any more famous prophet with a sword during Muhammad's time? The newly baptized Christian identifies the Arabian sword-holder as a false prophet because prophets do not use swords. This is one description of Muhammad by a non-Muslim.[3]

In another Greek source, a sermon in 634 by the patriarch of Jerusalem, Sophronius (d. ca. 639), we read of the Arab armed with "barbarians and godless" warriors, who "prevented [Christians] from entering Bethlehem." The description continues in another sermon by Sophronius dated to 636 or 637. He details "the Arabs' atrocities and victories" as they "overrun the places which are not allowed to them, plunder cities, devastate fields, burn down villages, set on fire the holy churches, overturn the sacred monasteries," identifying them as "the vengeful and God-hating" Arabs, "who insult the cross, Jesus and the name of God, and whose leader is the devil."[4] Sophronius's descriptions reflect the Arab Muslim conquests of Jerusalem. Sophronius describes the leader of those Arabs as the devil who insults the cross, Jesus, and God's name.

The importance of these two Greek references is that they are contemporary to the time of Muhammad's reported career in Arabia. Both of them describe active military forces under an Arabian leader flourishing around the year 634. From this same year, we have two important Syriac sources that mention Muhammad's name explicitly. The first, attributed to Thomas the Presbyter, connects Muhammad with the military activities of the time. This is, according to Robert Hoyland, "the first explicit reference to Muḥammad in a non-Muslim source, and its very precise dating inspires confidence that it ultimately derives from firsthand knowledge." The account—dated Friday, February 7, 634—refers to the "battle between the Romans and the Arabs of Muḥammad," in which "the Romans fled, leaving behind the patrician *bryrdn*, whom the Arabs

2. Hoyland, *Seeing Islam as Others Saw It*, 55.
3. Van der Horst, "Short Note on the *Doctrina Jacobi Nuper Baptizati*," 1–6.
4. Hoyland, *Seeing Islam as Others Saw It*, 72, 73.

killed. Some four thousand poor villagers of Palestine were killed there, Christians, Jews and Samaritans. The Arabs ravaged the whole region."[5] The explicit mention of "the Arabs of Muḥammad" and their treatment of non-Muslims strengthens the argument that the two Greek sources probably refer to the same Arabs and the same Muhammad and identify them in negative terms. In another Syriac source, dated to 637, we find Muhammad's name explicitly mentioned in a statement that the "Arab troops decisively defeated Byzantine forces" and "many villages were destroyed through the killing by [the Arabs of] Muḥammad."[6] The two Syriac sources support the evidence of the two Greek sources regarding the Christian—contemporary to Muhammad—description of Muhammad as a false prophet, devil, or God-hating Arab leading armed warriors. These sources originate from the first century of Islam. One may wonder, Did the non-Muslim views concerning Muhammad change over time?

In the first Islamic century, non-Muslims gradually developed their opinion of Muhammad. In the available reports, we find various descriptions of Muhammad. In some, he is portrayed as mainly an armed warlord or a conquest initiator; others describe him as a caravan trader with no religious significance whatsoever. Some speak of him as the king of the Arabs who controlled parts of Arabia; others depict him as a monotheist preacher and lawgiver—albeit with no specifics about his message. In general, many refer to him as a false prophet and sometimes as the beast of Revelation 13.[7] Most non-Muslim descriptions of Muhammad from the first century of Islam come from Christian writers. Because the Arab Muslim conquerors took over Byzantine Christian lands, Christian scholars had to wrestle with Islam and its claims. This is one reason why most depictions of Muhammad are not positive. Slowly, over time, non-Muslims became familiar with Islam and its developing tenets. Their views of Muhammad also developed gradually.

5. Hoyland, *Seeing Islam as Others Saw It*, 120.

6. Penn, *When Christians First Met Muslims*, 22–24; see also Hoyland, *Seeing Islam as Others Saw It*, 116–117.

7. Hoyland, "Earliest Christian Writings," 276–95. The Monophysite Coptic bishop John of Nikiu described Muslims as the followers of "the detestable doctrine of the beast, this is, Mohammed." See John of Nikiu, *Chronicle of John*, 201, 124ff. On John of Nikiu, see Gianfranco Fiaccadori, "John of Nikiou," in *Christian-Muslim Relations: A Bibliographical History*, ed. David Thomas et al., vol. 1 (Leiden: Brill, 2009), 209–18. See also Ibrahim, *Stated Motivations*, 186.

One of the most important contributors to the discussion surrounding Muhammad is John of Damascus (675–749), who is considered one of the fathers of the Eastern Orthodox Church. He is known as the first major Christian thinker to engage Islam and its claims in a detailed way. In Damascus, John worked under the Umayyad caliph as a tax official. By 730 he had left the caliphal court and become a monk. He spent the rest of his life writing for the Greek and Latin churches. In his Greek work *The Fount of Knowledge*, John dedicates an entire section to heresies from a Christian perspective, highlighting when they started and what they entailed. In one section he speaks of Islam as "the heresy of the Ishmaelites." He describes Muslims as Ishmaelites and Agarenes (or Hagarenes), because, John observes, Muslims are descendants from Ishmael and his mother, Hagar, Abraham's wife.[8] In evaluating Muslim practices of his time, John writes of the "people-deceiving practice of the Ishmaelites."[9] He lists Islam as a heresy and writes of "the superstition of the Ishmaelites which to this day prevails and keeps people in error, being a forerunner of the Antichrist." In his description of Muhammad, John classifies him as a false prophet: "From that time to the present a false prophet named Mohammed has appeared in their midst." John explains that Muhammad was exposed to the right biblical teaching but rejected it to live in heresy: "This man, after having chanced upon the Old and New Testaments and likewise, it seems, having conversed with an Arian monk, devised his own heresy."[10] Some scholars accuse John of being biased against Islam, but recent research emphasizes that John's view reflects a highly sophisticated understanding and analysis of Islam and its practices.[11] After John of Damascus, many Christians wrote about Islam in Greek but did not necessarily adopt his views of Islam and Muhammad. Theophanes the Confessor (760–818), for instance, did not identify Islam as a Christian heresy. He described Muhammad as a false prophet ruling over murderous Arabs and said that Muhammad's commanders were ruthless invaders of Christian lands.[12]

8. John of Damascus, *Writings*, 153.
9. Schadler, *John of Damascus and Islam*, 89.
10. John of Damascus, *Writings*, 153.
11. Schadler, *John of Damascus and Islam*, 97–139.
12. See Theophanes, *Chronicle of Theophanes*, 37–39. See Ibrahim, *Stated Motivations*, 186.

In 781, the Abbasid Caliphate was in its golden age, flourishing and enjoying stability three decades after overthrowing the Umayyads. The caliph of the time, Mahdi, held religious discussions in his court. During one of them, he reportedly debated with Patriarch Timothy I, head of the Church of the East. During a two-day period, they discussed common beliefs of Islam and Christianity while also emphasizing the stark differences. The patriarch defended his faith against Islamic charges regarding the Bible's corruption, the Trinity, and Jesus's divinity, among others. Although the debate was under a fierce Islamic caliphate, the patriarch demonstrated courage, respect, and insight. He said Muhammad "walked in the steps of the prophets."[13] Respectfully, he represented Muhammad as possibly seeking the true worship, but he never affirmed Muhammad's prophethood. This matches the earlier understanding of John of Damascus, that Muhammad might have been exposed to biblical teaching, but he later deviated from it. Unlike John of Damascus, Patriarch Timothy did not specifically refer to Muhammad as a false prophet—perhaps because he was in the presence of the caliph. However, Timothy emphatically rejected the assertion that Muhammad is mentioned in the Bible or was the foretold prophet coming after Jesus. Timothy explains the deficiency of Muhammad's teaching and concludes, "As to us we have not accepted Muhammad because we have not a single testimony about him in our Books."[14] This indicates Timothy's full trust in Christian scripture and complete denial of Muhammad's prophethood.

There are numerous examples of Christian-Muslim encounters. While John of Damascus was from the Eastern Orthodox Church and Patriarch Timothy I was from the Church of the East, we conclude with a final example from the Melkite Church. This church includes Christians who were in harmony with the decisions of the Council of Chalcedon in 451 concerning the two natures of Christ. They shared the Byzantine emperor's theological stance and were thus called Melkites, or royalists (the name Melkite means "king's people"). In 1216, another debate reportedly occurred between a Melkite Christian and a Muslim ruler, but this

13. See the translation of the entire debate in *Timothy's Apology for Christianity*. The quotation here is from p. 8.

14. *Timothy's Apology for Christianity*, 35. For an excellent discussion and analysis of the debate, see Neely, "Patriarch and the Insider Movement," 3–79.

time the ruler had several Muslims with him. The Christian was Jurji, a Syrian monk from the Monastery of Mar Simaan, near Antioch. The debate is described as a salon-like session in the caliph's court. It was a part of the intellectual life of medieval Islamic society. Like Patriarch Timothy, Jurji defends Christianity against Islamic charges and questions Islam and its tenets. In describing Muhammad, Jurji explains that, based on Muhammad's life and conduct, Christians of his church "do not assign Muhammad honor." For Jurji, Muhammad led pagans from worshiping idols to something different, but "not the true worship of God, because he wanted to rule over them." Jurji understands Muhammad as a man who had an encounter with some sort of truth when the monk Bahira educated him about Christianity. Bahira led Muhammad— says Jurji—out of paganism and against worshiping the Arabian idol al-Akbar; however, Muhammad was then afraid of his people and thus compromised the true worship and instructed them, "Worship Allah, and fear al-Akbar."[15] We notice here that Christians were considerate of their context and avoided outright condemnation of Muhammad as a false prophet, yet their descriptions maintained an understanding of Muhammad that was far from true prophethood.

In examining numerous medieval Syriac and Arabic Christian texts, Sidney Griffith (1938–) provides a compelling observation regarding the way Christians viewed Muhammad and his message in the early Christian-Muslim encounter: "It was not uncommon in Christian/Muslim debate texts in Syriac and Arabic from the early Islamic period for the question to arise about what status the Christian was prepared to accord to Muḥammad as a prophet, and to the Qur'ān as an inspired scripture. For the most part the answer was that, at best, Muḥammad was a little less than a prophet, and the Qur'ān not quite a book of divine revelation."[16] Therefore, while Muslims emphatically presented Muhammad as the final prophet sent by the deity, who earlier sent other prophets, including Jesus and Moses, non-Muslims, in general terms, were unwilling to grant Muhammad such a status based on what they knew of his deeds and teachings. What do we know about Muhammad's teachings? This is the discussion in the following section of the book.

15. Ibrahim and Hackenburg, *In Search of the True Religion.*
16. Griffith, "Qur'an in Arab Christian Texts," 204.

PART 2

MUHAMMAD'S MESSAGE

21

What Was Muhammad's Central Message?

Muslims believe Muhammad came as Allah's final prophet with one simple but powerful message: tawhid. The Arabic term *tawhid* refers to the belief and affirmation that Allah is one, and only one. It is a reference to strict monotheism, unitarianism, or divine unicity. In Allah there is no diversity, plurality, or multiplicity—only complete and strict unity. Tawhid stands in opposition to believing in many gods or associating partners with the one deity. While tawhid is the central message of Muhammad, neither the term itself nor its verbal form, "to believe in one deity," is ever mentioned in the Quran. Still, the concept of believing in one—and only one—deity appears in many verses in the Quran. "While the term *tawhid* is never mentioned in Islam's scripture, the concept of Allah's oneness appears in various verses—just as Christians find strong evidence of the Triune God in the Bible, although the term Trinity does not appear."[1] The Quran often repeats, "There is no deity other than he [Allah]." This important statement became the first part of the Islamic Shahada (creed, testimony, or profession of faith).

1. See Ibrahim, *Concise Guide to the Quran*, 90.

To show the importance of tawhid for Muslims, consider one example. One of the shortest suras (or chapters) in the Quran is sura 112.
Muslims refer to it by the Arabic title "al-Ikhlas" (the sincere devotion)
or "al-Tawhid" (the strict monotheism). This is one of the most concise
and important chapters of the Quran in describing the concept of tawhid, although the word itself is not explicitly mentioned. The chapter
reads, "In the name of Allah, the most gracious, the most merciful.
Declare: He is Allah; the One. He is the Absolute. He has not begotten
and has not been begotten. There is none like him" (Q 112:1–4). The
chapter emphatically declares that Allah is one and that he has no equal.
Many Muslim traditions were later written to establish a unique status
for this chapter in particular, as it distinguishes the Islamic tawhid. We
are told that Muhammad heard of a man who was reciting sura 112,
of which the first aaya (or verse) is "Declare: He is Allah." In response,
Muhammad told his companions to inform the man that "Allah loves
him."[2] Thus, Allah loves those who recite the tawhid sura. In another
tradition, Muhammad taught Muslims that this sura is unmatched in
importance. He asked his companions, "Is any one of you incapable of
reciting a third of the Qur'an in a night?" They wondered, "How could
one recite a third of the Qur'an" in one night? To this, Muhammad
declared that this chapter "is equivalent to a third of the Qur'an."[3] Nothing matches tawhid as Islam's central message. Similarly, Muhammad
once reportedly swore as an oath by Allah's name that "this Surah is
equal to one-third of the Qur'an."[4] Moreover, Muhammad reportedly
established that reciting this tawhid sura makes one's prayer acceptable
to Allah.[5] We are told that as Muhammad "went to bed every night, he
used to cup his hands together and blow over it after reciting [this sura]
. . . and then rub his hands over whatever parts of his body he was able
to rub, starting with his head, face and front of his body. He used to do
that three times."[6] Many Muslims imitate this very action attributed to
Muhammad as they seek prevention and protection from evils at night.
Muhammad reportedly told a Muslim that reciting this tawhid sura

2. Sahih Muslim, 4.1773.
3. Sahih Muslim, 4.1769; see also Bukhari, 6.61.534; and Jami' at-Tirmidhi,
5.42.2896.
4. Bukhari, 6.61.533; 8.78.638; 9.93.471; also Sunan an-Nasa'i, 2.11.996.
5. Sunan Abi Dawud, 8.1488; and Sunan Ibn Majah, 5.34.3857.
6. Bukhari, 6.61.536.

would protect and "serve [him] for every purpose."[7] When Muhammad met a Muslim who loved this sura, he promised him, "Your love for this Surah will make you enter Paradise."[8]

These traditions demonstrate to Muslims the utmost importance of one specific chapter in the Quran, mainly because it affirms and emphasizes tawhid. While one cannot be certain whether Muhammad made these statements, they have a great impact on the lives of Muslims. Some scholars argue that these hadiths were developed by later Muslims, who projected them back and attributed them to Muhammad for legitimacy. These traditions serve the purposes of their time of documentation rather than being an actual record of past words. One aim of these traditions is to establish a unique Muslim identity, in contrast to other religions, around the idea of tawhid. In the end, this concept, according to Muslims, is the central message of Muhammad. The logic is, "If there were two gods, [Muslims] assert, there would inevitably arise between them, at one time or another, a conflict of wills."[9]

Muslims believe that Muhammad's central message, tawhid, is the same message proclaimed by pre-Islamic prophets sent by Allah, including those from the Bible such as Moses, David, and Jesus. When the message of these earlier prophets was rejected, Allah sent his final prophet to proclaim the same message—only this time, Muslims believe, it would prevail. However, according to Muslim sources, one cannot be certain that Muhammad had always been a monotheist, as we mentioned earlier; he reportedly praised pagan goddesses and affirmed their intercession.[10] Nonetheless, Muslims are adamant about the importance of tawhid as Muhammad's central message. For Muslims, the worst transgression is believing in the opposite of tawhid, a concept they call shirk. The term *shirk* indicates the association of partners with the deity. It is polytheism, or better called associationism. If Muslims love and cherish tawhid, nothing is more awful or hated than shirk. Muslims boast of themselves as the people of tawhid and despise any hint of shirk or polytheism. Undoubtedly, these strong feelings about tawhid and shirk among Muslims are based on Quranic assertions. The

---

7. Sunan Abi Dawud, 42.5064; see also Jami' at-Tirmidhi, 6.46.3575.
8. Bukhari, 1.11.741.
9. Gimaret, "Tawḥīd," 10:389; see also Shatzmiller, "al-Muwaḥḥidūn," 7:801–7.
10. See question 11 above and Ibrahim, *Concise Guide to the Quran*, chap. 19.

Quran mentions the associators in multiple verses: "Slay the associators wherever you find them" (Q 9:5); "wage war on all of the associators as they are waging war on all of you" (Q 9:36). These verses are a sample that indicates how severe shirk is in Islam's scripture.

The Christian doctrine of the Trinity has puzzled Muslims for centuries. Most of them view it as shirk. Very few Muslims throughout history were able to accept the Christian understanding and, therefore, describe Christians as monotheists. The mere notion of three persons in one divine being is unfathomable for most Muslims because tawhid is understood as strict: there is only one deity, who has no partners. The Quran complains about Jews and Christians: "The Jews say, 'Uzayr is the Son of Allah,' while the Christians say, 'The Christ is the Son of Allah.' That is the utterance of their mouths, imitating the sayings of those unbelievers before them. Allah assail them! How they are perverted! They have taken their rabbis and their monks as lords instead of Allah, and the Christ, Mary's son. They were commanded to worship only one god. There is no god except he. Glory be to Him, above that they associate" (Q 9:30–31). These verses reject any association within the deity and deny that Allah has a son. In sura 5, multiple verses accuse Christians of twisting the true worship: "They are unbelievers who say, 'Allah is the Christ, the son of Mary'" (Q 5:72). This is followed by, "They are surely unbelievers who say, 'Allah is the third of three'" (Q 5:73). The Quran rejects the Trinity. These Quranic verses accuse Christians of making Allah one of three gods and state that those who adopt this belief are unbelievers. This is understood by the vast majority of Muslims as a claim that Christians have committed shirk.

Furthermore, the Quran directly addresses what appears to be a distorted form of a triune deity: "And Allah will say, 'O Jesus son of Mary, did you say to the people, "Take me and my mother as gods apart from Allah?"' Jesus will say, 'Glory be to you! It is not for me to say what I have no right to . . . I only told them what you commanded me: You shall worship Allah, my Lord and your Lord'" (Q 5:116–17). This passage clarifies the Quranic view of the Trinity. "It turns out that the Quran suggests another form of the Trinity: Allah, Mary, and Jesus. It assumes that Christians see Jesus and Mary as two gods to be worshiped beside Allah."[11] It is understandable that Muslims would consider this twisted

11. Ibrahim, *Concise Guide to the Quran*, 92.

Trinity to be shirk. This erroneous understanding of the Trinity advances Mary as a part of the triune God, implying that Allah married Mary and that together they had baby Jesus. Like Muslims, Christians would deny any such belief; they would emphatically reject it as blasphemous. "Although this is not what Christians believe, it is what the Quran claims about them," and this has influenced Muslim exegetes throughout centuries.[12] These Muslim interpreters of the Quran relied often on these verses and ascribed associationism to Christians. Scholars have always pondered the Quranic representation of the Trinity, especially as it differs from what Christians actually believe. Some scholars suggest that during Muhammad's time there was a heretical Christian group in Arabia that claimed Mary was part of the Trinity instead of the Holy Spirit. This, scholars claim, was the group that Muhammad encountered and rejected. However, this suggestion lacks evidence. Ultimately, based on the Quranic understanding of tawhid and shirk, Christianity emphatically denounces a twisted form of the Trinity. In the end, the Quran seems confused about the Trinity as including Mary. Christians know of the Trinity by revelation and Scripture. Muhammad, it appears, having rejected the Christian revelation, would not have understood the doctrine.

Muhammad's central message was calling people to tawhid. The term becomes synonymous with the followers of Islam, as they cherish being identified as ahl al-tawhid ("the people of tawhid"). It contrasts them with those who believe in many deities or who associate partners with the deity.[13] If Islam's central message is tawhid, who is the deity of whom Muhammad preached? Who is Allah? This is our next question.

12. Ibrahim, *Concise Guide to the Quran*, 92.
13. See Ibrahim, *Concise Guide to the Quran*, chap. 20.

22

Who Is Muhammad's Deity, Allah?

Muslims worship Allah. They view Allah as the only true existing deity. All other gods are false. For them, worshiping anyone but Allah is idolatry. He is the absolute and purest description of oneness, tawhid—that is, unitarianism or monotheism. The Quran presents Allah as unique and unmatched: he is the creator of the heavens and the earth, and there is nothing that equals him (Q 42:11). "Sights cannot attain him, but he comprehends them all" (Q 6:103). In the Quran, Allah is emphasized as absolute in his divine determination, both guiding and leading people astray.[1]

Four times in the Quran (7:180; 17:110; 20:8; 59:24), we read that Allah has the most beautiful names (al-asmaa' al-husnaa): "The most beautiful names belong to Allah. So, call upon him by them. Stay away from those who pervert his names. They will be punished for that which they used to do" (Q 7:180). In fact, these extraordinary and marvelous names of Allah are connected with his absolute oneness: "Allah, there is no god but he. The most beautiful names are his" (Q 20:8). Muslims think of these names as attributes of Allah—they are adjectives describing his majesty and nouns explaining his perfection. They also convey his just, wise, and merciful deeds toward humankind. If you want to

---

1. Reynolds, *Allah*, 49. On Allah leading people astray, see Nickel, *Quran with Christian Commentary*, especially the comments on Q 2:26; 4:88; 74:31.

know Allah, Muslims say, learn his names and repeat them in praise. This is why one can find Muslims, especially during fasting, sitting in mosques during prayer time, repeating Allah's names in a quiet voice like a murmur: "The place held by this recitation in Muslim piety gives it an outstanding importance."[2]

While the Quran emphasizes that Allah has the most beautiful names, it does not list or specify them. There is no way for a Muslim, based on the Quran alone, to identify these names or use them in worship. However, in the third century of Islam, a hadith attributed to Muhammad emerged, indicating Allah has ninety-nine extraordinary names: "Allah has ninety-nine names, i.e. one-hundred minus one, and whoever knows them will go to Paradise."[3] Through this hadith, Muslims know the number of Allah's names and the reward for knowing and memorizing them. Moreover, in another hadith, Muhammad reportedly conveyed why the number of Allah's names is odd, not even: since Allah is one, which is an odd number, he loves odd numbers. "There are ninety-nine names of Allah; he who commits them to memory would get into Paradise. Verily, Allah is Odd (He is one, and it is an odd number) and He loves odd numbers."[4] With these hadiths, the count of Allah's names is established and Muslims realize the religious significance of and reward for memorizing them. However, one does not learn what these names are. Since the Quran and the most trusted hadith collections do not specify the exact list of Allah's names, later traditions had to provide one.

Classical Muslim traditionist Tirmidhi (d. 892) is known among Muslims as one of the earliest to provide a list of Allah's ninety-nine most beautiful names.[5] Tirmidhi states that he heard the list from more than one Muslim authority, attributing it to Muhammad. The list includes adjectives about Allah that are comparable to divine attributes found in other faiths, such as Judaism and Christianity. Allah is generous; he is just and he is merciful. These are among his most beautiful names. Allah is also the king. He is the creator, the almighty, the powerful, the kind,

2. Gardet, "al-Asmā' al-Ḥusnā," 1:714.
3. Bukhari, 3.50.894; 8.75.419; 9.93.489; see also Jami' at-Tirmidhi, 6.45.3506, 3508; and Sunan Ibn Majah, 5.34.3860.
4. Sahih Muslim, 35.6475; see also a similar hadith in 35.6476.
5. The Sunni trusted collections, Sahih Bukhari and Sahih Muslim, do not include a list, only the total number of names. However, Tirmidhi provides the list in his Jami' at-Tirmidhi, 6.45.3507; see also a similar list in Sunan Ibn Majah, 5.34.3861.

the forgiver, the protector, the holy, the judge, the generous, the hearer, the watcher, and so forth. These attributes are shared between Islam and other faiths as descriptions of the deity. However, the ninety-nine names include some attributes that appear unique to Allah. We are told that he is the proud one (al-mutakabbir), the humiliater (al-mudhil), and the harmer (al-daar). While these are included in the list, many progressive Muslim thinkers reject some or all of them. One should also note that some of the names are repeated without any clear distinctions, such as al-ghaffar and al-ghafur, which both refer to the forgiver, and al-qadir and al-muqtadir, which both reflect Allah's almightiness.

Over the centuries, while Muslims cherished these names and continued using them in worship, some problems became apparent. Only some of the included names are based on the Quran; others never appear in Islam's scripture, such as the abaser (al-khafid), the causer of death (al-mumit), and the restorer of things (al-mu'id). The inclusion of names unsupported by the Quran brings the hadith—and the alleged list—into question. But this is not the only problem. The Quran also includes attributes of Allah (e.g., Q 2:19; 8:30; 11:92; 21:51, 81) that do not appear in the list given in the hadith. Thus, the entire tradition sits on shaky ground. Some scholars conclude that "the list was not always absolutely fixed and was liable to contain variants."[6] Muslims in different generations added and removed names from the list, to the extent that some Shiite scholars believe that the names of the imams are names of Allah; thus, Ali is claimed as one of Allah's names.[7] It appears that the choice to add or remove from the list depended on the sectarian and political preference of each Muslim. In a puzzling statement, the Muslim scholar Tirmidhi, who initially provided the list, seems to have been skeptical about it, as he includes a caveat after listing the names: "This hadith is strange (weak), and I heard it from more than one person."[8] Consequently, some Muslim authorities, including Ibn Taymiyya (d. 1328), rejected the list altogether, although it remained in use in popular Islam through the centuries.[9] In recent years, contemporary Egyptian Muslim

6. Gardet, "al-Asmā' al-Ḥusnā," 1:714.

7. Majlisi, Biḥār al-anwār, 83:221.

8. Book of Tirmidhi, Sunan, 5:530 (author's translation). In Arabic, the name Ali can mean "the highest one."

9. Ibn Taymiyya, Majmū' al-fatāwā, 6:379.

cleric Abd al-Raziq al-Radwani (1964–), a scholar of Islamic dogma, has made the argument that twenty-nine names from the list are incorrect and lack support from the Quran and sound traditions.[10]

Despite the disagreement surrounding the ninety-nine names, Muslims recite them repeatedly and cherish the mention of "Allah," as a name, quite often. It is central to one of the most important pillars of Islam, the Shahada, which is Islam's profession of faith. The first part states, "I testify that there is no god but Allah," and the second part declares the belief in Muhammad as Allah's messenger: "and Muhammad is Allah's messenger." This demonstrates the significance of Allah's name, which is also repeated many times during the ritual prayer practiced by devotees five times each day as the second pillar of Islam. The call to prayer, adhan, begins with the famous phrase "Allahu Akbar." This phrase means "Allah is greater," and it is repeated four times at the beginning of the adhan to call Muslims to ritual prayer as prescribed religious duty. The phrase is very important in Muslim daily life, as it signifies Allah's supremacy above all. While the phrase became well known after some used it in terrorist attacks, we should note that Muslims use it on various other occasions: "In celebration or rejoicing, in lifting a heavy weight or walking up a flight of stairs, in experiencing a severe catastrophe or expressing frustration, and in many other incidents."[11] Muslims love and revere the mention of Allah's name, as expressed in their utterance "Allahu Akbar."

It appears that the name of Islam's deity was well known before Muhammad. According to Muslim traditions, the name of Muhammad's father was Abdullah (Abd-Allah), meaning "slave of Allah." More importantly, some recent inscription discoveries from Saudi Arabia, dated back to the mid-sixth century, include a form of the name *Allah* in Arabic.[12] Thus, the proper name *Allah* appears to have been known in pre-Islamic times, although some may still argue that later Muslim traditions projected back the deity's name in Muhammad's family for legitimization. This logic suggests that through the incorporation of Allah in their names and the creation of stories about their reverence, these important figures in Muhammad's family are depicted as devoted

10. Radwani, *Asmā' Allāh al-ḥusnā al-thābita fī al-kitāb wa-l-sunna*.
11. See Ibrahim, "Why Do They Shout 'Allahu Akbar'?"
12. Nehmé, "New Dated Inscriptions," especially 133–36.

believers in Allah even before Muhammad was born. This appears, for instance, in the way Muhammad's grandfather is portrayed by Muslim traditions as a believer in Allah as the deity who protects the sacred house in Mecca.[13] This sacred house became the Sacred Mosque in Islam, the central place of worship.

Moreover, some scholars, relying on the Quran alone, argue that Allah was definitely known to the Arabs in pre-Islamic times. Pre-Muhammad Meccans believed in Allah as a high god and acknowledged him as one supreme god among other deities. Of course, being a supreme or high god clearly indicates he was not the sole or only deity. Even the major Muslim historian Tabari (d. 923) writes that "Allah had three daughters who were lesser deities, revered and honored by the pagans."[14] If this is true, some may question Islam's adoption of the name, especially as Muslim traditions indicate that "Arabs believed that the three female deities whom Muhammad praised were actually the daughters of Allah."[15] Other modern scholars examine the semantics of the Quran and conclude that this pre-Islamic polytheistic belief in Allah was "surprisingly close to the Islamic concept," to the extent that the Quran "sometimes even wonders why such a right understanding of God does not finally lead the disbelievers to acknowledging the truth of the new teaching."[16] This suggests that the advent of Islam did not change much from the pre-Islamic understanding of Allah. Thus, the Islamic deity Allah is not an Islamic creation—it was known before Muhammad.[17] With the advent of Islam, the supreme god who was high among many deities turned into "the affirmation of the Living God, the Exalted One."[18]

Today's Arabic-speaking Christians use the name *Allah* to refer to the deity they worship. Granted, what they believe about the deity differs

13. Ibn Hisham and Ibn Ishaq, *Life of Muhammad*, 26.

14. See the discussion and references in Ibrahim, *Concise Guide to the Quran*, 90. Some scholars suggest that pagans in Muhammad's days were monotheistic worshipers who thought of the goddesses as angels who could intercede. See Crone, "Religion of the Qur'ānic Pagans"; and Azmeh, *Emergence of Islam*, 267, 322–26; and Hawting, *Idea of Idolatry*, 1, 62–67.

15. Ibrahim, *Concise Guide to the Quran*, 90.

16. Izutsu, *God and Man in the Koran*, 98, 101. See also Watt, "Qur'ān and Belief in a 'High God'"; Crone, "Religion of the Qur'ānic Pagans"; and Wensinck, "Takbīr," 10:119.

17. Gardet, "Allāh," 1:406–17.

18. Gardet, "Allāh," 1:406.

significantly from the Islamic description of Allah. In fact, some research-ers of medieval Christianity argue convincingly that the term *Allah* was used by Arab Jews and Christians who lived in the Arabian Peninsula during pre-Islamic times.[19] This argument is plausible, although some challenge it by pointing to the scarcity of supporting evidence, especially as pre-Islamic Arab Jews and Christians are known to have used Hebrew and Syriac, respectively, in their worship.

In Islam, Allah is the one and only deity. His absolute oneness, tawhid, is the most important doctrine for Muslims. The opposite of tawhid is shirk, which is the most grievous of sins. Allah is known to Muslims through his most beautiful names, which are understood as his majestic and perfect attributes. These names convey to Muslims Allah's character and deeds. In their worship, Muslims use these names to praise and adore Allah. Although the Quran does not specify the names, later traditions list them with some variation. Some are comparable to what other faiths claim about their deities, while others seem distinct and exclusive to Islam. Allah's name is central in the daily life of a Muslim, as is evident in its repetition in the Shahada (profession of faith) and the adhan (call to ritual prayer).

19. See Shehadeh, *God with Us and without Us*, 94ff. This is also supported by recent inscription discoveries. See Nehmé, "New Dated Inscriptions," 121–64, especially 133–36.

23

What Is Muhammad's Message about Jesus?

Muhammad's message about Jesus can be found in various Muslim accounts, including the Quran, the sira, and the hadiths. In a previous publication, *A Concise Guide to the Quran*, I explore the Quran's claims about Jesus: "The Quranic Jesus is honored and highly esteemed but was not crucified. He performed miracles and knew the unseen future but was a mere human who prayed to Allah and ate food. He was one of the prophets sent by Allah to humankind. He was never God or his son. Jesus did not die." I conclude, "The Quranic Jesus was simply a messenger, not a savior."[1] Here, we focus on Muhammad's sira and his hadith collections and their descriptions of Jesus.

In Muhammad's sira, we encounter a strong connection between Muhammad and Jesus. In the conquest of Mecca in 630, Muhammad entered Mecca—eight years after he was forced to emigrate from there to Medina—victorious. One of the first things he did was destroy every idol and picture in the Ka'ba, with one exception. "The apostle ordered that the pictures should be erased except those of Jesus and Mary," although he added, "There is no God but Allah alone; He has no associate."[2] This appears to suggest that Muhammad held a strong affection for Jesus

1. Ibrahim, *Concise Guide to the Quran*, 108–15, quotes from p. 115.
2. Ibn Hisham and Ibn Ishaq, *Life of Muhammad*, 552, 774.

and Mary. We are told that Muhammad viewed himself as an answer to Abraham's prayer and a fulfillment of the good news of Jesus because Abraham was considered his father and Jesus his brother.[3] During his night journey from Mecca, Muhammad reportedly rode a flying, horse-like creature and, having landed at the temple of Jerusalem, "found Abraham, Moses, and Jesus among a company of the prophets," at which time Muhammad "acted as their imam in prayer."[4] While this report indicates Muhammad's superiority over previous prophets, it also describes a good tie between him and Jesus. Even though Muhammad and Jesus were separated by six centuries, the Muslim sources highlight their relationship as Allah's prophets. Muhammad describes Jesus's appearance in his sira: "Jesus, Son of Mary, was a reddish man of medium height with lank hair with many freckles on his face as though he had just come from a bath."[5]

Muhammad's sira explains that Muhammad never accepted Jesus as more than a prophet and messenger of Allah; he was "nothing but a slave" of Allah, who sent him as "an example to the children of Israel."[6] This is one reason why Muhammad reportedly rejected any claims of divinity attributed to Jesus. When some Christians asked, "Do you want us, Muhammad, to worship you as the Christians worship Jesus, Son of Mary?" Muhammad strongly denounced the idea and said, "God forbid that I should worship anyone but God or order that any but He should be worshipped. God did not send me and order me to do that."[7] Muhammad's message in the sira repeatedly and emphatically denies that Jesus was anything other than human. He was like Adam in that both were created without a male father. As for his death, Jesus did not die but was rescued and taken up to heaven by Allah.[8] In the same vein, Muhammad reportedly rebuked Christians: "Do not praise me extravagantly as Jesus son of Mary was praised [by Christians] and say the servant and the apostle of God."[9] It is plausible to assume that these sira accounts follow the stream of the Quran, especially because—according to many

3. Ibn Hisham and Ibn Ishaq, *Life of Muhammad*, 72.
4. Ibn Hisham and Ibn Ishaq, *Life of Muhammad*, 182.
5. Ibn Hisham and Ibn Ishaq, *Life of Muhammad*, 183–84.
6. Ibn Hisham and Ibn Ishaq, *Life of Muhammad*, 164; see also 152, 155.
7. Ibn Hisham and Ibn Ishaq, *Life of Muhammad*, 261.
8. Ibn Hisham and Ibn Ishaq, *Life of Muhammad*, 276–77.
9. Ibn Hisham and Ibn Ishaq, *Life of Muhammad*, 685.

scholars—the sira was formed to explain the Quran and to reflect the sectarian rivalries of a later period, not to record an actual past.

Muhammad's hadith collections provide more descriptions of Jesus. According to Bukhari, Muhammad said, "Both in this world and in the Hereafter, I am the nearest of all the people to Jesus, the son of Mary," and explained that all "prophets are paternal brothers; their mothers are different, but their religion is one."[10] This hadith elaborates further on how the sira identifies Jesus and Muhammad as brothers. In another hadith, Muhammad describes his strong connection with Jesus even historically, to the extent that no other prophet was sent by Allah between their periods: "I am most akin to the son of Mary among the whole of mankind and the Prophets are of different mothers, but of one religion, and no Prophet was raised between me and him."[11] These hadiths describe Muhammad as one link in a chain of prophets sent by Allah, and they highlight the exceptional connection between Muhammad and Jesus in Islamic sources. Still, Jesus is not a god or a son of a god. Allah asked Jesus, "Did you say unto men 'Worship me and my mother as two gods besides Allah?'" Jesus denied: "Glory be to You! It was not for me to say what I had no right (to say)."[12] As in some accounts in the sira, we are told in the hadiths that Muhammad described the likeness of Jesus as "a medium-statured man with white and red complexion and crisp hair" and that Muhammad reportedly declared, "Do not praise me as the Christians praised [Jesus]. I am no more than the slave of Allah and His Messenger."[13] In these two hadiths, the sira and hadith accounts agree about Jesus.

In a unique hadith about Jesus, Muhammad is reported to have said, "When any human being is born, Satan touches him at both sides of the body with his two fingers, except Jesus, the son of Mary, whom Satan tried to touch but failed."[14] Muslims understand Satan's touching of every person at birth as the source of sin in humankind. This hadith declares the uniqueness of Jesus, as he was never touched by Satan. While it seems to elevate Jesus over all created people, even Muhammad, since he

10. Bukhari, 4.55.652; also Sahih Muslim, 30.5836.
11. Sahih Muslim, 30.5834.
12. Jami' at-Tirmidhi, 5.44.3062. This is similar to Q 5:116.
13. See Sahih Muslim, 1.317, and Musnad Ahmad, 2.71, respectively.
14. Bukhari, 4.54.506.

was not excluded from Satan's touch, other hadiths elevate Muhammad above all humankind, especially on the last day. Muhammad reportedly said about himself, "I will be the chief of all the people on the Day of Resurrection," and "I shall be pre-eminent amongst the descendants of Adam on the Day of Resurrection and I will be the first intercessor and the first whose intercession will be accepted (by Allah)."[15] So while the hadith on Jesus's uniqueness at birth is indeed unmatched, the overall hadith corpus does not support any description of Jesus as divine or a savior—not even remotely.

Still, other hadiths portray Jesus more favorably than other prophets sent by Allah. Toward the end of time, Jesus—not any other prophet—will descend from heaven to be the just judge on earth. Muhammad reportedly stated, "By Him in Whose hand is my life, the son of Mary will soon descend among you as a just judge. He will break crosses, kill swine and abolish Jizya and the wealth will pour forth to such an extent that no one will accept it."[16] This hadith seems to distinguish Jesus alone as the final just judge on earth, but it uses the statement as a polemic tool against Christians, who—according to Islamic claims—worship the cross and consume pork. The hadith warns that Jesus will break crosses and kill swine. He will also abolish the jizya—a tax forced by Muslims on Christians who did not convert to Islam—because the true religion will be one, Islam. There will be no more misguided Christians; Jesus will again speak the truth to them.

Muhammad's message about Jesus in the sira and the hadith traditions aligns with that of the Quran. While Jesus is honored and respected, he was not crucified, nor was he a god or a savior. He will come again as a last judge and will rebuke Christians who did not accept Muhammad. He will break the cross, because Christians worshiped it, and will kill swine, because—though it was forbidden—Christians consumed it. This Islamic Jesus differs from the biblical one, and the differences between the two depictions are crucial, definitive, and decisive. In examining what the sira and the hadiths say about Jesus and Muhammad, one repeatedly stumbles on two major claims: Jesus prophesied the advent of Muhammad, and Christian scriptures include an explicit mention of Muhammad. Where does the Bible mention Muhammad's name? This is our next question.

15. See Bukhari, 4.55.556, and Sahih Muslim, 30.5655, respectively.
16. Sahih Muslim, 1.287; also Bukhari, 3.34.425; 3.43.656.

24

Where Is Muhammad Mentioned in the Bible?

The biography of Muhammad refers to Christians who converted to Islam after they met Muhammad because they believed he was mentioned in their scriptures. We read of Bahira, the monk who met Muhammad and "looked at his back and saw the seal of prophethood between [Muhammad's] shoulders in the very place described in his book description (in the Christian books)."[1] Similarly, the Christian emperor Heraclius gathered his Roman generals and spoke with them about Muhammad: "By God, he is truly the prophet whom we expect and find in our books, so come and let us follow him and believe in him that it may be well with us in this world and the next."[2] Moreover, we are told that some Christians from Najran "used to inherit books from their predecessors. Whenever one chief died and authority passed to his successor he would seal those books with the seals that were before his time and not break them." The Christian chief contemporary with Muhammad said of him, "He is a prophet and his name is in the [Christian books]."[3] Even the Jews, we are told, find Muhammad's name in

1. Ibn Hisham and Ibn Ishaq, *Life of Muhammad*, 80.
2. Ibn Hisham and Ibn Ishaq, *Life of Muhammad*, 656.
3. Ibn Hisham and Ibn Ishaq, *Life of Muhammad*, 736–37.

the Torah: "O Jews, fear God and accept what He has sent you. For by God you know that [Muhammad] is the apostle of God. You will find him described in your Torah and even named."[4] In fact, according to the renowned Muslim historian Tabari (d. 923), when Muhammad seized a Jewish tribe, he instructed them, "Accept Islam, for you know that I am a prophet sent by God. You will find this in your scriptures and in God's covenant with you."[5]

While nowhere in these references do we discover which Jewish or Christian books specifically mention Muhammad's name, the Muslim claim is clear: Jews and Christians should accept Muhammad as a prophet because he is foretold in the Bible—both Gospels and Torah—and some have already acknowledged this in past generations. These historical references do not exist in a vacuum. Even the Quran asserts similar claims about some who follow Muhammad, "whom they find mentioned with them in the Torah and the Gospel" (Q 7:157). In fact, in the Quran, Jesus prophesies of Muhammad's advent and calls him Ahmad: "O sons of Israel, I am indeed Allah's messenger unto you, confirming the Torah, which is before me, and giving glad tidings of a messenger who will come after me, whose name will be Ahmad" (Q 1:6). Thus, Jesus gave Muhammad the name Ahmad—which Muslims claim to mean the "Praised One"—and foretold of his advent. Like the Quran, the hadith traditions refer to Muhammad: "Yes. By Allah, he is described in [the] Torah with some of the qualities attributed to him in the Qur'an."[6] However, a thorough search of the Bible does not yield any explicit mention of Muhammad. This is, in part, one reason for the emergence of the common Muslim claim that the Bible has been altered. Still, many Muslim apologists, past and present, endeavor to find Muhammad in various verses from the Old and New Testaments.

For instance, Muslims claim that Deuteronomy speaks of Muhammad: "The LORD came from Sinai and dawned from Seir upon us; he shone forth from Mount Paran; he came from the ten thousands of holy ones, with flaming fire at his right hand" (Deut. 33:2). Muslims argue that Paran in this verse refers to Muhammad's origin near Mecca, where he was born. While the verse and its context do not seem to hint

4. Ibn Hisham and Ibn Ishaq, *Life of Muhammad*, 241.
5. Tabari, *History*, 7:85.
6. Bukhari, 3.34.335.

in any way to the origin of a future prophet, this is what some Muslims believe. Similarly, some Muslims claim that Muhammad is mentioned in Genesis 25:13: "These are the names of the sons of Ishmael, named in the order of their birth: Nebaioth, the firstborn of Ishmael; and Kedar, Adbeel, Mibsam." Since Muhammad is the son of Ishmael and traces his lineage to Kedar, these Muslims believe the Bible mentions Muhammad here. Other Muslims find implied mentions of Muhammad in Isaiah: "The LORD goes out like a mighty man, like a man of war he stirs up his zeal" (Isa. 42:13), and "Let the desert and its cities lift up their voice, the villages that Kedar inhabits; let the habitants of Sela sing for joy, let them shout from the top of the mountains" (42:11). Muslims argue there were no other warriors like Muhammad who came through the mountains of Mecca. Some Muslims believe that because Muhammad preached against idols, no one else could fulfill Isaiah 42:17: "They are turned back and utterly put to shame, who trust in carved idols, who say to metal images, 'You are our gods.'" These are a sample of the many biblical passages that Muslims claim as references to Muhammad. They also emphatically suggest that Moses prophesied of Muhammad: "The LORD your God will raise up for you a prophet like me from among you, from your brothers—it is to him you shall listen" (Deut. 18:15). Some Muslims view this as a clear reference to Muhammad the Arabian prophet, despite the immediate context, which indicates that Moses was talking with the Jews about the awaited prophet from among them.

As for the New Testament, Muslims claim that Jesus prophesied of Muhammad clearly in the Gospel of John: "And I will ask the Father, and he will give you another Helper, to be with you forever, even the Spirit of truth, whom the world cannot receive, because it neither sees him nor knows him. You know him, for he dwells with you and will be in you" (John 14:16–17). For Muslims, the "Helper" (*paraklētos*) is Muhammad. Whereas Christians for two millennia have argued that the reference is to the Holy Spirit, the third person of the Trinity, as evidenced in other passages (14:26; 15:26; 16:7), Muslims view it as a biblical prophecy comparable to the verse in the Quran in which Jesus foretells of a prophet who will come after him named Ahmad. Of course, this claim is challenged by various details in the immediate context: Jesus speaks of a spirit, not a person; the prophesied spirit will not only remain forever among Christ's disciples but also dwell among them and be in them. Moreover, if Muslims insist that Muhammad is the "Helper" in the Gospel of John, then one implication is that Jesus himself sent Muhammad: "If I go, I will send him to you" (John 16:7). If Muslims truly believe Muhammad was sent by the deity, does this equate Jesus with the sending deity?

Finally, in their diligent pursuit to prove that Muhammad is mentioned in the Bible, some Muslims argue that the uncanonical Gospel of Barnabas tells of Muhammad. However, the authenticity of this alleged gospel is questioned by many Christians and Muslims alike. It refers to Muhammad as the Messiah, which contradicts the Quran itself (Q 3:45; 4:157, 171; 5:75). Scholars argue that it is a forgery from the Middle Ages, as they trace many problems in it—including passages that starkly contradict both the Bible and the Quran, historical and geographical errors, and ample anachronisms. Although it was common in the last century for Muslims to refer to the Gospel of Barnabas as proof of Muhammad's mention in the Bible, this argument has become rare—except among uninformed people—due to the document's textual and historical problems.

Faced with the challenge of finding Muhammad in the Bible, many classical Muslim exegetes argued that the Bible was corrupt, implying Jews and Christians had altered the text. This claim was carried throughout the centuries and became common. However, the Quran itself unequivocally denies any textual corruption of the Bible. The Quran states that no man can change divine words (Q 6:34) and instructs Muhammad to ask Christians and Jews if he is unaware of religious matters (Q 10:94). The Quran insists that the Torah is truthful and trustworthy (Q 5:43–44) and that the gospel contains guidance and light (Q 5:46). In fact, during Muhammad's time, Christians were commanded to follow Jesus's words in the gospel (Q 5:47). This indicates that the Bible was trusted at that time. It could not have been corrupted later because not only—according to Muslims—does Allah protect it but also "it is historically attested that the Bible was completely canonized, taught, quoted, documented, and circulated in various known lands (including within the superpowers of the Roman and Persian Empires) long before the advent of Muhammad in the seventh century."[7]

7. See the detailed discussion in Ibrahim, *Concise Guide to the Quran*, 101ff.; the quotation is from p. 106.

So was Muhammad mentioned in the Bible? Many Muslims believe he was, although there is no explicit reference, and the implied mentions are hardly plausible. From a critical standpoint, it appears that the Quran—in an attempt both to elevate Muhammad's prophethood and to dilute the Christian belief in the divinity of Jesus—advanced a claim that Jesus foretold of the final prophet and even named him. This was probably an attempt to convince Christians to believe in the one foretold by Jesus. To support the Quranic assertions, classical Muslim historians and exegetes created numerous accounts claiming that Jews and Christians met Muhammad and affirmed his prophethood, insisting that their respective scriptures included Muhammad's name. When this proved untrue in existing Jewish and Christian books, the claim of corruption emerged. Many cultural and religious Muslims still believe that the true Bible mentioned Muhammad but that the one used by Jews and Christians today is corrupt and does not include his name. Many progressive Muslims may rightly disagree with the claim that the Bible has been textually corrupted, but the case for the Bible mentioning Muhammad is still difficult to prove.

25

Where Are Muhammad's Sermons?

Muslims gather in the mosque each Friday to perform the ritual prayer (in Arabic, *salat*) at noon. Friday in Arabic is called *Jumu'a*, meaning "a gathering, assembling, or congregating." The ritual prayer on Friday is called the jumu'a prayer and is considered especially significant based on the Quran and traditions. In fact, there is a chapter in the Quran titled "The Jumu'a," in which Muslims are commanded, "O believers, when the call for prayer is made on Friday, go forth to Allah's remembrance and leave the trading aside" (Q 62:9). Some consider Friday the holiest day of the week.[1] It is the official Muslim holiday, although some Muslim-majority countries do not necessarily make it a day off. While Friday is important, the Friday ritual prayer at noon at the mosque and the Friday sermon are also of the highest significance in Islam. Before the Friday prayer, the imam of the mosque preaches two sermons. A sermon, or khutba, is the major source of Islamic teaching, especially for cultural and devoted Muslims, who understand that a prayer at the mosque

1. According to tradition, "The best day on which the sun has risen is Friday; on it Adam was created. On it he was made to enter Paradise, on it he was expelled from it. And the last hour will take place on no day other than Friday." Sahih Muslim, 4.1857; also 14.1384. See also Sunan an-Nasa'i, 2.14.1375.

receives a better reward from Allah than one performed at home.[2] The khutba serves as the formal public preaching of Islam. When preaching, an imam relies on the Quran and Muhammad's hadiths to exhort and warn Muslims regarding important matters. Additionally, the khutba is often an important venue for guiding Muslims concerning current political and social matters pertaining to Islam.

Most importantly, Muslims believe that the tradition regarding the Friday khutba can be traced back to Muhammad's day. He used to preach every Friday, as he reportedly cared for Muslims and their religious education. While he was in Mecca, Muslims claim, it was not possible for him to preach openly, due to the persecution from the pagans of Mecca. But at Medina, the situation changed. He was able to have his own mosque, which was basically the courtyard of his house. Every Friday he led the Muslims in their ritual prayer and conducted the khutba. This is a cherished belief among Muslims; however, there are unanswered questions. The Quran never mentions a khutba, and we do not have access to any khutba by Muhammad, except his final sermon as reported in later Muslim accounts.[3]

If Muhammad truly lived in Medina for over ten years, he would have delivered at least five hundred sermons. While we have tens of thousands of hadiths compiled centuries after his death and attributed to him, none of his Friday sermons have reached us. If the khutba was essential in teaching religious matters, it is puzzling that none of the major companions of Muhammad—who lived near him for years and often listened to him preach—endeavored to record, compile, or collect his sermons. This pressing question calls into doubt the importance of the traditions. Why did Muslims wait two centuries to record Muhammad's hadiths, while his most important sermons were never transcribed? Why didn't his first listeners gather his sermons? To what extent can one trust later sayings, if his immediate listeners never kept a record? These questions shed doubt on Muslim traditions in general, and many have questioned their reliability and validity.

2. Muhammad is reported to have said, "The reward of the prayer offered by a person in congregation is twenty-five times greater than that of the prayer offered in one's house or in the market (alone)." Bukhari, 1:11:620. In Sahih Muslim, the reward is more: "Prayer said in a congregation is twenty-seven degrees more excellent than prayer said by a single person." Sahih Muslim, 4.1365; also 4.1360. See also Sunan an-Nasa'i, 1.10.848.

3. Wensinck, "Khuṭba," 5:74–75.

In fact, in a so-called trusted hadith we are told that Muhammad himself forbade Muslims from writing traditions about him: "Do not take [literally, write] down anything from me, and he who took down anything from me except the Qur'an, he should efface [it]."[4] According to this hadith, Muhammad prohibited his immediate followers from writing his sayings and instructed them to erase anything they wrote about him except the Quranic statements. This may explain why his sermons were not recorded, but it does not reveal why later Muslims created collections of his alleged sayings. It is significant that this hadith appears in what Sunni Muslims commonly consider a sound and authentic hadith collection. In response to this hadith, Muslims had to consider why it was permissible for later generations to write down hadiths attributed to Muhammad after he had forbidden it. Some of today's Muslim clerics argue that Muhammad's early companions disagreed with each other regarding the transcription of his sayings—while many of them discouraged it, most allowed and authorized it. Some Muslim clerics—in supporting the validity of hadiths—claim that later Muslims *unanimously* agreed that it was permissible.[5] While the word *unanimously* may appear to some as an exaggeration, these claims provide no reason for the apparent violation of Muhammad's precise instruction, unless one considers his hadith a forgery. Thus, no one seems to have written down Muhammad's sermons while he lived, but centuries after his death, in an apparent violation of his instruction, Muslims gathered thousands of statements, attributed them to Muhammad, and claimed them as authentic and sound.

The matter of the existence or disappearance of Muhammad's sermons is important; without them how can one know Muhammad's teaching on a particular topic? He presumably delivered hundreds of sermons and taught Muslims what they needed to know about Islam. Although he accomplished this for ten years, none of his teachings have reached us. If one wants to learn what Muhammad taught, where should

4. Sahih Muslim, 42.7147.

5. See Islam Question & Answer, "Soundness of the Hadeeth." According to the official page, "Islam Q&A is an academic, educational, da'wah website which aims to offer advice and academic answers based on evidence from religious texts in an adequate and easy-to-understand manner. These answers are supervised by Shaykh Muhammad Saalih al-Munajjid."

one go? Muslim scholars point us to the Quran and Muhammad's hadiths. Since the Quran is often general and vague, Muslims rely heavily
on the hadiths, especially those identified by Muslim scholars as sound
and authentic collections. These scholars claim that the bulk of Muhammad's sermons are kept in his hadiths. Although eyewitnesses were not
permitted to write down Muhammad's words, later Muslims did, and
Muslims are invited to follow these words in religious matters. So what
did Muhammad teach about love, marriage, women, jihad, fighting,
slavery, homosexuality, prayer, and other matters? Muslims go to the
hadiths for these answers—after consulting the Quran. Since these are
sophisticated matters for cultural and even many religious Muslims, the
job of interpreting these texts lies mainly in the hands of Muslim jurists
and clerics. They supervise the flow of knowledge among the masses. As
for Muhammad's reported hadith forbidding the writing down of his
words, it appears to have sunk in an ocean of contradictory traditions,
resulting in an obliterated past.

26

What Did Muhammad Say about Loving One's Neighbors?

According to the Quran, Muhammad is the perfect example of conduct for Muslims to follow: "Indeed, you have had an excellent example in Allah's apostle" (Q 33:21). This reflects that Islam is a religion with two foundations: the Quran and Muhammad's example. The Muslim community follows the sacred text, the Quran, as it was reportedly lived and practiced by the excellent precedent, Muhammad. While this is generally true among all Muslims, Shiites add to these two foundations an extra layer: the example and teachings of the twelve infallible imams.

Muslims often claim that Muhammad changed many of the customs and practices of the pre-Islamic era, a period known as jahiliyya, meaning "age of ignorance." He set an example for his Muslim community in many aspects of life, including how he exemplified caring for one's neighbor. We are told that in pre-Islamic jahiliyya, people were wicked and would abuse and assault their neighbors. With Muhammad's advent, he set a new example of caring and valuing one's neighbor. Muhammad, Muslims claim, granted neighbors rights and forbade harming them or stealing from them. He reportedly strengthened and secured the Muslim society by establishing kindness and cooperation as societal foundations. In so doing, Muslims argue, Muhammad was an example of fulfilling the Quran, as it commands Muslims to demonstrate kindness and goodness to various people, including near and distant neighbors: "Worship Allah and associate none with him. Do good to parents, relatives, orphans; to the poor, the nearby neighbor, the foreign [or distant] neighbor" (Q 4:36). Some Muslims interpret this verse as commanding them to do good even to strangers.

Muhammad is reported to have said, "None amongst you believes (truly) until he loves for his brother—or he said 'for his neighbor'—that which he loves for himself."[1] Muslims often repeat this tradition as a basis for acting kindly and justly toward one's neighbor. Muhammad reportedly declared, "Gabriel impressed upon me (the kind treatment) towards the neighbor (so much) that I thought as if he would soon confer upon him the (right) of inheritance."[2] This is a divine prescription, through the archangel Gabriel, for Muslims to care for their neighbors in accordance with Muhammad's example. Muhammad reportedly instructed, "Whoever believes in Allah and the Last Day, should not hurt his neighbor and whoever believes in Allah and the Last Day, should serve his guest generously and whoever believes in Allah and the Last Day, should speak what is good or keep silent."[3] This hadith appears to call Muslims not to harm their neighbors but to treat them with dignity and respect. Muslims believe that Muhammad not only instructed so but also lived accordingly. Thus, hurting one's neighbor is against Muhammad's command. In the same vein, Muhammad warned Muslims not to act wrongly against their neighbors: "He will not enter Paradise whose neighbor is not secure from his wrongful conduct."[4] In effect, eternal bliss—according to this hadith—appears unattainable for Muslims who commit wrongdoings against their neighbors. In another hadith, Muhammad reportedly commanded Muslims to care for their neighbors—specifically, to feed their hungry neighbors, as no one is a true believer

1. Sahih Muslim, 1.72, 73; and Bukhari, 1.2.13. Needless to mention, this hadith has obvious similarities to the biblical statements of Jesus on loving one's neighbor (Matt. 22:39–40; Mark 12:31). This may reflect how later Muslim authors sought to present Muhammad and his teachings to Christians in the conquered lands. See Ibrahim, *Stated Motivations*, 91.

2. Sahih Muslim, 32.6356.

3. Bukhari, 8.73.158; see also similar accounts in Bukhari, 7.62.114; 8.76.482; and Sahih Muslim, 1.76.

4. Sahih Muslim, 1.74.

who is well-fed while their neighbors are hungry.[5] For many Muslims, this means treating a neighbor like a family member.

Muhammad reportedly warned Muslim women, "O Muslim women! None of you should look down upon the gift sent by her female neighbor even if it were the trotters of the sheep (fleshless part of legs)."[6] In this hadith, Muhammad emphasized the value of respecting one's neighbor. It forbids Muslims from looking down on neighbors and their gifts. According to tradition, a Muslim man came to Muhammad and asked, "I have two neighbors! To whom shall I send my gifts?" Muhammad responded, "To the one whose gate is nearer to you."[7] Moreover, in matters of property selling, Muhammad is said to have granted the neighbor the right of preemption—that is, the primary right to its purchase: "The neighbor is most entitled to the right of pre-emption, and he should wait for its exercise even if he is absent, when the two properties have one road."[8] This rule is practiced in many Muslim-majority countries and is based on Muhammad's reported command to favor one's neighbor over others.

These hadiths provide a compelling instruction for Muslims regarding the treatment of their neighbors. In their attempt to follow these traditions, Muslims are not supposed to attack, harass, or harm their neighbors. Rather, they are exhorted to care for them and protect their possessions. While the Muslim histories include examples of some who acted wrongly against their non-Muslim neighbors, these traditions seem to command the opposite. Some claim that these hadiths were reported in a community full of Muslims, so they do not apply when the neighbor is not Muslim. However, for the vast majority of Muslims today, caring for one's neighbor is a religious duty, a highly commended social action, and a well-known cultural trait. Among cultural Muslims in particular, there is a popular saying: "Muhammad commanded us to take good care of our seventh neighbor." The point is that if you care for your seventh neighbor, you should also care for the six nearer to you. While this is not an actual hadith that one can locate in Muhammad's compiled

5. Sahih Muslim, 32.6357, 6358.

6. Bukhari, 3.47.740; 8.73.46; see also Sahih Muslim, 5.2247.

7. Bukhari, 3.35.460; 8.73.49.

8. Sunan Abi Dawud, 23.3511. See also Sunan Ibn Majah, 17.2589: "The neighbor has more right to preemption of his neighbor, so let him wait for him even if he is absent, if they share a path."

traditions, it is popularly attributed to him and widely circulates among Muslims, driving their commendable deeds toward their neighbors.[9]

Did Muhammad really say these hadiths? This is an important question because it has significant implications. The answer determines a great deal concerning the authority, reliability, and application of these hadiths in Muslim communities. Each statement receives its authority from the status of the one who said it. A statement from Muhammad receives much more authority among Muslims than one from anyone else. The acceptance of these traditions as morally true is not contentious. In the end, everyone hopes to live in peace and harmony with their neighbors. And whether Muhammad stated them or not, these hadiths have become a significant part of the religious and cultural Muslim identity. But what about some other controversial hadiths from the same collections? If some trust and apply the hadiths regarding caring for one's neighbors, what should one do with the others that seem to command the opposite? What about the hadiths attributed to Muhammad regarding apostasy from Islam, fighting the non-Muslims, slavery, and homosexuality? These are contentious topics. Are people supposed to pick and choose from the pool of thousands of hadiths, claiming some are reliable while others are not? These are indeed significant questions with substantial consequences.

9. For some resources, see Rosenthal, "Stranger in Medieval Islam"; Siddiqui, *Hospitality and Islam*, 20–71; and Bakalla, *Arabic Culture through Its Language and Literature*, especially chap. 1.

27

How Does Muhammad's Tradition Treat Apostasy from Islam?

When Muhammad died in 632, according to Muslim traditions, many Muslims abandoned Islam. Muhammad's successor, Caliph Abu Bakr, decided to wage wars against all these ex-Muslims.[1] The Muslim tradition calls these wars the Apostasy Wars, in which Abu Bakr appears as a hero who defends Islam's purity and fulfills Muhammad's commands. Some of these ex-Muslims declared themselves prophets, and others refused to pay the zakat, an obligatory religious tax paid by Muslims to the Muslim ruler. Abu Bakr believed that whether one abandoned Islam as a whole or simply abandoned one of its tenets, one was an apostate. In one account, Abu Bakr is reported to have stated, "By Allah, if they refuse to give me even a tying rope which they used to give to Allah's Messenger, I would fight them for withholding it."[2] The wars succeeded in bringing some Muslims back to Islam, but many were killed. While Shiites often understand the Apostasy Wars as campaigns that Abu Bakr launched to secure his ruthless rule against those who rejected his

1. Tabari, *History*, 10:55ff.; and Baladhuri, *Origins of the Islamic State*, 143–59. See the detailed discussion in Ibrahim, *Stated Motivations*, 130ff.
2. Bukhari, 9.92.388; also Sahih Muslim, 1.29.

145

leadership after Muhammad's death, many Sunnis view the caliph as a devoted Muslim commander who was protecting Islam and following Muhammad's instruction: "Whoever changed his Islamic religion, then kill him."[3] This statement is attributed to Muhammad and appears in many trusted hadith collections.[4]

From a critical perspective, one cannot be certain whether Muhammad actually stated this hadith. Most scholars believe the statement more accurately reflects the political and religious requirements of the centuries following Muhammad's death. However, the implication—for those who believe Muhammad stated it and want to follow his example by applying it—is huge. One important consequence involves religious freedom. In a sense, non-Muslims are free to change religions as they please, but Muslims are not at liberty to embrace any other religion. Apostasy from Islam is, according to this hadith, punishable by death. Considering the example of Abu Bakr's Apostasy Wars, the stakes are even higher. Many believe he launched these wars to protect Islam. If Muslims admire Abu Bakr's example in waging war against the apostates and view it as a fulfillment of Muhammad's command, then they find it difficult to accept that a Muslim would abandon Islam. Thus, religious liberty is in jeopardy. In 2016, the Pew Research Center published the findings from its examination of apostasy policies around the world: "Laws restricting apostasy and blasphemy are most common in the Middle East and North Africa."[5] In the heartland of the Arab Muslim World, the majority of people can be punished for changing their religion or for questioning or insulting perceived sacred figures. Contemporary Muslim scholar Abdullah Saeed (1965–) explains the problem: "Today, Islam seems to be the only major religion to maintain that conversion away from the religion (apostasy) must be punished with death. In a number of Muslim-majority countries such as Saudi Arabia, apostasy laws and the associated death penalty still prevail."[6]

3. Bukhari, 9.84.57.
4. See, for instance, Bukhari, 4.52.260; Sunan an-Nasa'i, 5.37.4064: "Whoever changes his religion, kill him"; and Sunan Ibn Majah, 3.20.2535: "Whoever changes his religion, execute him." The same hadith can be found in several other collections: Sunan Abi Dawud, 39.4337; Jami' at-Tirmidhi, 3.15.1458; and Sunan an-Nasa'i, 5.37.4065, 4067.
5. Theodorou, "Which Countries Still Outlaw Apostasy and Blasphemy?"
6. Saeed, "Limitations on Religious Freedom in Islam," 369–70.

Saeed's statement reveals two competing paradigms within Islam: a traditional, literal application of Muhammad's commands, exemplified in Saudi Arabia's implementation of apostasy laws, and a progressive Muslim interpretation that seeks "to explore the issue of apostasy and ways of rethinking this in the context of Islam, as part of an argument for freedom of religion among Muslims."[7] Saeed is an example of a Muslim scholar who attempts to rethink and interpret Islam in today's world. He is an Australian citizen who teaches Islamic studies at the University of Melbourne. Saeed was born in the Maldives, which, according to its 2008 constitution, follows Sunni Islam as the state religion: "The Maldives is a sovereign, independent, democratic Republic based on the principles of Islam."[8] In the Maldives, the president—as well as any government official, member of the parliament, or professional within the judicial circle—must be "a Muslim and a follower of a Sunni school of Islam."[9] Saeed is viewed by many from his homeland as too progressive to return home. His attempts to rethink Muslim traditions contradict the literal interpretations of hadiths. For Saeed, "Islamic tradition is much more restrictive of religious liberty than modern norms, and this tradition still carries great weight and authority among the majority of Muslims today."[10] Saeed's statements reflect the growing dissonance within Islam—not only between traditional and progressive approaches to Islamic sacred texts but also between the conversations in Western academia and those in the heartland of Islam.

But there is a deeper problem: the hadith concerning killing those who abandon Islam is not singular. There are many others. If one rejects them, the inevitable consequence is the collapse of the entire tradition, or a poor methodology of cherry-picking as one pleases. In one hadith, we are told that Muhammad declared, "I have been commanded to fight against people so long as they do not declare that there is no god but Allah, and he who professed it was guaranteed the protection of his property and life on my behalf."[11] The literal reading of this hadith is troubling. If one seeks to follow Muhammad's example, one must fight

---

7. Saeed, "Limitations on Religious Freedom in Islam," 370.
8. Comparative Constitute Project, "Maldives 2008."
9. Comparative Constitute Project, "Maldives 2008."
10. Saeed, "Making the Islamic Case for Religious Liberty."
11. Sahih Muslim, 1.30.

people until they embrace Islam by professing the Shahada (profession of faith). This statement is repeated within many hadiths identified as sound and authentic by Muslim scholars. It also appears in a different form, in which Muhammad is reported to have said, "I have been ordered to fight the people till they say: 'None has the right to be worshipped but Allah.' And if they say so, pray like our prayers, face our Qibla and slaughter as we slaughter, then their blood and property will be sacred to us and we will not interfere with them except legally and their reckoning will be with Allah."[12] This hadith drives many of the atrocities committed by militant groups such as ISIS and Boko Haram. These groups interpret Islam literally: fighting non-Muslims is justified by Allah and in fulfillment of Muhammad's explicit commands. Non-Muslims, according to this literal reading, should be fought until they embrace Islam and its tenets.

But some Muslims today notice a major problem with hadiths such as these that call for forcing Islam on non-Muslims. These statements violate and oppose specific Quranic verses. In light of these explicit hadiths, it is unsurprising that some Quranic verses about tolerating non-Muslim faiths are dismissed as abrogated. Many extremists justify their atrocities by relying on explicit statements attributed to Muhammad and some matching Quranic verses rather than focusing on tolerant Quranic verses like "To you your religion and to me mine" (Q 109:6) and "There is no compulsion in religion" (Q 2:256). In the end, Muslims commonly understand the Quran to be the general, while hadiths are the precise; the former is usually interpreted by the latter. When the two contradict, the precise and explicit take priority, especially because Muhammad's precedent is greatly cherished among Muslims. This is why our initial question is crucial: Did Muhammad really say these hadiths? How reliable are they? If one believes that these hadiths were truly stated by Muhammad and that he is the best example for humankind, the implication is huge for many aspects of life, including religious liberty and mutual coexistence.

Muslim trust in the authority and reliability of Muhammad's hadiths—and their literal application—is at the center of an important question

12. Bukhari, 1.8.387. The hadith can be found repeatedly in many trusted collections. See Bukhari, 4.52.196; Sahih Muslim, 1.30, 32; Sunan Abi Dawud, 14.2634, 2635; and Sunan Ibn Majah, 1.1.71; 5.36.3927.

posed on a major Sunni website, IslamQA.info, which claims to be "an academic, educational, da'wa [Islamic preaching] website which aims to offer advice and academic answers based on evidence from religious texts in an adequate and easy-to-understand manner."[13] A majority of Sunnis consider this website one of the most educational in the Arab world. It provides religious rulings (fatwas) based on the Quran, Muhammad's hadiths, and trusted Sunni schools of thought. Under the title "Does Islam Affirm Freedom of Religion?" one Muslim asks, "If Islam has indeed embraced freedom of belief, why should it fight apostasy, paganism, and atheism?" A Muslim cleric responds, "Islam does not endorse religious freedom. Islam only commands the pure belief, demands it, and imposes it on people. It does not make them free to choose whatever they desire from available religions. To say that Islam permits religious freedom is wrong." The cleric adds, "There is no freedom in Islam in that way. A person must adhere to the correct belief and abandon what Allah has forbidden." He concludes, "Whoever changes his religion—the religion of Islam—with infidelity must be killed, if he does not repent. This way everyone knows that a Muslim has no freedom at all to leave the truth to take the falsehood."[14] This Muslim cleric appears to cherish and follow Muhammad's hadiths as reliable and valid instructions for all situations.

In another question, the same website criticizes article 18 of the Universal Declaration of Human Rights, which states, "Everyone has the right to freedom of thought, conscience and religion; this right includes freedom to change his religion or belief, and freedom, either alone or in community with others and in public or private, to manifest his religion or belief in teaching, practice, worship and observance."[15] In response, the cleric quotes various Quranic verses (Q 68:35, 36; 32:18; 38:28), rejects the human rights article, and claims, "It is a call to abolish the [Islamic] ruling on apostasy, and to openly flaunt the principles of kufr [unbelief] and heresy. It is a call to open the door to everyone who wants to criticize Islam or the Prophet of Islam Muhammad and to have the freedom to criticize and express oneself with no restrictions. These are

13. Islam Question & Answer, "About Our Site."
14. These are direct translations of question #129141, Islam Question & Answer.
15. See UN General Assembly, Resolution 217A, Universal Declaration of Human Rights, December 10, 1948, https://www.un.org/en/universal-declaration-human-rights/.

corrupt principles."[16] For this Muslim cleric and others like him, Muhammad's statements are reliable and authoritative.

In contrast to these literal applications of Muhammad's hadiths, progressive and modernist Muslims take different approaches. Two creative approaches are worth noting. Some accept the hadiths as reliable but understand them only as reflective of Muhammad's time, not as valid commands for all times and places. Others reject the entire hadith corpus, claiming it is a forgery, as they adhere only to the Quran. These approaches usually appear in Western circles and among scholars who aim to present Islam as a valid religious choice in pluralistic societies.

This progressive approach to Islamic matters, including religious freedom, appears in a recent example. In October 2018, Mustafa Akyol, a self-described Muslim modernist, presented a lecture at the University of Notre Dame titled "Religious Freedom in Islam." Akyol addressed Quranic verses and hadith statements on apostasy from Islam. He began his lecture by describing a troubling situation he experienced in Malaysia after he lectured on apostasy laws in the country. Apparently, the lecture displeased the authorities, because the Malaysian religious police arrested him and placed him in front of a sharia court. He was accused of illegally reciting the Quran without a religious permit but was later released. At Notre Dame, in making a case for religious freedom in Islam, Akyol argued for reinterpreting Islamic texts through historicism. For him, religious texts emerge within a specific historical context that reflects social and cultural features: "The best way to go about reinterpreting the Quran is through historicism, which focuses on divine intent in the context of the work's initial production."[17] While he speaks here of the Quran, his approach is clear and directly opposes the literal interpretation of Islamic texts. This Islamic modernist approach should prove helpful in addressing hadiths attributed to Muhammad on apostasy and religious freedom.

There are at least two competing paradigms in the Muslim world today. The first advocates for a traditional reading of Islamic texts. It calls for a literal interpretation and application of Muhammad's commands

16. This question is in the English section of the same website: Islam Question & Answer, "Western Human Rights Organizations."
17. See the report on Akyol's lecture in Murphy, "Lecture Explores Religious Freedom." See also Akyol, *Reopening Muslim Minds*, xxii–xxiv.

as found in the so-called trusted and authoritative hadith traditions. This paradigm explains the emergence of groups like ISIS and Boko Haram. The literal application of Muhammad's hadiths stems from an enthusiastic trust in their reliability and is encouraged by many who believe that the Quran is valid in all times and places and that Muhammad's commands are to be followed literally. The second paradigm distances itself from traditions, either by contextualizing and reinterpreting them or by dismissing them altogether and viewing them as later inventions. While this paradigm flourishes particularly in Western circles, it has a growing number of advocates in the heartland of Islam. Only one of these two paradigms can advance religious liberty and mutual coexistence. Still, the weight, reliability, and authority of Muhammad's hadiths are unmatched among the vast majority of cultural and religious Muslims. How long will this celebrated status endure among the masses? Only time will tell.

28

What Do the Hadiths Say about Jihad?

After the attacks of September 11, 2001, the word *jihad* became familiar in the West. While many non-Muslims view it as Islamic holy war against the infidels, a significant number of Muslims in the West insist that it has nothing to do with war and mainly refers to the struggle with oneself for piety and self-control. Indeed, the word is confusing to non-Muslims, but it has now become a part of the English language. In Islamic terminology, the word refers to struggling and striving to follow Allah's commands. While the Quran seems to treat jihad generally, the hadith traditions provide specifics. In my book *A Concise Guide to the Quran*, I focus on the meaning of jihad in the Quran. I explain that Islam's scripture provides at least two meanings for the concept of jihad. One refers to armed fighting (Q 8:72; 9:88; 49:15). The Quran has a specific term devoted to armed fighting with religious significance, *qital*, which refers to sacred fighting for Allah's cause. In examining the Quran's treatment of jihad and qital, I conclude, "Overall, while jihad has two meanings, qital has only one. While the former can be ambiguous, the latter is very clear. If people say that jihad is Islamic holy war, this can be right or wrong—but if they say that qital for Allah's sake is Islamic holy war, they are right. Jihad and qital are not synonymous, but they overlap in one area: fighting against non-Muslims."[1] While the Quran appears vague and ambiguous in its use of the term *jihad*, the hadiths are detailed and specific.

In Sahih al-Bukhari, an entire section is devoted to the term *jihad*.[2] Among the vast majority of Sunnis, this hadith collection is the most trusted Islamic source after the Quran. Sunnis commonly believe that Imam Bukhari "worked extremely hard to collect his [hadiths]. Each report in his collection was checked for compatibility with the Qur'an, and the veracity of the chain of reporters had to be painstakingly established."[3] This reflects the authoritative and prescriptive nature of the hadiths for most Muslims. For them, the hadith statements—especially those compiled by Bukhari—contain Muhammad's teaching on the topic of jihad. In his collection on jihad, Bukhari gathered more than 280 hadiths (with some obvious repetitions) and attributed them to Muhammad, affirming they were precisely stated by Islam's prophet centuries earlier.

According to Bukhari, a Muslim man asked Muhammad, "Instruct me as to such a deed as equals Jihad (in reward)," to which Muhammad replied, "I do not find such a deed."[4] In the same hadith, we are introduced to an important Islamic term, *mujahid*, which refers to the person who strives in jihad for Allah; it is translated in English by Bukhari's translator as "the Muslim fighter." We are told that "the Mujahid (i.e., Muslim fighter) is rewarded even for the footsteps of his horse."[5] According to Bukhari, Muhammad praised the example of a Muslim mujahid and said, "The example of a Mujahid in Allah's Cause—and Allah knows better who really strives in His Cause—is like a person who fasts and prays continuously. Allah guarantees that He will admit the Mujahid in His Cause into Paradise if he is killed, otherwise He will return him to his home safely with rewards and war booty."[6] Similarly, Muhammad is reported to have said, "Paradise has one-hundred grades which Allah has reserved for the Mujahidin [plural of Mujahid] who fight in His Cause, and the distance between each of two grades is like the distance between

---

1. See the discussion on Quranic jihad in Ibrahim, *Concise Guide to the Quran*, 126.
2. See https://sunnah.com/bukhari/56, where the title reads, "Fighting for the Cause of Allah (Jihaad)."
3. See the comments of the editor at Sahih Bukhari, https://www.sahih-bukhari.com/.
4. Bukhari, 4.52.44.
5. Bukhari, 4.52.44.
6. Bukhari, 4.52.46.

the Heaven and the Earth."[7] This suggests the remarkable incentive for a mujahid, a striver in Allah's path. This is also evident in a reported hadith by Muhammad: "Nobody who enters Paradise likes to go back to the world even if he got everything on the earth, except a Mujahid who wishes to return to the world so that he may be martyred ten times because of the dignity he receives (from Allah)."[8] These hadiths reflect the praiseworthy status of jihad and highlight the great reward awaiting a striver in battle for Allah's cause. They also indicate that there is a high status and reward for any martyr who dies in jihad. This may explain why many seek martyrdom for Allah's sake and cause.

In the same vein, Muhammad reportedly said that the best deed for a Muslim is to offer the ritual prayer at its divinely prescribed times, while the second best is to be good and obedient to one's parents, and the third is to "participate in Jihad in Allah's Cause."[9] Muhammad continued by explaining that there is no forced emigration (hijra) for Muslims since they conquered the pagans of Mecca, "but Jihad and good intention remain; and if you are called (by the Muslim ruler) for fighting, go forth immediately."[10] It appears that jihad in these hadiths is directly linked with fighting for Allah's cause, not simply indicating a self-piety and godliness. Muhammad reportedly declared, "Know that Paradise is under the shades of swords."[11] If a devoted Muslim perceives these statements as directly voiced by Muhammad, one inevitable reaction might be to seek the jihad of the sword for Allah's cause. Like the term *mujahid*, the hadith introduces another term, *ghazi*, which refers to a warrior or an invader in Allah's cause. Muhammad reportedly said, "He who prepares a Ghazi going in Allah's Cause is given a reward equal to that of a Ghazi."[12] The term *ghazi* is a noun derived from the Arabic verb *ghaza*, "to invade." According to Muhammad's reported statement, there is a great reward not only for a warrior but also for the one who prepares the warrior. In one battle led by Muhammad, the Muslims of Medina reportedly declared, "We are those who have sworn allegiance

7. Bukhari, 4.52.48.
8. Bukhari, 4.52.72.
9. Bukhari, 4.52.41.
10. Bukhari, 4.52.42, 79; 5.59.600; see also 4.52.311.
11. Bukhari, 4.52.73.
12. Bukhari, 4.52.96.

to Muhammad for Jihad as long as we live."[13] This hadith reflects jihad in connection to devotion to Muhammad. Even Muslim women, we are told, sought jihad in battle because of its status and reward. Nonetheless, according to the hadith, women are not expected to fulfill the jihad in battle, because their jihad is to perform pilgrimage: Muhammad's wife Aisha came to him and asked him to permit her to participate in jihad, but he responded, "Your Jihad is the performance of Hajj."[14]

These are only a sample of hadiths on jihad found in one compilation that is highly trusted by Sunnis. These hadiths indicate the high status, great reward, and importance of jihad for Muslims, especially for those who believe that these statements came directly from Muhammad. The examination of these hadiths also highlights how they are clearer and more direct than many Quranic statements about jihad. This is one reason why the hadith corpus is so dear and close to the hearts of Muslims. If a Muslim seeks to obey Allah and Muhammad, they will inevitably attempt to follow these statements to the letter. But did Muhammad really say these hadiths? It might be better for a religiously pluralistic world if he did not. In fact, today a growing number of non-Muslim and Muslim thinkers question the long-standing authority of the hadith traditions. From a critical standpoint, many scholars—particularly in the West—view the hadith statements as a product of their time of documentation, not as words said by Muhammad. When these hadiths were being compiled, Muslims were asking political and religious questions that did not concern Muslims during Muhammad's time. It seems to have been convenient for many Muslims to forge accounts and simply attribute them to the most authoritative man in Islam, Muhammad. Once attributed to Muhammad, the collection only needed to be declared authentic and reliable in order to chastise any Muslim who questioned it. While this line of argument flourishes among non-Muslim scholars, a growing number of Muslims have adopted it as well by showing dissatisfaction with the entire tradition. Some identify these Muslims as "hadith-rejecters" in contrast to "the people of the hadith." Who are these hadith-rejecters, and why do they reject the hadiths? How can Islam maintain its core without the huge reliance on Muhammad's traditions? We will discuss these matters in the next two questions.

13. Bukhari, 4.52.208.
14. Bukhari, 4.52.127, 128.

29

Who Are the Hadith-Rejecters among Muslims?

In 833, there was a significant conflict between two Muslim groups. The first was made up of religious scholars, known as the lovers of the hadiths or the people of the hadiths. They cherished and highly respected the hadiths as a reliable corpus of Muhammad's traditions. These Muslims were also known as traditionists. The second group was made up of freethinking Muslims—highly influenced by Greek philosophy—who questioned the reliability of the hadith traditions and demanded rigorous scrutiny in separating the sound from the fabricated. This second group was known as the Mu'tazilites. A Mu'tazilite was a Muslim who thought critically about religious matters and sought to make sense of traditional answers. While Mu'tazilites were indeed rationalists, they were still fully committed to most traditional Islamic doctrines and to the defense and expansion of Islam. They questioned the hadiths and their authority, but they were certainly committed Muslims, and some of them wrote anti-Christian treatises.[1]

---

1. Reynolds, *Muslim Theologian in a Sectarian Milieu*, chap. 1. For the conflict between the two groups, see Ibrahim, *Conversion to Islam*, chaps. 3–4.

The traditionists were growing in power as they developed numerous hadiths. Many of the traditionists were getting paid to write hadiths, and most Muslims revered them as the advocates of Muhammad's traditions. Their growing influence threatened the caliph's religious authority; therefore, the caliph at the time, Ma'mun, wanting to maintain authority over religious matters, demanded that the traditionists submit to his power as the religious arbiter of the caliphate. The traditionists were stubborn, but the caliph instructed them to accept the Mu'tazilite belief that the Quran had not eternally existed with Allah and was instead created at a certain point in time. If the traditionists did not comply, said the caliph, they would face death. This became known as the Muslim inquisition (in Arabic, *mihna*, "trial"). The conflict was initiated, sponsored, and supervised by the Muslim caliph himself, although he was not actually fond of the Mu'tazilite doctrinal positions. He simply sought to maintain power over religious matters among Muslims. Consequently, he forced the scholars of the hadiths to forsake their support of the traditions, which would cause them to lose the authority they had obtained from elevating these traditions. For the Mu'tazilites, it did not make sense that the Quran was eternal—how could there be two eternal beings, Allah and the Quran? For traditionists, the Quran was absolutely uncreated—it had been eternal with Allah. One reason for their strong belief was the hadiths themselves: the hadith tradition emphatically presented an eternally existing Quran in a celestial tablet, and the traditionists cherished and revered that tradition. Four months later, the caliph died. His successors continued to enforce the inquisition for some time, but they eventually grew tired of the resistance from the traditionists. A few years later, the inquisition was abolished, and thus the traditionists were victorious. They became the earliest manifestation of Sunnism, which highly esteems and relies on Muhammad's hadiths. As for the Mu'tazilites, their approach and rationalistic arguments soon faded, although some Muslims remained dedicated to this vision within Islam.[2]

This event reveals why the people of the hadiths continued to grow in power and influence up to the present. They—not the rationalists who question traditions and their reliability—won the fight. Whether

2. For a background and scholarly analysis of the Muslim inquisition, see Ibrahim, *Conversion to Islam*, chap. 4, where a list of valuable studies and primary sources is offered.

the hadith collections are reliable or not, hadith scholars have been for centuries the arbiters of religious matters in Islam. Why were they so powerful? One reason is that hadiths are not merely statements found in books; they are far more. Hadiths are the core of everything we know about Islam. All historical accounts on Muhammad and early Islam are formed from consecutive hadiths. All that we know about Quranic exegesis is also a series of hadiths. Ibn Ishaq, Ibn Hisham, Tabari, and all those who followed them in later generations—the renowned classical Muslim writers—were actually scholars of hadiths. They were from the people of the hadiths. They controlled the knowledge of Islam's origins, which was supported by hadiths. These scholars influenced all aspects of Muslim life, as they used hadiths to prescribe religious rulings. Their power relied on the status of the hadiths. If the reliability of hadiths vanished, the authority of hadiths would collapse, and the entire historical and exegetical Islamic corpus would be in jeopardy. This is one reason why many Muslims today are adamantly against attempts to question the hadith material.

According to Muslim sources, some of these hadith scholars made their living through narrating hadiths as they worked for different caliphs. To establish legitimacy, these scholars also advanced a major claim: the hadiths are the second authoritative source in Islam—only next to the Quran. This claim established more power for their position as the people of the hadiths. To support such a claim, they argued that the Quran called Muslims to follow the hadiths: "Say, if you love Allah, follow me. Allah will then love you and forgive your sins. Allah is all-forgiving and all-merciful. Say, obey Allah and the messenger. However, if you turn your backs, Allah does not love the unbelievers" (Q 3:31–32). Relying on this passage, hadith scholars claim that Allah instructed them to follow Muhammad's hadiths. However, we should note that the Quran is not specific in these two verses, and it does not refer to the hadiths. It mainly invites Muslims to follow Allah and the messenger. Even if we assume the messenger here is Muhammad, these verses do not explicitly specify the hadiths, especially as the hadith corpus was created centuries after Muhammad. Hadith scholars point to another verse: "Those who obey Allah and the messenger will be with those blessed by Allah" (Q 4:69). Still, this verse does not specify the hadith corpus in particular; yet it is quoted by hadith scholars to claim authority. Their logic: the Quran instructs Muslims to follow Muhammad, and the scholars provide his trusted hadiths.

For centuries, Sunni Muslims did not dare to question the hadiths, especially those compiled by Bukhari. In fact, there is a popular saying in the Arab World: "Are you faulting Bukhari?" The point of the saying is that you cannot question a highly respected person. When an esteemed figure is being questioned about any matter, one may use this saying to indicate the difficulty of questioning a person of this status. Throughout history, a few hadith-rejecters emerged, but they always remained on the margins of Islamic thought. Today there is a noticeable dissonance in Islam regarding Muhammad's hadiths. We can identify a growing number of hadith-rejecters among Muslims. They dismiss the hadiths partially or completely. They question the classical assumption of the halo surrounding the hadith collections. These hadith-rejecters are either skeptics or deniers of the reliability and authority of Muhammad's hadiths. While this growing trend does not necessarily label itself Mu'tazilite, it critically evaluates the so-called Muslim traditions. The remarkable observation is that the hadith-rejecters are currently flourishing everywhere, even in the Arab Muslim World.

Among Muslims today, one of the clearest examples of the hadith-rejecters is the group self-identified as "The People of the Quran." Some call them Quranists. For them, "Allah's laws can be obtained from the Quran, as Allah's message is complete, reliable, and eternal," and they "distrust the authenticity and reliability of Muhammad's hadiths, and all traditions in general."[3] While the hadith scholars argue that the Quran needs exegetical works to interpret its verses, the hadith-rejecters—such as the Quranists—view the Quran as the best tool to interpret itself. They view these hadiths as forgeries since they were created centuries after Muhammad's time and were fabricated for religious and political reasons. In our day, a well-known Quranist is Ahmed Sobhy Mansour (1949–), who received his doctorate at the prestigious Azhar University in Cairo. After he taught for years in Egypt, focusing on the Quran alone, he was marginalized and harassed for his views as a hadith-rejecter. He was considered a heretic and subsequently imprisoned. He was later forced into exile, at which time he moved to the United States and began teaching

---

3. Ibrahim, *Concise Guide to the Quran*, 134.

his views openly. Before Mansour, the Quranist movement was influenced by Ghulam Ahmad Parwez (1903–1985), who was born in India and later became a resident of Pakistan. Parwez challenged Sunnism by adopting and applying rationalism in interpreting religious matters. Relying on the Quran alone and rejecting the so-called trusted hadiths, Parwez questioned foundational Islamic matters related to some pillars of Islam, including the ritual prayer, almsgiving, and the performance of the pilgrimage to Mecca. His important book *Islam: A Challenge to Religion*, published in Lahore, Pakistan, in 1968, is considered by some to be one of the most influential religious works in Pakistani history.

The question remains: Why is there a growing number of Muslims who currently reject the hadiths? Is it due only to the late date of compilation of the hadith corpus? This is what scholars call the external evidence, and while this may be one reason, there is more to it. What about the internal evidence—that is, the content of the hadiths? Are the so-called trusted hadith collections really compelling and convincing in what they say about Muhammad, Allah, and Islam? What drives some Muslims to strongly reject the hadiths today? We turn to these matters in the next question.

30

Why Are the Hadith-Rejecters Growing in Number?

In past centuries, Muslims would travel to Islamic libraries in remote places to access manuscripts of early Arabic sources in order to learn and excel in Islamic dogma. Today numerous sources are available online, and many of them are translated. Everyone questions everything, especially what used to be called sacred. In the past, Muslims tended to rely on what the imam of their local mosque said about Muhammad's hadiths. Today everyone can access the Islamic primary sources, especially the so-called sound and trusted hadith collections, and search their contents in different languages. Today's Muslims have access to a tremendous amount of knowledge, far beyond what was available to past generations. Muslims began to read the hadiths for themselves. Many questions arose due to the unrealistic nature of some hadiths or the unfavorable way they presented both Islam and Muhammad. This, among other factors, resulted in a growing number of hadith-rejecters. Even in the heartland of Islam, the Middle East and North Africa, the news of hadith-rejecters is now a growing trend. For instance, among the hadith-rejecters from Morocco are Ahmed Assid, Mohamed Lamsiah, and Rachid Aylal, and among those from Egypt are Islaam Behery, Khaled Muntaser, Ibrahim Eissa, and Ahmed Abdo Maher. All are quite active on social media and quite vocal in their criticism of the hadiths. They are gaining a wide audience because their cases seem compelling to many Muslims. In essence, the hadith-rejecters believe a great number of the so-called sound hadiths are no longer defensible in modern discussions. Some hadiths contradict the Quran, while others are illogical or unacceptable in that they are offensive to Islam and quite degrading of Muhammad.

Hadith-rejecters point to many hadiths that clearly contradict the Quran. For instance, consider the hadith statements that force people to believe in Islam. The two hadiths mentioned earlier—"Whoever changed his Islamic religion, then kill him" and "I have been commanded to fight against people so long as they do not declare that there is no god but Allah"—both clearly violate the Quran, which contains the following statements: "There is no compulsion in religion" (Q 2:256); "I do not worship what you worship. Nor do you worship whom I worship. . . . To you your religion, and to me my religion" (Q 109:3–6); Allah "causes to stray whoever he wills and guides whoever he wills" (Q 16:93); "Whoever wants to believe, let him believe, and whoever wants to unbelieve, let him unbelieve" (Q 18:29). While the Quran, in these verses, seems to allow people to choose their religion and to reject coercion in matters of beliefs, the hadiths clearly oppose the Quranic commands and support fighting and killing anyone who does not choose Islam. In this example, a hadith seems to violate a Quranic command, but others stand in direct contradiction of the Quran.

The Quran states, "Behold, your Lord is Allah, who created the heavens and the earth in six days, and then settled on the throne" (Q 7:54), while the hadiths list seven days of creation and indicate what Allah created during each of them.[1] But the matter is more problematic: while Muslims insist that the Quran is preserved from error and that it is the exact copy of a celestial tablet, the hadith traditions indicate that the Quran is not complete but reflects corruption and alteration. According to the trusted collection of Bukhari, the second caliph, Umar, stated that "among what Allah revealed, was the Verse of the Rajam (the stoning of a married person) who commits illegal sexual intercourse, and we did recite this Verse and understood and memorized it. Allah's Messenger did carry out the punishment of stoning and so did we after him."[2] This

1. Sahih Muslim, 39.6707.
2. Bukhari, 8.82.817; and Sahih Muslim, 17.4194.

so-called Stoning Verse does not exist at all in today's Quran. In fact, the Quran is clear that the punishment for adultery is a hundred lashes, not stoning: "The woman and the man guilty of illegal sexual intercourse, flog each of them with a hundred lashes" (Q 24:2). Still, another hadith insists that there was a Stoning Verse but that, according to Muhammad's wife Aisha, the verse was eaten by a sheep: "The verse of stoning and of breastfeeding an adult ten times was revealed, and the paper was with me under my pillow. When the Messenger of Allah died, we were preoccupied with his death, and a tame sheep came in and ate it."[3] Thus, the hadith traditions contradict the Quran and violate the sacredness of its preservation. Here lies one reason why hadith-rejecters dismiss the hadith collections as unreliable and untruthful.

Hadith-rejecters also question some illogical traditions. For example, according to Bukhari's collection, a she-monkey was surrounded by other monkeys and stoned for being adulterous.[4] Many wonder, How can a monkey be adulterous? This opposes logic. Muhammad is reported to have said, "When the call for the prayer is pronounced, Satan takes to his heels, passing wind with noise."[5] The hadith does not seem reasonable or logical. In the same vein, Muhammad, according to Bukhari, stated, "If a house fly falls in the drink of anyone of you, he should dip it (in the drink) and take it out, for one of its wings has a disease and the other has the cure for the disease."[6] Indeed, some Muslims reject these hadiths, claiming them unreasonable and illogical, but hadith advocates, even today, attempt to prove a scientific value for flies' wings in order to support Muhammad's reported statement. This is also evident in the case of conservative hadith scholars supporting a strange hadith attributed to Muhammad in which he instructed people to follow his camels and "drink their milk and urine."[7] The hadith is unacceptable for critical thinkers, although it is repeated many times in the so-called trusted collection of Bukhari.[8] Similarly, Muhammad is reported to have said, "If somebody takes some dates every morning, he will not be affected by

3. Sunan Ibn Majah, 3.9.1944.
4. Bukhari, 5.58.188.
5. Bukhari, 4.54.505; 1.11.582; 2.22.313, 323. See also Sahih Muslim, 4.756, 1162.
6. Bukhari, 4.54.537.
7. Bukhari, 7.71.590.
8. Bukhari, 2.24.577; 7.71.672; and Sahih Muslim, 16.4130, 4132.

poison or magic on that day till night."[9] Today there is a highly respected profession among conservative Muslims called "The Prophetic Medicine," in which medical advice is given based on Muhammad's hadiths above any nonreligious source.[10]

Some of the illogical hadiths portray Muhammad negatively. In one hadith, Bukhari portrays Muhammad as a hypocrite: "A man asked permission to enter upon Allah's Messenger. The Prophet said, 'Admit him. What an evil brother of his people or a son of his people.' But when the man entered, the Prophet spoke to him in a very polite manner."[11] This story depicts Muhammad as a two-faced liar who insults a man in his absence but speaks kindly to his face immediately afterward. A trusted hadith reports that Muhammad "had a female slave with whom he had intercourse."[12] Bukhari reports that a man successfully "worked magic" on Muhammad, until Muhammad "started imagining that he had done a thing that he had not really done."[13] If a person can successfully influence Muhammad with magic, to the extent that he would imagine things, how can Muslims trust his words or deeds? For hadith-rejecters, these are unacceptable depictions of Islam's prophet and cannot be considered trusted accounts.

In the same vein, there are ample illogical hadiths—claimed in the trusted and authentic collections—about the deity. We are told that "Our Lord, the Blessed, the Superior, comes every night down on the nearest Heaven to us when the last third of the night remains, saying: 'Is there anyone to invoke Me, so that I may respond to invocation? Is there anyone to ask Me, so that I may grant him his request? Is there anyone seeking My forgiveness, so that I may forgive him?'"[14] This hadith indicates that Allah descends every night from heaven to listen to prayers. Hadith-rejecters find various illogical elements in this hadith: Why does he need to come down? Can he not hear from heaven? More importantly, if he comes down when it is night on one half of the earth, it would be

9. Bukhari, 7.71.663.

10. See two classical Muslim sources on the topic, translated into English: Jawziyyah, *Medicine of the Prophet*; and Suyuti, *Medicine of the Prophet*.

11. Bukhari, 8.73.80; 8.73.152; and Sahih Muslim, 32.6268.

12. Sunan an-Nasa'i, 4.36.3411.

13. Bukhari, 7.71.658; and Sahih Muslim, 26.5428.

14. Bukhari, 2.21.246; 9.93.586; Sahih Muslim, 4.1656, 1657, 1658; and Sunan Abi Dawud, 5.1310.

morning on the other. Indeed, the hadith has various gaps and does not present a reasonable claim or a compelling case. Many Muslim thinkers find it embarrassing and thus completely reject it as a fabrication.[15] The problem is if you reject one hadith, how can you trust others in the same collection and consider them authentic?

Similarly, there are many illogical verses against other prophets, including Moses. In one of them, Bukhari reports, "The angel of death was sent to Moses and when he went to him, Moses slapped him severely, spoiling one of his eyes."[16] In another, "Moses went out to take a bath and put his clothes over a stone and then that stone ran away with his clothes. Moses followed that stone saying, 'My clothes, O stone!'"[17] Some scholars view these traditions about Moses as polemic tools against the Jews of the time; indeed, this may ring true. Whether Muhammad said them or not is impossible to determine. One concern is how their reliability and authority are viewed by the vast majority of Muslims. The collections of Imam Bukhari and Imam Muslim, in particular, are viewed by most Muslims as totally reliable and trustworthy.

But there is a deeper problem. Some hadiths question Muhammad's views of women and thus, again, present Muhammad negatively. Muhammad was reportedly asked about this Quranic verse: "Get, as witness, two witnesses from your men, and if there are not two men, then a man and two women" (Q 2:282). The verse indicates that in matters of legal witnessing, the witness of a woman is equal to half of that of a man. Muhammad, in interpreting this verse, reportedly said, "This is because of the deficiency of a woman's mind."[18] While hadith scholars may try to justify this hadith in its claim that women are deficient in their minds, hadith-rejecters may use it as a proof for the dismissal of the entire hadith corpus. They reject such hadiths, viewing them as a product of a male-dominant classical Islam and, therefore, incompatible with the modern day. For hadith-rejecters, it is a disgrace to associate Muhammad with such statements. But other hadiths seem to

---

15. In another hadith, Muhammad reportedly said, "The Hell Fire will keep on saying: 'Are there anymore (people to come)?' Till the Lord of Power and Honor will put His Foot over it . . . [and] its various sides will come close to each other (i.e., it will contract)." See Bukhari, 8.78.654.

16. Bukhari, 2.23.423.

17. Bukhari, 1.5.277.

18. Bukhari, 3.48.826.

degrade women even more. According to Bukhari, Muhammad was once asked the reason for women being consigned to hellfire, to which he replied, "I have not seen anyone more deficient in intelligence and religion than you [women]. A cautious sensible man could be led astray by some of you."[19] In the same hadith, Muhammad reportedly said, "O women! Give alms, as I have seen that the majority of the dwellers of Hell-fire were you (women),"[20] and in another hadith, "Amongst the inmates of Paradise the women would form a minority."[21] These do not seem to portray women positively. There are other, similar hadiths. Muhammad reportedly declared, "If there is evil omen in anything, it is in the house, the woman and the horse,"[22] and the "woman advances and retires in the shape of a devil."[23] In these two hadiths, women are depicted as evil omens and devils. When hadith-rejecters dismiss these negative traditions, they are actually attempting to protect Islam, as there are obvious problems in these hadiths. However, the people of the hadiths are adamant about the authority and status of Muhammad's hadiths.

Still, it is important to examine why the number of hadith-rejecters is growing among Muslims today. Many practices that seem supported by hadiths are unsuitable in the modern day. Consider child marriages in some Arab Muslim nations. The hadiths insist that Muhammad married Aisha when she was six or seven, that he consummated the marriage when she was nine, and that "her dolls were with her."[24] Some Muslims, even today, seek to follow Muhammad's example. A few years ago, the news erupted of a Yemeni child bride. She was eight years old, married to a man five times her age, and she died on her wedding night.[25]

19. Bukhari, 1.6.301.
20. Bukhari, 1.6.301.
21. Sahih Muslim, 36.6600.
22. Bukhari, 7.62.31; and Sahih Muslim, 26.5528.
23. Sahih Muslim, 8.3240.
24. Sahih Muslim, 8.3311. See also Sahih Muslim, 8.3309, where Aisha reports about marrying Muhammad, "I was at that time on a swing along with my playmates."
25. Elie, "Yemeni Child Bride.'" See also Khalife, "How Come You Allow Little Girls to Get Married?" This report states that "14 percent of girls in Yemen are married before reaching age 15, and 52 percent are married before 18." Another article gives similar statistics: "In some rural areas [in Yemen], girls as young as 8 are married. Girls are sometimes forced to marry much older men." Human Rights Watch, "Yemen: Child Marriage Spurs Abuse of Girls and Women."

Whether the Yemeni wedding was legal or not, some of the advocates of the hadiths may insist it was religiously justified. For hadith-rejecters, such claims and actions weaken Islam and show it in a dark light. By now, it is not difficult to trace numerous hadiths that appear to portray Muhammad and Islam in an unacceptable way for today's world. This is one reason for the growing number of hadith-rejecters. Nonetheless, I should warn the reader: while there is indeed a growing number of Muslim rejecters of the hadiths, this should by no means give the impression that this is a big movement in Islam. The hadith traditions continue to stand firm among Muslims, and the lovers and scholars of the hadiths remain significantly strong and remarkably powerful.

There are other Islamic practices that are highly problematic in our day but that appear supported by religious traditions. In addition to the examples discussed earlier—relating to apostasy, jihad, and marriage—there are troubling hadiths on slavery and homosexuality. Should we believe Bukhari's hadiths about Muhammad's slaves? Many Muslims today argue that Muhammad, as the best example of humankind, never owned slaves and freed all slaves with whom he met.[26] However, according to Bukhari, "Allah's Apostle was staying on a Mashroba (attic room) and a black slave of Allah's Apostle was at the top of its stairs."[27] While this hadith only describes a black slave of Muhammad, another hadith names this slave: "Allah's Apostle was on a journey and he had a black slave called Anjasha."[28] These hadiths indicate that Muhammad did not free all of his slaves, since at least one of them is identified. Similarly, Bukhari refers to a testimony by Umar, who became the second caliph in Islam. He came to visit Muhammad, and "a black slave of Allah's Apostle was (sitting) on the first step. [Umar] said to him, 'Say (to the Prophet) Umar bin Al-Khattab is here.'"[29] Some argue that when a hadith refers to "a black slave," this might imply that there were many of them, especially since we read that Muhammad reportedly sold two black slaves to purchase another one: "The Prophet said: 'Sell him to

26. See El Hamel, *Black Morocco*, 17–41. See also the Sunni article where the cleric writes, "When the question is asked: why does Islam permit slavery? We reply emphatically and without shame that slavery is permitted in Islam, but we should examine the matter with fairness." Islam Question & Answer, "Islam and Slavery."

27. Bukhari, 9.91.368.

28. Bukhari, 8.73.182.

29. Bukhari, 6.60.281.

me,' and he bought him for two black slaves."[30] According to this hadith, there seems to be evidence that Muhammad owned slaves. In a different hadith, a companion became sick, so Muhammad "sent a slave" with him to accompany him.[31] It appears that Muhammad owned his own slaves, as was the case with other Arabs of his time, and did not feel obliged to free them. In fact, Muhammad's daughter Fatima, we are told by Bukhari, stated that "she heard that the Prophet had received a few slave girls."[32] Muhammad reportedly once "went to (the house of) his slave tailor."[33] Even Muhammad's wife Aisha had "her slave girl."[34] One of Muhammad's companions declared, "Aisha the wife of the Prophet sent her slave girl Nukhayla to me yesterday."[35] Therefore, we know the name of Aisha's slave.

After we examine these hadiths, many of today's arguments about Muhammad freeing slaves collapse. Did Muhammad really own and sell slaves? Hadiths in Bukhari's collection indicate he did. Should Muslims accept them or become hadith-rejecters? The answer is consequential. This is one reason why some Muslims dismiss these hadiths completely. They want to identify them as unreliable so that they are no longer normative or prescriptive. Consider the fact that in some Arab Muslim countries today the practice of owning slaves still flourishes, although slavery was officially abolished in the last century. For those who own slaves today, one hadith is enough to justify their actions. They claim to follow in the footsteps of Muhammad.[36]

What do the hadiths say about homosexuality? They seem to follow the Quran in condemning it. Muhammad is reported to have instructed his followers, "Whoever you find doing the action of the people of Lot, kill the one who does it, and the one to whom it is done."[37] In main-

30. Sunan an-Nasa'i, 5.39.4189.
31. Bukhari, 6.60.274.
32. Bukhari, 7.64.274.
33. Bukhari, 7.65.344; 7.64.274.
34. Bukhari, 5.59.541.
35. Bukhari, 9.91.368.
36. See Clarence-Smith, *Islam and the Abolition of Slavery*, where he writes on the "embarrassing institution" of slavery in Islam in chapter 1 and details the disagreements among Sunni scholars over slavery in chapter 2. See the Muslim feminist perspective of Ali, *Marriage and Slavery in Early Islam*, 187ff.
37. Sunan Ibn Majah, 3.20.2561; and Jami' at-Tirmidhi, 3.15.1456. See also Sunan Abi Dawud, 39.4447.

stream Islam, homosexuality is punishable by death. For traditional Muslims, these hadiths are in harmony with Quranic verses that forbid homosexuality and describe it as the abhorrent sin of the people of Lot (Q 7:80–84; 15:74; 26:165–66; 27:58; 29:40). Thus, according to these verses and Muhammad's hadiths, it appears that a homosexual must be killed.[38] For conservative Sunni clerics, "the crime of homosexuality is one of the greatest of crimes, the worst of sins and the most abhorrent of deeds," and Muhammad's companions "unanimously agreed on the execution of homosexuals."[39] This claim describes the common Sunni views. However, many progressive Muslims have been attempting to amend this strict ultimatum as they seek to present Islam as a suitable religion in a multireligious modern world. Progressives read the Quran as ambiguous on the issue and indicate dissatisfaction with the hadiths.

This has resulted in examples of openly gay Muslims, even imams of mosques. Daayiee Abdullah (1954–) is a gay imam in Washington, DC. He studied Islam in the Middle East and openly criticizes the mainstream Sunni teaching against homosexuality. For him, this teaching must change, "or it will die from its harshness or rigidity," because the "way it is presently understood, it rots the heart and decays the brain."[40] Abdullah is an example of a scholar who relies on the Quran and rejects the hadiths. Ludovic-Mohamed Zahed (1977–) is a French-Algerian imam who, like Abdullah, is openly gay. He founded an inclusive mosque in Paris, France, with the stated aim of accommodating LGBT and feminist Muslims.[41] In response to Zahed and his inclusive mosque, the Paris Grand Mosque issued an unambiguous condemnation: "[This] is something that's outside the Islamic community. The Koran condemns homosexuality. It is banned."[42] The Paris Grand Mosque, it appears, cherishes and follows Muhammad's traditions as if they are prescriptive commands. Zahed, on the other hand, seems to follow an Islam uniquely tailored to fit his paradigm and the requirements of the modern day.

38. See Islam Question & Answer, "Why Does Islam Forbid Lesbianism and Homosexuality?," where the answer provides several references from Muslim authorities forbidding homosexuality as the sin of the people of Lot.
39. See Islam Question & Answer, "Punishment for Homosexuality."
40. Markoe, "Muslim Attitudes about LGBT Are Complex."
41. Zahed, "Why I Want to Open a Gay-Friendly Mosque in Paris."
42. Banerji, "Gay-Friendly 'Mosque' Opens in Paris."

These examples highlight many hadith-rejecters and a few reasons for their rejection. In the earlier discussion of jihad, apostasy, marriage, slavery, and homosexuality, the question was, Should one consider Muhammad's hadiths reliable and follow them, or dismiss them due to their later date or contradicting contents? The answer is far-reaching, and the question is complex. Can one dismiss some hadiths and keep others, or should all be ignored as unreliable? It is noteworthy that every statement we examined is claimed by Sunni Muslims to be part of the most trusted hadith collections. If we dismissed these, nothing remaining would be more reliable. A more problematic question is this: If Muslims dismiss the hadiths as forgeries, can they still trust the knowledge they have had for centuries about Islam's history and Quranic exegesis? In the end, all of these Muslim sources rely on hadiths. Most of what we know about Islam's practices and tenets comes from the hadiths, not the Quran. In recent years, some Muslim academics, particularly in the West, have been wrestling with ways to continue appreciating the hadiths as they advance notions of hadith criticism and apply selective jurisprudence tools to navigate through the hadith corpus.[43] This is a clear example of how foundational the tradition is for many Muslims. They want to shield and revive it in the face of numerous charges and accusations.

Today we witness a dissonance within the Muslim community. Most Muslims still revere the authority of Muhammad's hadiths, but some are swimming against the current—just as the Mu'tazilites of the ninth century did when they believed in the power of reason and opposed the hadith party. This growing criticism of the hadiths is occurring not only in the West. Even in the Arab World, the heartland of Islam, the number of hadith-rejecters is increasing. They have been asking daring questions, and some have totally abandoned the tradition to focus only on the Quran. Still, the tradition and its traditionists are highly influential. What is the future of the hadiths? Will the hadith-rejecters grow more in number, at the expense of the traditionists? Will the hadiths continue to

43. See the attempts of Muslim scholar Jonathan A. C. Brown in *Misquoting Muhammad*, chaps. 2–3; and *Hadith*, 15–122, 240ff. Brown (1977–) converted to Islam from Christianity in 1997. He currently teaches Islamic studies at Georgetown University. Brown is devoted to Sunni Islam. His remarks about slavery, as documented in Muslim traditions and Islamic history, went viral and were condemned by many scholars, Muslims and non-Muslims alike, as they appeared to support the evil practice.

be trusted among Muslims, especially in a modern society that knows no limit of questions and has no boundaries in respecting the sacred? As we think about jihad, religious freedom, blasphemy laws, apostasy, women's rights, slavery, and the treatment of homosexuals, the answers to these questions will determine a great deal concerning Islamic rulings. Whatever a Muslim chooses, it will be highly consequential—both for Islam and for the entire world.[44]

44. For arguments by hadith-rejecters, see the religious rulings and teaching on the official website of the People of the Quran and Ahmed Subhy Mansour: https://www.ahl-alquran.com/.

Appendix A

Muslim Primary Sources in English

Balādhurī, Aḥmad ibn Yaḥyā al-. *The Origins of the Islamic State*. Translated by Francis Murgotten and Philip Khuri Hitti. New York: AMS Press, 1968.

Ibn Hishām, ʿAbd al-Malik, and Muḥammad Ibn Isḥaq. *The Life of Muhammad*. Translated by Alfred Guillaume. Oxford: Oxford University Press, 1967; 13th reprint, 1999.

ʿIbn Kathir, Ismāʿīl ibn ʿUmar. *The Life of the Prophet Muḥammad: Al-Sira al-Nabawiyya*. Translated by Trevor Le Gassick. 4 vols. Reading, UK: Garnet, 1998.

Ibn Khaldūn. *The Muqaddimah: An Introduction to History*. Translated by Franz Rosenthal. Abridged and edited by N. J. Dawood. Princeton: Princeton University Press, 1989.

Ibn Qutayba al-Dīnawarī. *The Excellence of the Arabs*. Edited by James Montgomery and Peter Webb. Translated by Sarah Savant and Peter Webb. New York: New York University Press, 2017.

Ibn Rāshid, Maʿmar, and ʿAbd al-Razzāq al-Ṣanʿānī. *The Expeditions: An Early Biography of Muhammad*. Edited and translated by Sean W. Anthony. New York: New York University Press, 2014.

Khalīfa ibn Khayyāṭ. *Khalifa ibn Khayyat's "History" on the Umayyad Dynasty, 660–750*. Edited by Robert G. Hoyland. Translated by Carl Wurtzel. Liverpool: Liverpool University Press, 2016.

Ṭabarī, Abū Jaʿfar Muḥammad ibn Jarīr al-. *The History of al-Ṭabarī*. 40 vols. Edited by C. E. Bosworth et al. New York: State University of New York Press, 1980–99.

Wāqidī, Abū ʿAbdullāh ibn ʿUmar al-. *The Life of Muḥammad: Al-Wāqidī's "Kitāb al-Maghāzī."* Edited by Rizwi Faizer. Translated by Rizwi Faizer, Amal Ismail, and Abdul Kader Tayob. London: Routledge, 2011.

Appendix B

Helpful Websites on Islamic Primary Sources

1. www.sunnah.com

   The website identifies itself as "The Hadith of the Prophet Muhammad at your fingertips." It includes fifteen trusted Sunni collections of Muhammad's sayings, known as hadith traditions. Muslims believe that the most trusted collections among these are those by Imam Bukhari (d. 870) and Imam Muslim (d. 875). Two wonderful features of this website are (1) that readers can do a word search and (2) that each hadith is presented in Arabic and English next to each other. The word *Sunnah* in the title refers to Muhammad's example, conduct, and pattern of life.

2. www.sahih-bukhari.com

   This is an English translation of the most authoritative hadith collection in Sunni Islam. It is known as Sahih al-Bukhari. The word *sahih* means "sound and reliable." Unlike the website www.sunnah.com, this one provides only Imam Bukhari's collection, and only in English. The website claims that "Imam Bukhari lived a couple of centuries after the Prophet's death and worked extremely hard to collect his [hadiths]. Each report in his collection was checked for compatibility with the Qur'an, and the veracity of the chain of reporters had to be painstakingly established." The website concludes, "Bukhari's collection is recognized by the overwhelming majority of the Muslim world to be one of the most authentic collections of the Sunnah of the Prophet."

3. qb.gomen.org/QuranBrowser

   This is a helpful Quran browser that provides access to ten different English translations of the Arabic Quran. The translations are classified by the website as orthodox Muslim, nonorthodox Muslim, and non-Muslim translations. While the categories can be questionable, having ten translations in one place is helpful for non-Arabic speakers attempting to understand the Arabic Quran.

4. www.searchtruth.com

   This website has various features. The most important for our purposes is the option to search the Quran and the sayings of Muhammad (hadiths). One can search the Quran in Arabic, English, French, and other languages. As for the hadiths, one can search only in English, but there are four available collections of hadiths. Under the Quran tab, the website provides a modern commentary on the Quran by Islamist Abu al-A'la al-Mawdudi (1903–1979), a well-known Indian-Pakistani fundamentalist theologian whose views include implementation of the sharia by the government, since political power should serve the Islamic legal and moral code.

5. www.altafsir.com

   Since the Quran is often difficult for even Arabic-speaking Muslims to understand, they usually use a commentary (tafsir). This website offers seven Quran commentaries in English. One can specify the verse and choose a specific commentary to see an explanation of the verse. This website offers translations of the Quran in twenty-four languages.

6. www.al-islam.org and www.shiasource.com

   These are two important websites that provide Shiite perspectives on Islamic matters. Both include numerous articles and digitalized books on Shiite Islam. They aim to spread the teachings of Islam as explained by Shiites past and present. You can search an item and get various results on both sites. In particular, these

two sources are important because they present Shiite perspectives
that contrast with the dominant Sunni narrative.

7. www.ahl-alquran.com

While most Muslims cherish Muhammad's traditions and value
them as second in authority after the Quran, some Muslims disre-
gard them—partially or completely—and focus only on the Quran.
These Muslims are usually known as "The People of the Quran"
(in Arabic, *ahl al-Quran*). This is an important website for them
that "is committed to spreading a vision of Islam that is true to the
letter and spirit of the Quran and that focuses on the consistency
between the word of God and democracy and human rights."

8. islamqa.info/en/about-us

This is a missional website that aims to answer questions from
a Sunni perspective, particularly the conservative understanding
(in Arabic, *salafi*) within Islam. The website aims to "spread Islam
and call people to it," to "spread Islamic knowledge and dispel
ignorance among Muslims," and to "refute the specious arguments
of doubters about Islam."

9. www.kalamullah.com

This is a huge Sunni library. It offers classical primary sources
and modern secondary studies, all in English. Some are searchable,
and others are downloadable. The site adopts a strict conservative traditional approach to Islamic matters. Its title, Kalamullah,
means "Allah's speech, or word." The website is important for
researchers, both in its ideology and in the wealth of resources
it provides.

10. corpus.quran.com

This website is helpful to researchers of the Quran, especially
those interested in word-search, annotation, and linguistic and
grammar matters. It offers helpful tools on syntax and morphology
for every Quranic word. It also includes several English translations
of the meaning of the Quran.

Glossary

Each term has a concise definition, followed by a more detailed explanation.

abd: slave of. The word appears as the prefix of some names, especially in relation to Allah's attributes. The name Abd-Allah means "slave of Allah." The name Abd al-Rahman means "slave of the merciful."

Abd al-Muttalib: Muhammad's grandfather. Abd al-Muttalib (d. 578) was the son of Hashim, the progenitor of the respected Hashemite clan, within which Muhammad was born in the tribe of Quraysh. The Hashemite clan and the Umayyad clan were cousins and had always fought for power in Arabia. Muslim sources portray Abd al-Muttalib as a monotheist—even before Muhammad was born—who never worshiped idols. He appears as a hero, believing in Allah and defending the Ka'ba against the Christian army's invasion in the Year of the Elephant—the year of Muhammad's birth. All that we know about Abd al-Muttalib comes from Abbasid sources, which aim to establish the legitimacy of the Abbasids (part of the Hashemite clan).

Abraha: a Christian governor of Yemen. We know about him from the Muslim sources, which portray him as an extreme Christian who

---

Some entries in this glossary are adapted from Ayman Ibrahim, *Concise Guide to the Quran: Answering Thirty Critical Questions* (Grand Rapids: Baker Academic, 2020).

was jealous of Mecca and wanted to destroy the Ka'ba. He governed San'aa in Yemen on behalf of the Christian emperor of Abyssinia (roughly Ethiopia and Eritrea today). Muslims believe that Abraha was envious of the beauty of the Ka'ba and therefore built a marvelous cathedral in San'aa and asked people to travel to it. He was furious when no one cared to heed his invitation, and later he launched an army, some riding elephants, to conquer Mecca and destroy the Ka'ba. Ironically, at that time the Ka'ba—according to Muslim sources—was full of idols. Still, Muslims claim that Allah protected it by sending an army of birds that threw stones against Abraha's army. Eventually, Abraha and his army were defeated, and the year became known as the Year of the Elephant, during which Muhammad was born.

abu: father of. Arabs address a man by referring to his sons or firstborn son. So the name Abu Bakr means "father of Bakr."

Abu Bakr: an early follower of Islam and a senior companion of Muhammad. He became the first caliph (successor of Muhammad) on the day of Muhammad's death. He was known as "the faithful" because he was one of the earliest believers of Muhammad's message. He was also the father-in-law of Muhammad, as his daughter, Aisha, was the youngest wife of Muhammad. Abu Bakr died of fever in 634, but some claim he was assassinated by opponents among the Meccan leaders (specifically by Umar, because he sought power).

adhan: the formal call to ritual prayer. It is called out by a person—always a man with a clear, strong, loud voice—whose task is to serve at the mosque by reciting the adhan in a melodic manner. In the Muslim world, the adhan is amplified by loudspeakers placed on the minarets of mosques. The adhan includes several phrases: "Allah is greater" (four times), "I testify that there is no god but Allah" (twice), "I testify that Muhammad is Allah's messenger" (twice), "Come [or hurry or hasten] to prayer" (twice), "Come to success" (twice), "Allah is greater" (twice), and "There is no god but Allah." Shiite Muslims follow the same adhan but add two statements. First, they chant, "I testify [or bear witness] that Ali is Allah's representative [or vice-regent]." This sentence is repeated twice after the sentence that describes Muhammad as Allah's messenger. It is their testimony of Ali's highest esteem as Muhammad's successor and Allah's representative. Second, toward the end of the adhan, before "Allah is greater," Shiites add, "Come to [or hurry toward] the best of deeds."

Aisha: Abu Bakr's daughter and Muhammad's favorite wife. Muhammad married her when she was six or seven years old and consummated the marriage when she was nine. She was his favorite wife, according to many traditions. Sunnis hold her in high esteem, but Shiites believe she was wicked and that she cheated on Muhammad. In Sunni traditions, Aisha reported and transmitted many of Muhammad's hadiths, but Shiites believe it was actually Muhammad's daughter Fatima who better transmitted Muhammad's hadiths. Historically, Aisha played a significant role in military battles against the fourth caliph, Ali, in 656.

al-: the Arabic definite article. It often precedes Arabic words transliterated into English (e.g., al-Azhar University, meaning "the Azhar University").

al-asmaa' al-husnaa: most beautiful names. The Arabic word *asmaa* means "names," while *husnaa* means "most beautiful." Muslims believe that Allah has ninety-nine names or attributes. These are adjectives describing his majesty and nouns explaining his perfection. They also convey his just, wise, and merciful deeds toward humankind. Some of the asmaa echo biblical references about the God of the Bible, while others appear to be exclusively Muslim. We know about the names from hadiths written centuries after Muhammad. Some Muslims dispute many of the names, arguing that they portray Allah negatively and do not appear in the Quran. Other Muslims claim that the Quran contains many attributes of Allah that do not appear in the list of ninety-nine names.

Ali: the fourth caliph in Islam. He was Muhammad's cousin and son-in-law. Shiites believe he was the rightful successor of Muhammad but that the three preceding caliphs stole the succession because of their lust for power and worldly dominion. Ali is also considered the first of a chain of twelve infallible imams who were faithful teachers of the Muslims.

Allah: the Islamic deity. The word *Allah* was known in Arabia before Islam. Today it is the standard Arabic word for the deity. Arabic-speaking

Jews and Christians use the term to refer to Elohim of the Bible. The most important aspect of the Islamic deity is his singularity and oneness, tawhid. There are reports, however, that in pre-Islamic Arabia Allah had three daughters who were lesser deities. These are the goddesses praised by Muhammad in the infamous incident of the satanic verses.

Aqsa: a holy site and mosque in Jerusalem. This mosque did not exist during Muhammad's time. It was reportedly built as a small prayer room by the second caliph on top of the Temple Mount after Muslims conquered Jerusalem. After being destroyed many times and neglected for decades, the mosque was renovated, rebuilt, and expanded by the Umayyad caliph Abd al-Malik (d. 705). The holy status of the mosque is mainly established based on the Muslim belief that Muhammad flew from Mecca to this site during his night journey. This belief has also established a strong Muslim claim on Jerusalem, which has long been the holiest city for Christians and Jews.

Baladhuri: a renowned Muslim historian of the Islamic conquests. He was a major Muslim historian from Iraq (d. 892). Baladhuri was a drinking peer and sitting companion of several Abbasid caliphs and served at the Baghdad caliphal court. This indicates his strong connection with the Abbasids and suggests some of his biases in history writing. One of his major works is *Futuh al-buldan* (The conquests of the lands). It details the Muslim conquests, categorized by lands conquered, from the time of Muhammad and under the early caliphs. A translation of it from the original Arabic into English was published in a two-volume critical scholarly edition in 1916 and 1924 titled *The Origins of the Islamic State*.

black stone: a sacred stone inside the Ka'ba. Muslims believe it is the most sacred stone on earth and that it dropped from heaven. It was white, but the sins of humans turned it black. Muhammad is reported to have placed it in its location inside the Ka'ba. During the Muslim pilgrimage, Muslims seek to touch or kiss the stone for blessing and healing. They venerate the stone and its divine power—a mere touch of the stone abolishes one's sins. Although Muslims believe that the black stone in the Ka'ba today is the original stone that fell from heaven, Muslim history itself reveals that the stone was removed many times and was actually stolen for decades by Shiites. Even the Ka'ba itself, according to Muslim histories, was completely demolished many times.

Bukhari: the most important hadith collector for Sunnis. He is called Imam Bukhari (810–870) by Sunnis. Muslims say that Bukhari was pious and devoted to Islam and that he traveled for sixteen years to collect about six hundred thousand of Muhammad's hadiths. After praying and seeking Allah regarding every single hadith, Bukhari concluded that only about seven thousand were authentic and the rest were forgeries. Sunnis consider his collection of hadiths to be the most truthful and second in authority, after the Quran. Shiite and liberal Muslims, however, reject his collection and regard some of its statements as illogical, unscientific, and disgraceful.

Buraq: a winged, horse-like creature. Muslim accounts describe it as something between a mule and a donkey. Muhammad rode it from Mecca to Jerusalem, then from Jerusalem to heaven, all in one night. Some Muslims believe the creature is real, while others argue that Muhammad was dreaming.

da'wa: the act of calling people to Islam. It is a form of Islamic preaching aimed at calling individuals and communities to accept Islam and follow Allah's precepts and Muhammad's teachings. Da'wa is thus a missionary activity. It is a duty for every Muslim. In the earliest centuries of Islam, the faith spread among non-Muslims through the da'wa of Arab merchants trading in non-Muslim lands as well as following the military raids led by Muslim armies. Coercive conversion was only one way of accepting Islam. After the Muslim conquests, many non-Muslims accepted the da'wa and converted to Islam, sometimes in an attempt to join the ruling elite of the land.

fatwa: a religious ruling on faith matters. It is an opinion provided by an educated Muslim cleric or scholar to answer a question posed by a layperson. Since Islamic texts are complex, Muslims need scholars' opinions on religious matters. Sometimes a fatwa is not requested but provided by Muslim scholars in urgent situations. When Salman Rushdie published his book on Muhammad's satanic verses in 1988, Muslims were furious. Iranian ayatollah Khomeini accused Rushdie of blasphemy and issued a fatwa demanding that Muslims kill him.

A fatwa receives its authority from the status and level of education of the scholar who issues it. In Muslim-majority countries, the government usually controls the issuing of fatwas by establishing an official House of Fatwa, which serves as a government advisory council for religious matters.

futuh: conquests, with a religious motive. These are military conquests of non-Muslim lands, including those of the Byzantine and Persian empires, led by Muhammad's successors (caliphs). The Arabic term literally means "openings." It describes the conquests not as invasions but as acts of "opening" and liberating the non-Muslim lands from the darkness by introducing the light of Islam. The term also identifies a genre of written traditions—composed of consecutive hadiths—named the futuh literature, which details the Muslim wars accomplished by Arab commanders after Muhammad's death.

ghazi: an invader. The Arabic noun *ghazi* is derived from the verb *ghaza*, "to invade." In Islam, a ghazi is a warrior or invader, portrayed as conquering for Allah's cause and rewarded with paradise.

hadith: a saying, deed, or teaching, especially attributed to Muhammad. It is a tradition telling of something Muhammad said or did. A hadith usually follows this basic form: "It is narrated on the authority of so-and-so that so-and-so heard the Apostle of Allah (Muhammad) say such and such." The strength of a hadith depends on the so-and-so part, specifically the person who heard or saw Muhammad and the informants who reported what was said or done throughout the generations. For Muslims, this is the second authority, after the Quran. The word *hadith* is singular, and its plural is *ahadith*; however, in English the plural is usually rendered *hadiths*. There are numerous collections of hadiths. Sunni and Shiite Muslims do not trust the same collections. Problematically, none of the available collections come from the time of Muhammad. In fact, there is no extant collection of hadiths from the first two centuries of Islam. Later, some Muslims collected hundreds of thousands of hadiths. After inspecting them, they narrowed down the collection to a few thousand, claiming the rest were forgeries. The two most trusted collections among Sunni Muslims are the one attributed to Bukhari (810–870) and the collection of his disciple Imam Muslim (821–875).

Hafsa: Umar's daughter and Muhammad's wife. After she lost her husband in battle, Mahammad married her, then divorced her, then remarried her. She received the collection of pages including the Quranic revelations when Abu Bakr ordered the first collection of the Quran. She kept them at her home during the caliphate of her father, Umar, and then gave them to Uthman for the second collection of the Quran. She died in 665.

hajj: pilgrimage. This is one of the duties for all Muslims. It is known as the fifth pillar of Islam. Hajj is an annual pilgrimage to Mecca, which Muslims (especially Sunnis) consider the holiest place on earth. The rituals of hajj are not based on the Quran but are detailed in later Muslim texts, especially the hadiths. While Muslims believe that the hajj is exclusively Islamic, scholars find that in pre-Islamic pagan Arabia, Arabs performed pilgrimages similar in many aspects to the rituals adopted by Islam.

hanif: a pre-Islamic monotheist. Linguistically, the term *hanif* refers to a person who was devoted to Allah's worship in pre-Islamic times. The term excludes Christians and Jews. Before receiving the alleged divine revelation, Muhammad was identified as a hanif because he reportedly rejected polytheism to adhere to the worship of Allah. Muslims say that Abraham was also a hanif and that the religion followed by any hanif is actually the religion of Abraham.

hijra: emigration. This is a remarkable event in Islamic history that occurred in 622, when Muhammad took his followers (about thirty) from his hometown, Mecca, to reside in Medina. This event later marked the beginning of the Islamic lunar calendar. Muslims claim that Muhammad's hijra to Medina was due to severe persecution in Mecca because of his prophetic preaching. He spent thirteen years preaching in Mecca, then emigrated to Medina, where he lived for ten years until his death. Muslims believe that the Quran corresponds to Muhammad's life. It has two major parts—those chapters revealed in Mecca and those revealed in Medina. The Meccan chapters are generally viewed as more peaceful than those of Medina, since the Medinan period was colored by raids and expeditions led or commissioned by Muhammad.

ibn and bint: son and daughter. In Arabic, people are usually known by association to their father or family. For instance, the name Ibn

Hisham literally means "son of Hisham." Similarly, Hafsa bint
Umar means "Hafsa, daughter of Umar." The plural of *ibn* is *banu*,
which means "sons of." So the tribe of Banu Hashim refers to the
"sons of Hashim."

Ibn Ishaq: the writer of the earliest biography of Muhammad. His name
means "son of Isaac" and is pronounced "Is" plus "haq," not "Ish"
plus "aq." The grandson of a captured slave, Ibn Ishaq died in
Baghdad in 767 (about 120 years after Muhammad). A few years
before Ibn Ishaq's death, the Abbasid caliph instructed him to write
Muhammad's biography. It was meant to serve the caliph's legitimacy as a ruler over the Muslims. After Ibn Ishaq wrote it, it was
lost. His disciple Ibn Hisham found a copy, edited it, and omitted
disgraceful accounts from it. This censored version is the copy we
have today of Muhammad's biography, which is respected by most
Muslims as the truthful account of their prophet. While some consider Ibn Ishaq a trustworthy narrator, many consider him a forger
of hadiths and a liar.

imam: a Muslim leader in the general sense of the word. Commonly, the
term refers to the person who leads the ritual Muslim prayers in a
mosque. Traditionally, it must be a man, but in recent years many
liberal and feminist Muslims have advocated for female imams in
Western countries (e.g., Germany and the United States). Among
the Shiites, however, the term holds significant meaning, as it refers
to the twelve infallible imams who came from the household of Muhammad. The first imam was Ali, Muhammad's cousin who married
his daughter Fatima. After Ali, his two sons became the second and
third imams, followed by various imams until the twelfth, who was
called Mahdi. Mahdi, according to Shiites, did not die. He went into
occultation in the year 940. Shiites believe he is alive and waiting for
the moment of resurgence to restore order and justice and establish
Allah's rule on earth. He is their major eschatological savior and the
final imam. For Shiites, Muhammad and their twelve imams, plus
Fatima, are the inerrant source of faithful teaching of the religion
of Allah. They are referred to as "The Household of Muhammad."

isma: infallibility and immunity from error. In Islam, prophets are infallible and unable to sin. They are given isma by Allah. The isma

concept indicates that a divinely sent person is immune from errors. Some Muslims claim that the isma is given only in matters of divine revelations, but most Muslims believe that prophets can never err in any area. This is one reason why the biblical story of David committing adultery with Bathsheba is unfathomable in Islamic theology. Shiite Muslims believe that the isma was also given to the twelve imams, Ali and his male descendants.

Isra and Mi'raj: Muhammad's night journey. Muslims believe this is one of Muhammad's miracles. The journey includes two parts, the Isra followed by the Mi'raj. In the Isra, Muhammad—accompanied by Gabriel—rides a winged horse-like creature from Mecca to Jerusalem, where they land at the Temple Mount and meet a few pre-Islamic prophets. In the Mi'raj, Muhammad ascends from Jerusalem to heaven. Again, he meets previous prophets, leads them in a Muslim ritual prayer, then meets Allah in person before descending back to earth. While both parts form the night journey, Muslims sometimes refer to the Isra as the night journey and the Mi'raj as the ascension. Muslims, past and present, are divided as to whether the journey was physical or merely a dream.

jahiliyya: Arabic for "age of ignorance." These were the days before the advent of Muhammad. Muslims claim that, before Muhammad, Arabs lived in a state of ignorance, worshiping idols until the light of Islam came. Today some Muslims refer to any ungodly way of life as jahiliyya. For instance, a Muslim may claim that the immorality and sexual revolution advanced by Hollywood is a jahiliyya.

jizya: a special tax paid by Christians and Jews to Muslim rulers. This is a tax based on religious identification. Since Muslims are the rulers who protect non-Muslims, particularly Christians and Jews, the reasoning is that these non-Muslims must pay tribute in return for protection. The jizya is supported by the Quran, which says the people who received "the Book" (usually understood as Christians and Jews) must pay the jizya while humiliated (Q 9:29).

Ka'ba: the most sacred place in Islam. Located in Mecca, in today's Saudi Arabia, this is a cubic structure covered in black cloth that serves as a shrine. Muslims consider it Allah's house. It is where millions gather every year for the ritual hajj (pilgrimage), during which Muslims walk around the Ka'ba several times in addition to performing other rituals. Some traditions claim that the Ka'ba was built by Abraham and his son Ishmael; according to other traditions, it was built by Adam. In the eastern wall is a black stone that allegedly fell from heaven. Muslims believe the stone has religious power and miraculous abilities. During the ritual pilgrimage, millions of Muslims every year attempt to touch—or even kiss—this black stone.

Khadija: Muhammad's first wife. She was a wealthy merchant in Mecca, praised and respected by all in the tribe. Muhammad worked for her, managing caravan trades in Northern Arabia. When she was forty, she proposed to and married Muhammad after losing her two previous husbands. Muhammad was twenty-five when they married. Her cousin, Waraqa, was Christian. He assured Muhammad of the call to prophethood after hearing the first verse of the Quran proclaimed by Muhammad. Muhammad never married another woman while Khadija was alive. After her death in 619, Muhammad had many other wives and concubines.

khutba: a sermon. In Arabic, the word *khutba* means "sermon," "exhortation," or "speech." It usually refers to the sermon given by the mosque's imam—or any religious leader—to inform Muslims of religious or political matters. It often relies on the Quran and Muhammad's hadiths. Muhammad is reported to have presented many of these sermons. To Muslims, the most important khutba is the one presented each Friday, when they gather to listen and pray in the mosque. Although Muslims recorded thousands of Muhammad's hadiths centuries after his death, none of his Friday sermons have been preserved. The only khutba we have for Muhammad is the one he preached before his death. Muslims call it the Farewell Sermon. We know about it not from eyewitnesses but from later hadith traditions.

maghazi: Muhammad's raids. The Arabic word is plural and literally means "campaigns" or "incursions." It refers to Muhammad's raids or to a genre of writing about his military campaigns. Early Muslims used the term to refer to Muhammad's life and career—not only his raids—but later, narratives collected under the heading maghazi developed to become sira, meaning "biography." A maghazi account is often composed of consecutive hadiths, describing Muhammad's conduct as a prophet and statesman.

Maria: a Christian wife or concubine of Muhammad. She was an Egyptian who was sent as a gift to Muhammad, along with her sister, from the Byzantine patriarch of Alexandria. Some claim Muhammad married her, while others identify her as a slave concubine.

Mecca: Muhammad's birthplace and the holiest city in Islam. Mecca is mentioned once in the Quran (Q 48:24) and perhaps hinted at in Q 3:96. We know about Mecca only from later Muslim traditions, which claim that Mecca was a major city for pagan worship because it was on a famous trade route. These claims are challenged, as Mecca was not found on any major map during the seventh century. Even after the birth of Islam, the city did not seem to maintain any commercial significance. Mecca flourished mainly in the 1950s with the discovery of oil reserves. Many non-Muslim scholars are thus skeptical that Mecca was the birthplace of Islam. In recent research, scholars examined Quranic references and advanced archaeological findings and concluded that Muhammad may have pursued his career in other locations, including the region of Petra in Jordan.

mujahid: a fighter in jihad. The Arabic term *mujahid* refers to a man struggling and striving in jihad for Allah's cause. Its plural form is *mujahidun* or *mujahidin*. Many Muslims view a mujahid as a religious fighter following Allah's path. The term appears in the Quran and in ample hadiths. If killed in war, a mujahid is considered a martyr and is assured of being admitted into paradise.

mushrik: a polytheist. In Islam, a mushrik is someone who commits the greatest sin in Islam: shirk—that is, associating partners or equals with Allah. A mushrik is among the unbelievers and thus is also a kafir (an unbelieving infidel). Since polytheists believe in many gods, a mushrik is better labeled an "associator."

Mu'tazilite: a rationalist Muslim. This is a Muslim who adopts rational arguments to make sense of theological matters. In early Islam, the Mu'tazilites opposed the people of the hadiths and rejected most traditions attributed to Muhammad. The hadith scholars (traditionists) eventually won the intellectual battle against the Mu'tazilites due to caliphal support, and they became known as the adherents of the hadiths, or Sunnis.

qibla: the direction of Islamic ritual prayer. It is now Mecca, precisely the Ka'ba. In their ritual prayer, Muslims must face the Ka'ba as their divinely designated direction of prayer. The qibla was not always Mecca or the Ka'ba. In the earliest years of Islam, it was Jerusalem. For thirteen years, Muhammad preached in Mecca, and his qibla was Jerusalem. Even after he and his followers emigrated from Mecca to Medina, their qibla was still Jerusalem. But this was the same qibla used by the Jews in their rituals. As the clash between Muslims and Jews grew in Medina, Muhammad received a revelation from Allah with the instruction to change the qibla from Jerusalem to Mecca (Q 2:144). This was toward the end of his second year in Medina.

Quran: Islam's scripture and most holy book. It is perceived by Muslims as the literal Word of Allah, revealed to Muhammad through an angelic mediator named Gabriel (in Arabic, Jibril). The revelation was through dictation. It has 114 chapters, called suras, with each chapter divided into verses, called aayas. Muslims believe that the Quran has only one author: Allah. While non-Muslim scholars argue it might have had many authors, including Muhammad himself, and that it has been developed as a text over time, Muslims are adamant about the authorship, attributing it to no one but Allah.

Quraysh: Muhammad's tribe. This tribe was a major one in Mecca. According to tradition, it controlled the caravan trade throughout Mecca as well as the revenue of the pilgrims to the Ka'ba. The vast majority of its members opposed Muhammad, rejected his message, and persecuted him and his followers. This led to his emigration from Mecca to Medina. Some of Muhammad's relatives in the tribe were given incentives to accept his preaching and convert to Islam.

Safiyya: Muhammad's wife from a Jewish background. Safiyya was a seventeen-year-old Jewish girl from Khaybar. She was a new bride when her husband died in the raid led by Muhammad against Khaybar. Bukhari reports that after the battle the beauty of Safiyya was mentioned to Muhammad, and he selected her as a wife. She is identified in hadith traditions as a slave girl. It is reported that because of her beauty, Muhammad gave up seven female slaves for her.

Safwan: a fighter in Muhammad's army accused of having an affair with Aisha. He was a companion of Muhammad and was accused—but later acquitted by Allah—of having an affair with Muhammad's wife Aisha. The alleged affair occurred after a military raid led by Muhammad, when Aisha and Safwan were separated from the caravan of Muhammad.

Sahifa: a treaty of alliance between Muslims and Jews. The Arabic term *sahifa* means "scroll" or "book." The Sahifa is known as "The Charter of Medina" or "The Constitution of Medina." It refers to a treaty that allegedly created an alliance between the Muslims (Meccans and Medinans) and some Jews in Medina. The alliance aimed to defend Medina against external aggression. Muslims celebrate the Sahifa as evidence that Muhammad was a prophet of peace. We know about the Sahifa only from Muslim sources written centuries after Muhammad. Scholars have always doubted not only its issuance in the first place but also its scope and application. The Muslim histories themselves suggest it was rarely applied, as evidenced by the expulsion of the Jews from Medina and the confiscation of their property by the Muslims.

sahih: sound and authentic. The Arabic term *sahih* means "correct, right, reliable, and authentic." It describes what Muslims believe to be sound and trustworthy from Muhammad's traditions (hadiths). Although these traditions were compiled centuries after his lifetime, Muslims believe that a set of collections is sahih—that is, authentic and to be trusted. For Sunnis, there are nine sahih collections, among which two are acclaimed as the most reliable—the collection by Imam Bukhari and that of his disciple Imam Muslim. Muslims claim that a hadith is sahih based on its chain of transmitters or informants, which links the hadith statement (documented, say, in the tenth century) back to Muhammad himself (in the seventh century). The Arabic word for chain of transmitters is *isnad*. If the isnad is rigorous, Muslims claim, the hadith is reliable and truly traces back to Muhammad.

salat: a Muslim ritual prayer. Five times each day, Muslims perform a ritual prayer, called *salat* in Arabic. This is a duty for Muslims. It is one of the Five Pillars of Islam: Shahada, or profession of faith;

salat, or ritual prayer; zakat, or almsgiving; sawm, or fasting; and hajj, or pilgrimage.

Saqifa: a small Bedouin home. In this roofed structure in Medina, on the day of Muhammad's death, Muslims quarreled among themselves regarding Muhammad's successor. The Medinan Muslims lost the dispute, as the Meccan Muslims advanced Abu Bakr to be the caliph. According to Shiite Muslims, Muhammad clearly appointed Ali as his successor, but Abu Bakr and other Meccans seized power without even considering the fact that Muhammad had just died.

satanic verses: nondivine words interjected into the Quran. This refers to an incident during Muhammad's time in Mecca. Early Muslim historians claim that he longed in his heart for less tension with the pagans of Mecca. Satan used this opportunity to place words into Muhammad's mouth that praised three pagan goddesses as effective in their intercession. The satanic words made their way into the Quran but were later annulled by Allah. While early Muslims told the story as fact, many later Muslims denied it ever happened. The term *satanic verses* was used as the title of a controversial novel by Salman Rushdie in 1988. In response to the novel, the Iranian ayatollah Khomeini issued a fatwa (religious ruling) calling for Rushdie's death.

Shahada: the Islamic creed or profession of faith. The Arabic word *Shahada* means "testimony" or "declaration." The Shahada states, "I testify that there is no god but Allah, and Muhammad is Allah's messenger." This is the declaration one makes to join the religion of Islam. The public statement of its two parts is mandatory for anyone wishing to become a Muslim. Whether the person wholeheartedly believes the declaration or not, the mere pronouncement of the creed makes one Muslim. This is why many distinguish between "faith" and "declaring Islam." The former refers to a true and deep conviction, while the latter might simply involve making the statement unaccompanied by true faith.

sharia: Islamic law prescribed by Allah. This is Allah's will and law for humankind. There is no book in Islam titled *Sharia*. It is a collection of rules on worship and practices compiled by medieval Muslim scholars from what was described in the Quran and Muhammad's traditions (hadiths, biographies, etc.). The rules cover daily aspects of every Muslim's life, including religious, political, social, and even personal matters. Many Muslims find it difficult to find answers to contemporary questions, so they rely heavily on Muslim clerics and jurists because the so-called sharia is found in sophisticated jurisprudence writings. When the Quran and Muhammad's words provide no solution for a legal question, Muslim scholars attempt to use analogy and a complex process of legal reasoning and interpretations to establish a law for the Muslims. The rules of the sharia are not identical between Sunnis and Shiites. Overall, Muslims trust that Muhammad applied Allah's sharia in Medina. Just like he did, Muslims believe they are called to establish Islamic states applying the sharia's principles in all life matters.

shirk: the sin of association. The term is used in the Quran to condemn unbelievers who worship any deity besides Allah. Shirk is the greatest unforgivable sin in Islam, defined as associating gods or partners with Allah, in contrast to pure and strict monotheism. Committing shirk makes one a mushrik. The opposite of shirk is tawhid, strict monotheism. The Quran refers to some Christians who consider Jesus and Mary to be gods and warns against this erroneous belief. Some Muslim scholars accuse Christians of shirk because of the doctrines of the Trinity and the incarnation.

sira: a biography, particularly that of Muhammad. The earliest biography of Muhammad was written by Ibn Ishaq about 120 years after Muhammad's death. This sira is now lost. However, a disciple of Ibn Ishaq named Ibn Hisham allegedly found a copy. He arranged and edited it, removing sensitive material in what many call a censorship process. This is now the sira we have for Muhammad. It was translated into English by British scholar Alfred Guillaume (1888–1965) and published by Oxford University Press in 1955.

Sunna: Muhammad's collective tradition. There is no book or set of books titled *Sunna*. Sunna refers to a group of classical writings that include thousands of traditions about Muhammad's life, teachings, and deeds. Sunna thus refers to traditions about Muhammad written by Muslims who lived centuries after his death. Hadiths are part of the Sunna. Muhammad's biographical deeds

are part of the Sunna. Descriptions of his raids and expeditions as
well as reports of his treatment of anyone or his behavior in any
situation are parts of the Sunna. Sunni Muslims follow the Sunna
of Muhammad—that is, his life, conduct, and teachings. From a
critical standpoint, most of these traditions cannot be supported
by evidence. They were documented to address the political and
social requirements at the time of their writing. This is why many
scholars established that the vast majority of these traditions are
forgeries.

**Sunni and Shiite (also Shia and Shi'a): the two main sects or branches
of Islam.** Sunni Muslims constitute about 80 to 85 percent of Muslims worldwide, while Shiite Muslims make up about 10 to 13 percent. The disagreements between the two groups are religious and
political. Shiites believe that the first three successors of Muhammad stole the succession after Muhammad's death from the rightful
leader, Muhammad's cousin and son-in-law Ali. Shiites have always
been the minority among Muslims. Thus, most Islamic writings have
not been in their favor. Sunni Muslims, on the other hand, have held
the power through the majority of Islamic history. They rely on the
Sunna—that is, Muhammad's alleged traditions and teachings—as
the main guide to life and practice after the Quran. These Sunna
writings were, of course, written mostly under the instruction of
the ruler of the day. Shiites have their own traditions and sets of
hadiths, which they attribute to Muhammad and his faithful family
and household, called the imams. In the West, Sunnis and Shiites
appear to live in harmony, since they constitute a slight minority,
but the case is different in the Muslim world. Clashes between the
two groups often occur to the extent that a 2012 Pew Research study
revealed that 40 percent of Sunnis from the Middle East and North
Africa do not consider Shiites to be Muslims.

sura: a chapter in the Quran. This is one solid unit in the Quran, which
contains 114 units (chapters) total. The suras are not arranged
chronologically in order of revelation. They are organized roughly
by length, from longest to shortest. However, sura 1 is not the longest. It is placed first as the opening sura of the Quran. The longest
sura is the second chapter, titled "The Cow." The shortest is the
108th sura, not the 114th. The suras were arranged in medieval

times, centuries after the alleged proclamation and compilation of the text. Muslims wholeheartedly believe that the order of the suras—as well as the verses—was prescribed by Allah and no one else. The order of the suras, Muslims claim, matches the order of the celestial tablet. Each sura has a title in Arabic ("Table," "Cattle," "Thunder," etc.). Suras are numbered from 1 through 114. Muslims, especially Arabs, prefer to use the Arabic titles, while non-Arabic speakers usually refer to a sura by its number. While Muslims insist that the Quran is written in perfectly clear Arabic, many scholars suggest that the word *sura* is not originally Arabic; it is either from a Hebrew word meaning "row" or from a Syriac word referring to writing.

Syriac: a Semitic language. In the seventh century, when Muhammad lived in Arabia, Christians used Syriac in their liturgy and writing. It is a dialect of Aramaic (the language Jesus spoke). Scholars believe that the Quran borrowed many words from Syriac liturgical texts.

Tabari: a renowned Muslim historian and Quran commentator. He was born in today's Iran in 839 and died in Baghdad in 923. He wrote a long book of Islamic history as well as a Quran commentary. The two works include a wealth of information on the history and scripture of Islam and became the foundation for future historical and exegetical works.

tarikh: history or historiography. The Arabic word *tarikh* means "history"—that is, the past. It also refers to any writing about the past—that is, historiography. The Muslim tarikh, as we know it today, is a product of the Abbasid Caliphate, which came to power in 750. All historical writings before the Abbasids are now lost. While some early Muslims seem to have paid attention to history writing, no Muslim historical witness comes from Muhammad's time or from the first two caliphates of Islam—the Rashidun and the Umayyads. The Abbasid caliphs sponsored the writing of historical accounts about centuries past. To emphasize and establish their legitimacy as pious rulers of Islam, they hired Muslim writers to create historical accounts that advanced Abbasid claims for power by emphasizing the caliphs' descent from Muhammad and depicting their rivals, the Umayyads, as impious and worldly.

tawhid: strict and absolute monotheism. The Arabic word *tawhid* is better—though uncommonly—translated as "unitarianism." This is the most important belief in Islam. It is the opposite of shirk. It even opposes the Christian doctrine of the Trinity. Although the word *tawhid* never appears in the Quran, Muslims believe that tawhid is the central belief that sets Islam apart from any other religion or faith. Problematically, Muslim tradition refers to an incident when Muhammad did not seem to be a monotheist. He endorsed seeking intercessory prayer from three pagan deities. The incident is infamously known as the satanic verses. The verses were included in the Quran for a time but later abrogated when Gabriel rebuked Muhammad. We know of the incident from Muslim traditions. It is unlikely that someone invented this story, as it portrays Muhammad unfavorably.

traditionist: a scholar of the hadiths. A hadith is a tradition by or about Muhammad. A traditionist is a hadith scholar and, in some sense, a lover of traditions. In medieval Islam, traditionists became greatly powerful and formed the core of what is known today as Sunni Islam. Their power grew rapidly because most Muslim writings were a form of hadith; thus, hadith scholars became indispensable. Muslim writers not only reported traditions but also invented them to advance their religious views and political claims for power. During this time, some Muslim writers made their living by generating or forging traditions. Thus, even today many Sunni hadiths contradict Shiite hadiths.

Umar: the second caliph in Islam. He was a strong Meccan leader who supported Muhammad and succeeded Abu Bakr as caliph. He was assassinated in 644. He introduced the Islamic calendar and was a crucial dispatcher of the armies during the Muslim conquests of Syria, Iraq, Egypt, and North Africa.

umma: the unified Muslim community. The term appears in the Quran and describes Muhammad's followers as the best umma—that is, one united and unified community (Q 3:110). It is a cherished term for Muslims, identifying them as a unique and unmatched community, united under Muhammad's leadership and unified by the strong religious ties of monotheism.

Uthman: the third caliph in Islam. He succeeded Umar and was assassinated in 656. Uthman married two daughters of Muhammad. He was instrumental in collecting the corpus of Quranic revelations into one book around the year 650. Muhammad reportedly promised ten of his male companions a place in paradise; Uthman was one of them.

Sources Consulted

Question 1. Who Was Muhammad?

For studies on Muhammad's life and career, see Ibrahim, *Stated Motivations*, 66–119; F. Buhl et al., "Muḥammad," in *Encyclopaedia of Islam*, ed. P. J. Bearman et al., 2nd ed., 12 vols. (Leiden: Brill, 1960–present), hereafter *EI2*, 7:360–76; Haykal, *Life of Muḥammad*; Rodinson, *Muhammad*; Watt, *Muhammad at Medina*; Watt, *Muhammad at Mecca*; Andræ, *Mohammed*; Gabriel, *Muhammad*; Clinton Bennett, *In Search of Muhammad* (London: Bloomsbury Academic, 1998); Martin Lings, *Muhammad: His Life Based on the Earliest Sources* (Rochester, VT: Inner Traditions International, 1983); and Ali Dashti, *Twenty-Three Years: A Study of the Prophetic Career of Mohammad* (London: Routledge, 2013). See also the collection of articles on Muhammad in Ibn Warraq, ed., *The Quest for the Historical Muhammad* (New York: Prometheus Books, 2000).

Question 4. What Is So Unique about Muhammad's Birth Year?

Ibn Hisham and Ibn Ishaq, *Life of Muhammad*, 21ff.; J. Ruska and Ch. Pellat, "Fīl," in *EI2*, 2:892–93; Irfan Shahīd, "People of the Elephant," in *Encyclopedia of the Quran*, ed. Jane Dammen McAuliffe, 6 vols. (Leiden: Brill, 2001–2006), hereafter *EQ*, 4:44–46; A. F. L. Beeston, "Abraha," in *EI2*, 1:102–3; Jane Dammen McAuliffe, "Abraha," in *EQ*, 1:4–5; Tabari, *History*, 5:285; Abū al-Fidā' Ismā'īl Ibn Kathīr, *Al-Sīra al-nabawiyya*, ed. Muṣṭafā 'Abd al-Wāḥid, 4 vols. (Beirut: Dār al-ma 'rifa, 1976), 1:215ff., and 1:206 on the light emitting from Muhammad's mother upon his birth; and Ibn Kathīr, *Al-Bidāya wa-l-nihāya*, ed. Ḥanān 'Abd al-Mannān, 15 vols. (Beirut: Bayt al-afkār, 2004), 2:268ff.

Question 5. What Is Significant about Muhammad's Genealogy?

A. J. Wensinck and J. Jomier, "Ka'ba," in *EI2*, 4:317ff.; and Reuven Firestone, "Ishmael," in *EQ*, 2:563–64. The tradition of Abraham and Ishmael building the Ka'ba is found in Bukhari, 4.55.583. Muḥammad ibn Sa'd, *Kitāb al-ṭabaqāt al-kabīr*, ed. Muḥammad 'Abd al-Qādir 'Aṭā, 8 vols. (Beirut: Dār al-kutub al-'ilmiyya, 1990), 1:47; Abū al-Ḥasan al-Mas'ūdī, *Murūj al-dhahab*, ed. Kamāl Ḥasan Mar'ī, 4 vols. (Beirut: Al-maktaba al-'aṣriyya, 2005), 2:211; Abū al-Ḥasan al-Mas'ūdī, *Kitāb al-Tanbīh wa-l-ishrāf*, ed. 'Abdullāh al-Ṣāwī

(Cairo: Dār al-Ṣāwī, n.d.), 195; and Aḥmad ibn Ḥusayn al-Bayhaqī, *Dalā'il al-nubuwwa*, ed. ʿAbd al-Muʿṭī Qalʿajī, 7 vols. (Beirut: Dār al-kutub al-ʿilmiyya, 1984), 1:180. For scholarly studies on the contradictory reports about the Kaʿba and its history, see F. E. Peters, *The Muslim Pilgrimage to Mecca and the Holy Places* (Princeton: Princeton University Press, 1996), 3–41, especially p. 14 regarding the stone; and G. R. Hawting, "The Origins of the Muslim Sanctuary at Mecca," in *Studies on the First Century of Islamic Society*, ed. G. H. A. Juynboll (Carbondale: Southern Illinois University Press, 1982), 23–48.

Question 6. What Do Muslims Believe about Muhammad's Attributes?

See the valuable study Tarif Khalidi, *Images of Muhammad: Narratives of the Prophet in Islam across the Centuries* (New York: Crown, 2009), in which he explores the various Muslim depictions of Muhammad. Sahih al-Bukhari has a section devoted entirely to Muhammad's qualities titled "Virtues and Merits of the Prophet," which includes the chapter "The Description of the Prophet." For examples, see the following hadiths on the valuable website www.sunnah.com: Bukhari, 4.56.747, 751, 756; 7.72.793. See also Sahih Muslim, 30.5776, 5789. On Muhammad's reported care for people in general, see Bukhari, 8.73.2; and Sahih Muslim 32.6181. For the traditions on Muhammad smiling and taking care of children, see Bukhari, 1.9.495; Sahih Muslim, 31.5954; Sunan Ibn Majah, 1.1.144; and Sunan an-Nasa'i, 2.12.1142. For secondary studies, see F. Buhl et al., "Muḥammad," in *EI2*, 7:360ff.; and Uri Rubin, "Muḥammad," in *EQ*, 3:440ff. For a valuable resource on Muhammad's life, see Haykal, *Life of Muḥammad*, 70ff. For the important role of Muhammad in the everyday lives of Muslims, see Annemarie Schimmel, *And Muhammad Is His Messenger: The Veneration of the Prophet in Islamic Piety* (Chapel Hill: University of North Carolina Press, 2014), chaps. 2–3.

Question 7. Was Muhammad a Real Historical Figure?

On folk Islam, see Colin Chapman, *Cross and Crescent: Responding to the Challenge of Islam* (Downers Grove, IL: InterVarsity, 2012), chap. 12; Nabeel Jabbour, *The Crescent through the Eyes of the Cross: Insights from an Arab Christian* (Colorado Springs: NavPress, 2008), chap. 11; and Bill Musk, *The Unseen Face of Islam: Sharing the Gospel with Ordinary Muslims at Street Level* (Grand Rapids: Kregel, 2004). On the historical Muhammad, see Ibrahim, *Concise Guide to the Quran*, chap. 6; and Hoyland, "Earliest Christian Writings," 276–95. For an argument that Muhammad never existed, see Yehuda Nevo and Judith Koren, *Crossroads to Islam: The Origins of the Arab Religion and the Arab State* (Amherst, NY: Prometheus Books, 2003), 8, 347, 348. For non-Muslim sources on Muhammad and Islam, see Hoyland, *Seeing Islam as Others Saw It*; Penn, *When Christians First Met Muslims*; James Howard-Johnston, *Witnesses to a World Crisis: Historians and Histories of the Middle East in the Seventh Century* (Oxford: Oxford University Press, 2010); and Andrew Palmer, *The Seventh Century in the West-Syrian Chronicles*, trans. and annotation by Andrew Palmer (Liverpool: Liverpool University Press, 1993).

Question 8. What Do We Know about Mecca, Muhammad's Birthplace?

J. Chabbi, "Mecca," in *EQ*, 3:337–41; W. Montgomery Watt et al., "Makka," in *EI2*, 6:144–87; Gibson, *Qur'ānic Geography*; and Gibson, *Early Islamic Qiblas*. Gibson has his own channel on YouTube that includes many films explaining his arguments: https://www.you tube.com/c/DanGibsonFilms. See a negative response to Gibson's arguments in David A. King, "Review of Dan Gibson's *Early Islamic Qiblas*," *Suhayl* 16–17 (2018–2019): 347–66. For somewhat positive reviews of Gibson's findings, see W. Richard Oakes, "Review of

Qur'anic Geography," *Muslim World* 105 (2015): 423–26; and Daniel C. Waugh, "Review of *Qur'anic Geography*," *Silk Road* 10 (2012): 201.

Question 9. What Is the Black Stone in the Ka'ba?

A. J. Wensinck and J. Jomier, "Ka'ba," in *EI2*, 4:317ff.; and G. R. Hawting, "Pilgrimage," in *EQ*, 4:91–100. On the hajj and the black stone, see F. E. Peters, *The Muslim Pilgrimage to Mecca and the Holy Places* (Princeton: Princeton University Press, 1996), 3–41, especially p. 14 regarding the stone; G. R. Hawting, "The Origins of the Muslim Sanctuary at Mecca," in *Studies on the First Century of Islamic Society*, ed. G. H. A. Juynboll (Carbondale: Southern Illinois University Press, 1982), 23–48; Gerald Hawting, ed., *The Development of Islamic Ritual* (London: Routledge, 2017), especially chap. 14 by C. Snouck Hurgronje, "The Meccan Feast," and chap. 15 by Hava Lazarus-Yafeh, "The Religious Dialectics of the Hadjdj"; and M. Gaudefroy-Demombynes, *Le pèlerinage à la Mekke: Étude d'histoire religieuse* (Paris: n.p., 1923). On the circumambulation as a ritual found in other non-Muslim traditions before Islam, see F. Buhl, "Tawāf," in *EI2*, 10:376.

Question 10. What Do We Know about Muhammad's Wives and Their Roles in Islam?

See Barbara Stowasser, "Wives of the Prophet," in *EQ*, 4:506–21; Stowasser, "Khadīja," in *EQ*, 3:80–81; F. Buhl et al., "Muhammad," in *EI2*, 7:360–76; and Watt, "'Ā'isha Bint Abī Bakr," 1:307–8. For a general overview, see Barbara Freyer Stowasser, *Women in the Qur'an, Traditions, and Interpretation* (Oxford: Oxford University Press, 1996); see chaps. 8–9 on Muhammad's wives in the Quran and the hadiths. For negative Shiite views on Aisha, see the Shiite contemporary study Habib, *Obscenity*. For a study on Muhammad's wives, see Bint al-Shāti', *The Wives of the Prophet*, trans. Matti Moosa and Nicholas Ranson (Lahore: Sh. Muhammad Ashraf, 1971; repr., Piscataway, NJ: Gorgias Press, 2006); and Ashley Manjarrez Walker and Michael A. Sells, "The Wiles of Women and Performative Intertextuality: 'Ā'isha, the Hadith of the Slander, and the Sura of Yusuf," *Journal of Arabic Literature* 30, no. 1 (1999): 55–77. On Zayd and Zaynab, see David S. Powers, *Zayd* (Philadelphia: University of Pennsylvania Press, 2014). On Safiyya, see Ibrahim, *Stated Motivations*, 66–119; Ibrahim, *Conversion to Islam*, chap. 2; Nicholas Awde, *Women in Islam: An Anthology from the Qur'ān and Hadīths* (New York: Routledge, 1999), 10, 58–59, 85–90; and Reuven Firestone, "The Prophet Muhammad in Pre-Modern Jewish Literatures," in *The Image of the Prophet between Ideal and Ideology*, ed. Christiane J. Gruber and Avinoam Shalem (Berlin: de Gruyter, 2013), 33. See also Haykal, *Life of Muhammad*, 386–404.

Question 11. Was Muhammad Always a Monotheist?

W. Montgomery Watt, "Hanīf," in *EI2*, 3:165–66; and Uri Rubin, "Hanīf," in *EQ*, 2:402. On the connection between Abraham's religion and Muhammad, see F. E. Peters, *Muhammad and the Origins of Islam* (New York: State University of New York Press, 1994), 120–25. On isma, see Madelung and Tyan, "'Isma," in *EI2*, 4:182–84; and Paul E. Walker, "Impeccability," in *EQ*, 2:505–7. For the episode of the satanic verses in traditional sources, see Tabari, *History*, 6:107ff.; and Ibn Hisham and Ibn Ishaq, *Life of Muhammad*, 165–67. For secondary studies on the satanic verses, see Ibrahim, *Concise Guide to the Quran*, chap. 19; Ahmed, *Before Orthodoxy*; Ahmed, "Satanic Verses," in *EQ*, 4:531ff.; Watt, *Muhammad at Mecca*, 103; Watt, *Muhammad: Prophet and Statesman*, 61; and Gabriel Said Reynolds, *The Emergence of Islam: Classical Traditions in Contemporary Perspective* (Minneapolis: Fortress, 2012), 24, 139–42.

Question 12. What Is Muhammad's Night Journey to Jerusalem and Heaven?

Ibn Hisham and Ibn Ishaq, *Life of Muhammad*, 181ff.; Michael Sells, "Ascension," in *EQ*, 1:176–81; N. J. Johnson, "Aqsā Mosque," in *EQ*, 1:125–27; and B. Schrieke et al., "Mi'rādj," in *EI2*, 7:97–105. See also the thorough edited volume Mohammad Ali Amir-Moezzi, ed., *Le voyage initiatique en terre d'islam* (Leuven: Peeters, 1996). For a detailed hadith on the ascension to heaven and Muhammad's meetings with previous prophets, see Bukhari, 1.8.345; and Sahih Muslim, 1:313. For more on Muhammad's lack of miracles, see the detailed explanation in Ibrahim, *Concise Guide to the Quran*, chap. 25; and Denis Gril, "Miracles," in *EQ*, 3:392ff. For Muslims who deny Muhammad's miracles, see the study of Iranian rationalist Ali Dashti, *Twenty-Three Years: A Study of the Prophetic Career of Mohammad* (New York: Routledge, 2013), chap. 2, where he dismisses Muhammad's signs and wonders and presents the Quran as the only miracle. For recent secondary studies, see Frederick S. Colby, *Narrating Muhammad's Night Journey: Tracing the Development of the Ibn 'Abbās Ascension Discourse* (New York: State University of New York Press, 2008), 13–64; Ronald Paul Buckley, The Night Journey and Ascension in Islam: The Reception of Religious Narrative in Sunni, Shi'i and Western Culture (London: I. B. Tauris, 2013); and Christiane J. Gruber and Frederick Stephen Colby, eds., *The Prophet's Ascension: Cross-Cultural Encounters with the Islamic Mi'rāj Tales* (Bloomington: Indiana University Press, 2010).

Question 13. Why Did Muhammad Strike a Peace Treaty with the Jews?

For a primary source for the Sahifa, see Ibn Hisham and Ibn Ishaq, *Life of Muhammad*, 231–33. For a secondary study, see the important work by Lecker, "*Constitution of Medina*," 1–78, in which he translates the Sahifa and provides details about its documentation and content. See also Wensinck, *Muhammad and the Jews of Medina*; and Gil, *Jews in Islamic Countries*, chap. 2. On how conversion to Islam in the earliest period seems to have been merely a tribal submission to a powerful leader, see Ibrahim, *Stated Motivations*, 119, 156.

Question 14. Why Did Muhammad Raid the Pagans of Mecca?

On Muhammad's raids, see Ibrahim, *Stated Motivations*, 66–119; Gabriel, *Muhammad*, 86ff.; Francis E. Peters, *Muhammad and the Origins of Islam* (New York: State University of New York Press, 1994), 211ff.; and Peters, *Islam: A Guide for Jews and Christians* (Princeton: Princeton University Press, 2009), 68ff. For a secondary study on Badr, see Gabriel, *Muhammad*, 86–107.

Question 15. Was There Ever a Truce between Muslims and Meccans?

Ibn Hisham and Ibn Ishaq, *Life of Muhammad*, 499ff.; Tabari, *History*, 8:67ff.; W. M. Watt, "al-Hudaybiya," in *EI2*, 3:539; Francis E. Peters, *Muhammad and the Origins of Islam* (New York: State University of New York Press, 1994), 228ff.; and Asma Afsaruddin, *The First Muslims: History and Memory* (Oxford: Oneworld, 2008), 10ff.

Question 16. Did Muhammad Really Fight the Jews?

For Muslim primary sources on the raids against the Jews, see Bukhari, 1.8.367; 3.39.519; 4.52.153 (on how the properties were given to Muhammad); 4.53.357; 5.59.362, 447 (on the judgment of Sa'd against the Qurayza); 5.59.366; 6.60.406, 407; and Sahih Muslim, 19.4364, 4324, 4325, 4347 (on how Muhammad kept all properties for himself). See also Sunan Abi Dawud, 19.2995. See also Sunan Ibn Majah, 3.20.2541, which states concerning the killed men of the Qurayza, "Those whose pubic hair had grown were killed, and those whose pubic hair had not yet grown were let go"; also a similar account in Jami' at-Tirmidhi, 3.19.1584. For secondary studies, see Francis E. Peters, *Muhammad and the Origins of Islam* (New York: State University of New York Press, 1994), 211ff.; and Peters, *Islam: A Guide for Jews and Christians* (Princeton: Princeton University Press, 2009), 68ff.

Question 18. Who Killed Muhammad?

For primary sources on Muhammad's death, see Tabari, *History*, 9:163ff.; and Ibn Hisham and Ibn Ishaq, *Life of Muhammad*, 678ff. For secondary studies, see Shoemaker, *Death of a Prophet*, 73ff.; and Madelung, *Succession to Muhammad*, 356–59. See also the famous modern biography of Muhammad by the Egyptian historian Haykal, *Life of Muhammad*, 386ff., 524ff.; and Michael Muhammad Knight, *Muhammad's Body: Baraka Networks and the Prophetic Assemblage* (Chapel Hill: University of North Carolina Press, 2020), 137–39. For a Muslim argument that evil Jews poisoned Muhammad, see Islam Question & Answer, "The Jews' Attempts to Kill the Prophet," December 18, 2002, https://islamqa.info/en/answers/32762/the-jews-attempts-to-kill-the-prophet-peace-and-blessings-of-allaah-be-upon-him. This article, written from a conservative Muslim perspective and based on Muslim classical sources, discusses several attempts by the Jews to kill Muhammad. For non-Muslim studies, see Watt, *Muhammad at Medina*, 54, 234; Rodinson, *Muhammad*, 254; and Szilágyi, "After the Prophet's Death."

Question 19. Did Muhammad Appoint a Successor?

On appointing Ali at Ghadir Khumm and on the details of the incident, see L. Veccia Vaglieri, "Ghadīr Khumm," in *EI2*, 2:992–93; Mahmud Shahabi, "The Roots of Shi'ism in Early Islamic History," in *Shi'ism: Doctrines, Thought, and Spirituality*, ed. Seyed Vali Reza Nasr et al. (New York: State University of New York Press, 1988), 15–16; David Waines, *An Introduction to Islam* (Cambridge: Cambridge University Press, 2003), 155ff.; and Daniel W. Brown, *A New Introduction to Islam* (Malden, MA: Wiley-Blackwell, 2009), 131.

Question 20. What Are Some of the Early Non-Muslim Views on Muhammad?

See the valuable resource Mark Beaumont, ed., *Arab Christians and the Quran from the Origins of Islam to the Medieval Period* (Leiden: Brill, 2018); Charles Tieszen, *The Christian Encounter with Muhammad: How Theologians Have Interpreted the Prophet* (New York: Bloomsbury Academic, 2020); John Tolan, *Faces of Muhammad: Western Perceptions of the Prophet of Islam from the Middle Ages to Today* (Princeton: Princeton University Press, 2019), 1–43; and Tolan, ed., *Medieval Christian Perceptions of Islam* (London: Routledge, 2013), xi–84. On John of Damascus, see John W. Voorhis, "John of Damascus on the Moslem Heresy," *Muslim World* 24, no. 4 (1934): 391–98; Daniel J. Sahas, *John of Damascus on Islam: The "Heresy of the Ishmaelites"* (Leiden: Brill, 1972), 67–97, especially 77; and Daniel Janosik, *John of Damascus, First Apologist to the Muslims: The Trinity and Christian Apologetics in the Early Islamic Period* (Eugene, OR: Pickwick Publications, 2016). On Theophanes, see Maria Vaiou, "Theophanes the Confessor," in *Christian-Muslim Relations: A Bibliographical History*, ed. David Thomas et al., vol. 1 (Leiden: Brill, 2009), 426–36.

Question 21. What Was Muhammad's Central Message?

For a Muslim perspective on tawhid, see Fazlur Rahman, *Major Themes of the Qur'an* (Chicago: University of Chicago Press, 2009), 1–16; and Rahman, *Islam* (1966; repr.

Chicago: University of Chicago Press, 2020), 11–29. For secondary studies on tawhid and its opposite, see D. Gimaret, "Shirk," in *EI2*, 9:485ff; and Gimaret, "Tawḥīd," in *EI2*, 10:389ff. For the Quranic accusations against Jews and Christians associating partners with the deity, see Nicolai Sinai, "The Unknown Known: Some Groundwork for Interpreting the Medinan Qur'an," *Mélanges de l'Université Saint-Joseph* 66 (2015–16): 49ff.; Mun'im Sirry, *Scriptural Polemics: The Qur'ān and Other Religions* (Oxford: Oxford University Press, 2014), 33ff.; and Nicolai Sinai, *The Qur'an: A Historical-Critical Introduction* (Edinburgh: Edinburgh University Press, 2018), 83ff.

Question 22. Who Is Muhammad's Deity, Allah?

In addition to the references mentioned in the chapter, see Reynolds, *Allah*, 11, 46–49, 94–95, 105, 131–32, 177, 272n6; and Shems Friedlander, Muzaffer Ozak, and Hamid Amidi, *Ninety-Nine Names of Allah: The Beautiful Names* (Grand Rapids: HarperCollins, 1993).

Question 23. What Is Muhammad's Message about Jesus?

For more on Jesus in Islam, see Gabriel Said Reynolds, *The Qur'ān and the Bible: Text and Commentary* (New Haven: Yale University Press, 2018), 109ff., 473ff.; Reynolds, *Allah*, 81–85, 126–27, 204, 262; Nickel, *Quran with Christian Commentary*, 78ff., 85–86, 144, 164, 313; Tarif Khalidi, *The Muslim Jesus: Sayings and Stories in Islamic Literature* (Cambridge, MA: Harvard University Press, 2001), 6–46; Neal Robinson, *Christ in Islam and Christianity* (New York: State University of New York Press, 1991), 3–22; Timothy George, *Is the Father of Jesus the God of Muhammad? Understanding the Differences between Christianity and Islam* (Grand Rapids: Zondervan, 2002), 55–104; Carlos Andrés Segovia, *The Quranic Jesus: A New Interpretation* (Berlin: de Gruyter, 2018), chaps. 1–2; and Mona Siddiqui, *Christians, Muslims, and Jesus* (New Haven: Yale University Press, 2013).

Question 24. Where Is Muhammad Mentioned in the Bible?

On the Gospel of Barnabas, see Jan Joosten, "The Gospel of Barnabas and the Diatessaron," *Harvard Theological Review* 95 (2002): 73–96; Sidney H. Griffith, *The Bible in Arabic: The Scriptures of the "People of the Book" in the Language of Islam* (Princeton: Princeton University Press, 2013), 175ff.; Gerard A. Wiegers, "Muhammad as the Messiah: A Comparison of the Polemical Works of Juan Alonso with the *Gospel of Barnabas*," *Bibliotheca Orientalis* 52 (1995): 245–91; Jan Slomp, "The 'Gospel of Barnabas' in Recent Research," *Islamochristiana* 23 (1997): 81–109; and Slomp, "The Gospel of Barnabas," in *Christian-Muslim Relations, 1600–1700* (Brill: Leiden, 2017), 9:671ff. See also Gordon D. Nickel, *The Gentle Answer to the Muslim Accusation of Biblical Falsification* (Calgary: Bruton Gate, 2014); David Sox, *The Gospel of Barnabas* (London: George Allen & Unwin, 1984); Norman L. Geisler and Abdul Saleeb, *Answering Islam: The Crescent in Light of the Cross* (1993; repr. Grand Rapids: Baker Books, 2002), 303–8; Theodore Pulcini, "In the Shadow of Mount Carmel: The Collapse of the 'Latin East' and the Origins of the Gospel of Barnabas," *Islam and Christian-Muslim Relations* 12 (2001): 191–209; and M. De Epalza, "Le milieu hispano-moresque de l'Évangile islamisant de Barnabe," *Islamochristiana* 8 (1982): 159–83. For Muslim apologetic works alleging various Islamic charges against Christianity, see Ahmed Deedat, *What the Bible Says about Muhammad* (Chicago: Kazi Publications, 1982); Deedat, *The Choice: Islam & Christianity* (New Delhi: Adam Publishers & Distributors, 2012); Deedat, *Is the Bible God's Word?* (Durban, South Africa: Islamic Propagation Centre, 1981); Deedat, *The God That Never Was* (Durban, South Africa: Islamic Propagation Centre, 1983); and Deedat, *Crucifixion or Cruci-Fiction*

(Durban, South Africa: Islamic Propagation Centre, 1984). For a Christian discussion, see Nickel, *Quran with Christian Commentary*, 189–90, 564–65.

Question 25. Where Are Muhammad's Sermons?

For a critical assessment of Muslim tradition and its reliability, see Crone, *Slaves on Horses*; Crone, *Meccan Trade and the Rise of Islam*; and Crone, *Medieval Islamic Political Thought* (2004; repr. Edinburgh: Edinburgh University Press, 2014). See also Robinson, *Islamic Historiography*; Robinson, *Empire and Elites after the Muslim Conquest*; Erling Ladewig Petersen, *ʿAlī and Muʿāwiya in Early Arabic Tradition: Studies on the Genesis and Growth of Islamic Historical Writing until the End of the Ninth Century*, trans. P. Lampe Christensen (Copenhagen: Aarhuus Stiftsbogtrykkerie, 1964); and Herbert Berg, ed., *Method and Theory in the Study of Islamic Origins* (Leiden: Brill, 2003).

Question 27. How Does Muhammad's Tradition Treat Apostasy from Islam?

For discussions on apostasy in Islam, see Wael Hallaq, "Apostasy," in *EQ*, 1:119–22; W. Heffening, "Murtadd," in *EI2*, 7:635–36; and Abdullah Saeed and Hassan Saeed, *Freedom of Religion, Apostasy and Islam* (London: Taylor & Francis, 2017), chaps. 1–8. For the treatment of the term *apostasy* in the Quran, see Toshihiko Izutsu, *Ethico-religious Concepts in the Qurʾān* (1959; repr. Montreal: McGill-Queen's University Press, 2002), 119–54. For examples and testimonies of apostates from Islam, see Ibn Warraq, ed., *Leaving Islam: Apostates Speak Out* (New York: Prometheus Books, 2009).

Question 28. What Do the Hadiths Say about Jihad?

The literature on jihad is immense. See Ella Landau-Tasseron, "Jihād," in *EQ*, 3:35ff.; David Cook, *Understanding Jihad* (Berkeley: University of California Press, 2005), 5–8; Mateen A. Elass, "Four Jihads: Jihad Means More than Warfare, but the Sword Is Central to Islam's Texts, Its History, and Its Founder," *Christian History* 21, no. 2 (2002): 35–38; Reuven Firestone, *Jihad: The Origin of Holy War in Islam* (New York: Oxford University Press, 1999), 17ff.; Michael David Bonner, *Jihad in Islamic History: Doctrines and Practice* (Princeton: Princeton University Press, 2006), 1–18; and Asma Afsaruddin, *Striving in the Path of God: Jihad and Martyrdom in Islamic Thought* (New York: Oxford University Press, 2013).

Question 29. Who Are the Hadith-Rejecters among Muslims?

For studies on hadith-rejecters, see Ibrahim, *Concise Guide to the Quran*, 134ff.; Gabriel Said Reynolds, *The Emergence of Islam: Classical Traditions in Contemporary Perspective* (Minneapolis: Fortress, 2012), 43, 91–92, 207–8; and Ali Usman Qasmi, *Questioning the Authority of the Past: The* Ahl al-Qurʾan *Movements in the Punjab* (Karachi, Pakistan: Oxford University Press, 2011).

Question 30. Why Are the Hadith-Rejecters Growing in Number?

For a helpful discussion of sex slaves in early Islam, see Salma Saad, "The Legal and Social Status of Women in the Hadith Literature" (PhD thesis, University of Leeds, 1990). See also Pernilla Myrne, *Female Sexuality in the Early Medieval Islamic World: Gender and Sex in Arabic Literature* (London: I.B. Tauris, 2019), chaps. 1–3; and Myrne, "Slaves for Pleasure in Arabic Sex and Slave Purchase Manuals from the Tenth to the Twelfth Centuries," *Journal of Global Slavery* 4, no. 2 (2019): 196–225. See the valuable study Clarence-Smith, *Islam and the Abolition of Slavery*, chap. 1, where he writes on the "embarrassing institution" of slavery in Islam, and chap. 2, on the contradictions and fragile Sunni consensus over slavery. For a modern Muslim perspective, see Ali, *Marriage and Slavery in Early Islam*. On slavery and slaves among Arabs in history until today, see Bernard Lewis, *Race and Slavery in the Middle East: An Historical Enquiry* (Oxford: Oxford University Press, 1990); Jonathan A. C. Brown, *Slavery and Islam* (Oxford: Oneworld, 2020); Thomas Sowell, *Black Rednecks and White Liberals* (San Francisco: Encounter Books, 2006); and Sowell, *The Thomas Sowell Reader* (New York: Basic Books, 2011). We are told that in 2018, "The African Union has reprimanded Mauritania for failing to take action against widespread slavery within its borders and ordered the government to give financial compensation to two child slaves who were failed by its legal system." See Annie Kelly and Kate Hodal, "Mauritania Failing to Tackle Pervasive Slavery, Says African Union," *Guardian*, January 29, 2018, https://www.theguardian.com/global-development/2018/jan/29/african-union -mauritania-failing-to-tackle-pervasive-slavery. Libya has the same problem as Mauritania. See Martin Plaut, "Libya's Slave Markets Are a Reminder That the Exploitation of Africans Never Went Away," *New Statesman*, February 21, 2018, https://www.newstatesman.com /world/africa/2018/02/libya-s-slave-markets-are-reminder-exploitation-africans-never-went -away. On the history and current affairs regarding slavery in Muslim countries, see "Slavery in Islam," BBC, September 7, 2009, https://www.bbc.co.uk/religion/religions/islam /history/slavery_1.shtml. See also "Slavery in the 21st Century: Estimated 27 Million Live in Slavery around the World," NPR, August 27, 2003, https://www.npr.org/templates /story/story.php?storyId=1408233.

Bibliography

Diacritics included in names to assist with phonetics have been excluded in the text and notes.

Adang, Camilla. *Muslim Writers on Judaism and the Hebrew Bible: From Ibn Rabban to Ibn Hazm*. Leiden: Brill, 1996.

Ahmad, Barakat. *Muhammad and the Jews*. New Delhi: Vikas, 1979.

Ahmed, Shahab. *Before Orthodoxy: The Satanic Verses in Early Islam*. Cambridge, MA: Harvard University Press, 2017.

Akyol, Mustafa. *Reopening Muslim Minds: A Return to Reason, Freedom, and Tolerance*. New York: St. Martin's Press, 2021.

Ali, Kecia. *The Lives of Muhammad*. Cambridge, MA: Harvard University Press, 2014.

———. *Marriage and Slavery in Early Islam*. Cambridge, MA: Harvard University Press, 2010.

Andræ, Tor. *Mohammed: The Man and His Faith*. 1936. Reprint, London: Taylor & Francis, 2013.

ʿAyyāshī, Muḥammad ibn Masʿū al-. *Tafsīr*. 2 vols. Tehran: al-Maṭbaʿa al-ʿilmiyya, 2001.

Azmeh, Aziz al-. *The Emergence of Islam in Late Antiquity: Allah and His People*. Cambridge: Cambridge University Press, 2014.

Azraqī, Abū al-Walīd al-. *Akhbār Makka*. Edited by Rushdī al-Ṣāliḥ Malḥas. Beirut: Dār al-Andalus, 1983.

Bakalla, Muhammad Hassan. *Arabic Culture through Its Language and Literature*. London: Kegan Paul, 1984.

Bakhit, M. A. "Tabūk." In *Encyclopaedia of Islam*, edited by P. J. Bearman et al., 10:50–51. 2nd ed. 12 vols. Leiden: Brill, 1960–present.

Balādhurī, Aḥmad ibn Yaḥyā al-. *The Origins of the Islamic State*. Translated by Francis Murgotten and Philip Khuri Hitti. New York: AMS Press, 1968.

Banerji, Robin. "Gay-Friendly 'Mosque' Opens in Paris." *BBC World Service*. November 30, 2012. https://www.bbc.com/news/world-europe-20547335.

Beck, Daniel. *Evolution of the Early Quran: From Anonymous Apocalypse to Charismatic Prophet*. New York: Peter Lang, 2018.

Berg, Herbert. "Competing Paradigms in Islamic Origins." In *Method and Theory in the Study of Islamic Origins*, edited by Herbert Berg, 259–92. Leiden: Brill, 2003.

———. *The Development of Exegesis in Early Islam: The Authenticity of Muslim Literature from the Formative Period*. Surrey, UK: Curzon, 2000.

Book of Tirmidhi. *Sunan*. Edited by Aḥmad Shākir et al. 5 vols. Cairo: Maktabat Muṣṭafā al-Ḥalabī, 1975.

Brown, Jonathan A. C. *Hadith: Muhammad's Legacy in the Medieval and Modern World*. Oxford: Oneworld, 2009.

———. *Misquoting Muhammad: The Challenge and Choices of Interpreting the Prophet's Legacy*. Oxford: Oneworld, 2014.

Buhl, F. "Mu'ta." In *Encyclopaedia of Islam*, edited by P. J. Bearman et al., 7:757–59. 2nd ed. 12 vols. Leiden: Brill, 1960–present.

Clarence-Smith, W. G. *Islam and the Abolition of Slavery*. Oxford: Oxford University Press, 2006.

Comparative Constitute Project. "Maldives 2008." Constitute. https://www.constituteproject.org/constitution/Maldives_2008?lang=en.

Crone, Patricia. *Meccan Trade and the Rise of Islam*. Princeton: Princeton University Press, 1987.

———. "The Religion of the Qur'ānic Pagans: God and the Lesser Deities." *Arabica* 57 (2010): 151–200.

———. *Slaves on Horses: The Evolution of the Islamic Polity*. Cambridge: Cambridge University Press, 1980.

———. "What Do We Actually Know about Mohammed?" *Open Democracy*. June 10, 2008. https://www.opendemocracy.net/en/mohammed_3866jsp/.

Dagorn, René. *La geste d'Ismael d'après l'onomastique et la tradition arabe*. Paris: Librairie Champion, 1981.

Donner, Fred. "The Historical Context." In *The Cambridge Companion to the Qur'ān*, edited by Jane Dammen McAuliffe, 23–40. Cambridge: Cambridge University Press, 2006.

———. *Narratives of Islamic Origins: The Beginnings of Islamic Historical Writing.* Princeton: Darwin Press, 1998.

Duri, Abd al-Aziz. *The Rise of Historical Writing among the Arabs.* Edited and translated by Lawrence I. Conrad. Princeton: Princeton University Press, 1983.

El Hamel, Chouki. *Black Morocco: A History of Slavery, Race, and Islam.* Cambridge: Cambridge University Press, 2014.

Elie, Janise. "Yemeni Child Bride, Eight, 'Dies on Wedding Night.'" *Guardian.* September 11, 2013. https://www.theguardian.com/global-development/2013/sep/11/yemen-child-bride-dies-wedding.

Faizer, Rizwi Shuhadha. "Ibn Isḥāq and al-Wāqidī Revisited: A Case Study of Muḥammad and the Jews in Biographical Literature." PhD diss., McGill University, 1995.

Gabriel, Richard A. *Muhammad: Islam's First Great General.* Norman: University of Oklahoma Press, 2014.

Gardet, L. "al-Asmā' al-Ḥusnā." In *Encyclopaedia of Islam.* edited by P. J. Bearman et al., 1:714. 2nd ed. 12 vols. Leiden: Brill, 1960–present.

———. "Allāh." In *Encyclopaedia of Islam*, edited by P. J. Bearman et al., 1:406–17. 2nd ed. 12 vols. Leiden: Brill, 1960–present.

Gibson, Dan. *Early Islamic Qiblas: A Survey of Mosques Built between 1 AH/622 C.E. and 263 AH/876 C.E.* Vancouver: Independent Scholars Press, 2017.

———. *Qur'ānic Geography: A Survey and Evaluation of the Geographical References in the Qur'ān with Suggested Solutions for Various Problems and Issues.* Saskatoon, SK: CanBooks, 2011.

Gil, Mose. *Jews in Islamic Countries in the Middle Ages.* Leiden: Brill, 2004.

Gimaret, D. "Tawḥīd." In *Encyclopaedia of Islam*, edited by P. J. Bearman et al., 10:389. 2nd ed. 12 vols. Leiden: Brill, 1960–present.

Goldziher, Ignaz. *Mohammed and Islam.* Translated by Kate Chambers Seelye. New Haven: Yale University Press, 1917.

———. *Muslim Studies.* Edited by S. M. Stern. Translated by C. R. Barber and S. M. Stern. 2 vols. Albany: State University of New York Press, 1969–71.

Griffith, Sidney. "The Qur'an in Arab Christian Texts: The Development of an Apologetical Argument; Abū Qurrah in the Maǧlis of al-Ma'mūn." *Parole de l'Orient* 24 (1999): 203–33.

Gruber, Christiane Jacqueline. "The Prophet Muḥammad's Ascension (*Mi'rāj*) in Islamic Art and Literature, ca. 1300–1600." PhD diss., University of Pennsylvania, 2005, https://repository.upenn.edu/dissertations /AAI3179741/.

Guillaume, Alfred. *Islam*. Baltimore: Penguin Books, 1956.

Habib, Yasser. *Obscenity: The Other Face of Aisha*. London: Khuddam al-Mahdi Organisation, 2010.

Hawting, G. R. *The Idea of Idolatry and the Emergence of Islam: From Polemic to History*. Cambridge: Cambridge University Press, 1999.

Haykal, Muhammad Husayn. *The Life of Muḥammad*. Kuala Lumpur: Islamic Book Trust, 1994.

Horovitz, Josef. *The Earliest Biographies of the Prophet and Their Authors*. Edited by Lawrence I. Conrad. Princeton: Darwin Press, 2002.

Hoyland, Robert. "The Earliest Christian Writings on Muḥammad: An Appraisal." In *The Biography of Muḥammad*, edited by Harald Motzki, 276–97. Leiden: Brill, 2000.

———. *Seeing Islam as Others Saw It*. Princeton: Darwin Press, 1997.

Human Rights Watch. "Yemen: Child Marriage Spurs Abuse of Girls and Women." December 8, 2011. https://www.hrw.org/news/2011/12/08 /yemen-child-marriage-spurs-abuse-girls-and-women.

Ḥusayn, Ṭāhā. *Fī al-shi'r al-jāhilī*. 1926. Reprint, Susah, Tunisia: Dār al-ma'rif li-l-ṭibā'a wa-l-nashr, 1997.

Ibn Ḥazm. *Al-Muḥallā*. 12 vols. Beirut: Dār al-fikr, n.d.

Ibn Hishām, 'Abd al-Malik, and Muḥammad Ibn Isḥaq. *The Life of Muḥammad*. Translated by Alfred Guillaume. Oxford: Oxford University Press, 1999.

Ibn Qayyim al-Jawziyyah. *Medicine of the Prophet*. Translated by Penelope Johnstone. Cambridge: Islamic Texts Society, 1998.

Ibn Rāshid, Ma'mar, and 'Abd al-Razzāq al-Ṣan'ānī. *The Expeditions: An Early Biography of Muhammad*. Edited and translated by Sean W. Anthony. New York: New York University Press, 2014.

Ibn Taymiyya, Taqī al-Dīn. *Majmū' al-fatāwā*. Edited by 'Abd al-Raḥmān ibn Muḥammad. 37 vols. Medina: Mujamma' al-malik Fahd li-l-ṭibā'a wa-l-nashr, 1995.

Ibrahim, Ayman S. *A Concise Guide to the Quran: Answering Thirty Critical Questions*. Grand Rapids: Baker Academic, 2020.

———. *Conversion to Islam: Competing Themes in Early Islamic Historiography*. New York: Oxford University Press, 2021.

———. *The Stated Motivations for the Early Islamic Expansion (622–641): A Critical Revision of Muslims' Traditional Portrayal of the Arab Raids and Conquests*. New York: Lang, 2018.

———. "Why Do They Shout 'Allahu Akbar'?" *First Things*. September 20, 2016. https://www.firstthings.com/blogs/firstthoughts/2016/09/why-do -they-shout-allahu-akbar.

Ibrahim, Ayman S., and Clint Hackenburg. *In Search of the True Religion: Monk Jurjī and Muslim Jurists Debating Faith and Practice*. Piscataway, NJ: Gorgias Press, 2022.

Islam Question & Answer. "About Our Site." https://islamqa.info/en/about -us.

———. "Islam and Slavery." January 4, 2008. https://islamqa.info/en/answers /94840/islam-and-slavery.

———. "The Jews' Attempts to Kill the Prophet." December 18, 2002. https://islamqa.info/en/answers/32762/the-jews-attempts-to-kill-the -prophet-peace-and-blessings-of-allah-be-upon-him.

———. "The Punishment for Homosexuality." March 13, 2006. https://islamqa .info/en/answers/38622/the-punishment-for-homosexuality.

———. Question #129141. March 28, 2009. https://islamqa.info/ar/answers /129141/.

——— "The Soundness of the Hadeeth 'Do Not Write Anything from Me . . .' and Explanation of What It Means." June 2, 2001. https://islam qa.info/en/answers/22394/the-soundness-of-the-hadeeth-do-not-write -anything-from-me-and-explanation-of-what-it-means.

———. "Western Human Rights Organizations and the Ruling on Referring to Them for Judgement." April 13, 2007. https://islamqa.info/en/answers /97827/western-human-rights-organizations-and-the-ruling-on-referring -to-them-for-judgement.

———. "Why Does Islam Forbid Lesbianism and Homosexuality?" April 4, 2009. https://islamqa.info/en/answers/10050/why-does-islam-forbid -lesbianism-and-homosexuality.

Izutsu, Toshihiko. *God and Man in the Koran*. Tokyo: Keio Institute of Cultural and Linguistic Studies, 1964.

John of Damascus. *Writings*. Translated by Frederic Hathaway Chase. Fathers of the Church. Washington, DC: Catholic University of America Press, 1958.

John of Nikiu. *The Chronicle of John, Bishop of Nikiu: Translated from Zotenberg's Ethiopic Text*. Translated by Robert Henry Charles. 1916. Reprint, Merchantville, NJ: Evolution, 2007.

Kennedy, Hugh. *The Great Arab Conquests: How the Spread of Islam Changed the World We Live In*. New York: Da Capo, 2008.

Khalife, Nadya. "'How Come You Allow Little Girls to Get Married?': Child Marriage in Yemen." Human Rights Watch. December 7, 2011. https://www.hrw.org/report/2011/12/07/how-come-you-allow-little-girls-get-married/child-marriage-yemen.

Kister, M. J. "The Massacre of the Banū Qurayẓa: A Re-examination of a Tradition." *Jerusalem Studies in Arabic and Islam* 8 (1986): 61–96.

Kuiper, Matthew J. *Da'wa: A Global History of Islamic Missionary Thought and Practice*. Edinburgh: Edinburgh University Press, 2021.

———. *Da'wa and Other Religions: Indian Muslims and the Modern Resurgence of Global Islamic Activism*. London: Routledge, 2017.

Lecker, Michael. *The "Constitution of Medina": Muḥammad's First Legal Document*. Princeton: Darwin Press, 2004.

Madelung, Wilferd. *The Succession to Muḥammad: A Study of the Early Caliphate*. Cambridge: Cambridge University Press, 2006.

Madelung, W., and E. Tyan. "'Iṣma." In *Encyclopaedia of Islam*, edited by P. J. Bearman et al., 4:182. 2nd ed. 12 vols. Leiden: Brill, 1960–present.

Majlisī, Muḥammad Bāqir al-. *Biḥār al- anwār*. Edited by 'Abd al- Raḥīm al-Shīrāzī et al. 110 vols. Beirut: Dār iḥyā' al- turāth, 1983.

Markoe, Lauren. "Muslim Attitudes about LGBT Are Complex, Far from Universally Anti-Gay." *USA Today*. June 17, 2016. https://www.usatoday.com/story/news/world/2016/06/17/muslim-lgbt-gay-views/86046404/.

Moosa, Matti. *Extremist Shiites: The Ghulat Sects*. Syracuse: Syracuse University Press, 1987.

Murphy, Thomas. "Lecture Explores Religious Freedom in Islam." *Observer*. October 24, 2018. https://ndsmcobserver.com/2018/10/lecture-explores-religious-freedom-in-islam/.

Nagel, Tilman. *Muhammad's Mission: Religion, Politics, and Power at the Birth of Islam*. Translated by Joseph S. Spoerl. Boston: de Gruyter, 2020.

Neely, Brent. "The Patriarch and the Insider Movement: Debating Timothy I, Muhammad, and the Qur'an." In *Muslim Conversions to Christ*, edited by Ayman Ibrahim and Ant Greenham, 3–79. Bern: Lang, 2018.

Nehmé, Laïla. "New Dated Inscriptions (Nabataean and Pre-Islamic Arabic) from a Site Near al-Jawf, Ancient Dūmah, Saudi Arabia." *Arabian Epigraphic Notes* 3 (2017): 121–64.

Nickel, Gordon D. *The Quran with Christian Commentary: A Guide to Understanding the Scripture of Islam*. Grand Rapids: Zondervan Academic, 2020.

Ouardi, Hela. *Les derniers jours de Muhammad*. Paris: Albin Michel, 2016.

Penn, Michael. *When Christians First Met Muslims: A Sourcebook of the Earliest Syriac Writings on Islam*. Oakland: University of California Press, 2015.

Pierce, Matthew O. "Remembering the Infallible Imams: Narrative and Memory in Medieval Twelver Shi'ism." PhD diss., Boston University, 2013. https://open.bu.edu/handle/2144/13153.

Qummī, 'Alī ibn Ibrāhīm al-. *Tafsīr al-Qummī*. 2 Vols. Edited by al-Sayyid al-Mūsawī al-Jazā'irī. Qum, Iran: Mu'assasat dār al-kitāb, 1967.

Raḍwānī, 'Abd al-Rāziq al-. *Asmā' Allāh al-ḥusnā al-thābita fī al-kitāb wa-l-sunna*. 2 vols. Cairo: al-baṣīra l-il-taswīq, 2005.

Reynolds, Gabriel Said. *Allah: God in the Qur'ān*. New Haven: Yale University Press, 2020.

———. *A Muslim Theologian in a Sectarian Milieu: 'Abd Al-Jabbār and the Critique of Christian Origins*. Leiden: Brill, 2004.

Rippin, Andrew. "Literary Analysis of Qur'ān, Tafsīr, and Sīra: The Methodologies of John Wansbrough." In *Approaches to Islam in Religious Studies*, edited by Richard C. Martin, 151–63. Tucson: University of Arizona Press, 1985.

Robinson, Chase F. *Empire and Elites after the Muslim Conquest*. Cambridge: Cambridge University Press, 2000.

———. *Islamic Historiography*. Cambridge: Cambridge University Press, 2003.

Rodinson, Maxime. *The Arabs*. Chicago: University of Chicago Press, 1981.

———. *Muhammad: Prophet of Islam*. London: I.B. Tauris, 2002.

Rosenthal, Franz. "The Stranger in Medieval Islam." *Arabica* 44 (1997): 35–75.

Saeed, Abdullah. "Limitations on Religious Freedom in Islam." In *Routledge Handbook of Law and Religion*, edited by Silvio Ferrari, 369–80. New York: Routledge, 2015.

————. "Making the Islamic Case for Religious Liberty." *Current Trends in Islamist Ideology* 21 (2017). https://www.hudson.org/research/13022 -making-the-islamic-case-for-religious-liberty.

Schadler, Peter. *John of Damascus and Islam: Christian Heresiology and the Intellectual Background to Earliest Christian-Muslim Relations.* The History of Christian-Muslim Relations 34. Leiden: Brill, 2018.

Schumm, Walter R. "How Accurately Could Early (622–900 C.E.) Muslims Determine the Direction of Prayers (Qibla)?" *Religions* 11 (2020): 1–16. https://www.mdpi.com/2077-1444/11/3/102/htm.

Sellheim, Rudolf. "Prophet, Chalif und Geschichte: Die Muhammed-Biographie des Ibn Isḥāq." *Oriens*, nos. 18–19 (1965): 33–91.

Shatzmiller, M. "al-Muwaḥḥidūn." In *Encyclopaedia of Islam*, edited by P. J. Bearman et al., 7:801–7. 2nd ed. 12 vols. Leiden: Brill, 1960–present.

Shehadeh, Imad. *God with Us and without Us: Oneness in Trinity versus Absolute Oneness.* Carlisle, UK: Langham Global Library, 2018.

Shoemaker, Steven J. *The Death of a Prophet: The End of Muhammad's Life and the Beginnings of Islam.* Philadelphia: University of Pennsylvania Press, 2012.

Siddiqui, Mona. *Hospitality and Islam: Welcoming in God's Name.* New Haven: Yale University Press, 2015.

Suyuti, Jalal al-Din al-. *Medicine of the Prophet.* Edited by Ahmad Thomson. Rev. ed. London: Ta-Ha, 2015.

Szilágyi, Krisztina. "After the Prophet's Death: Christian-Muslim Polemic and the Literary Images of Muhammad." PhD diss., Princeton University, 2014. https://dataspace.princeton.edu/handle/88435/dsp01j9602077x.

Ṭabarī, Abū Jaʿfar Muḥammad ibn Jarīr al-. *The History of al-Ṭabarī.* 40 vols. Edited by C. E. Bosworth et al. New York: State University of New York Press, 1985–1999.

Theodorou, Angelina E. "Which Countries Still Outlaw Apostasy and Blasphemy?" Pew Research Center. July 29, 2016. https://www.pewresearch .org/fact-tank/2016/07/29/which-countries-still-outlaw-apostasy-and -blasphemy/.

Theophanes. *The Chronicle of Theophanes: Anni Mundi 6095–6305 (A.D. 602–813).* Edited and translated by Harry Turtledove. Philadelphia: University of Pennsylvania Press, 1982.

Timothy's Apology for Christianity. In *Woodbrooke Studies: Christian Documents in Syriac, Arabic and Garshūni.* Vol. 2, *Timothy's Apology for Christianity; The Lament of the Virgin; The Martyrdom of Pilate*, translated by Alphonse Mingana. Cambridge: W. Heffer and Sons, 1928.

Vacca, V. "Sawda bt. Zamʿa." In *Encyclopaedia of Islam*, edited by P. J. Bearman et al., 9:89–90. 2nd ed. 12 vols. Leiden: Brill, 1960–present.

van der Horst, Pieter W. "A Short Note on the *Doctrina Jacobi Nuper Baptizati.*" *Zutot* 6, no. 1 (2009): 1–6.

Wansbrough, John E. *Qurʾānic Studies: Sources and Methods of Scriptural Interpretation*. Oxford: Oxford University Press, 1977.

———. *The Sectarian Milieu: Content and Composition of Islamic Salvation History*. Oxford: Oxford University Press, 1978.

Watt, William Montgomery. "ʿĀʾisha Bint Abī Bakr." In *Encyclopaedia of Islam*, edited by P. J. Bearman et al., 1:307–8. 2nd ed. 12 vols. Leiden: Brill, 1960–present.

———. *Muhammad at Mecca*. Oxford: Oxford University Press, 1953.

———. *Muhammad at Medina*. Oxford: Clarendon, 1956.

———. *Muhammad: Prophet and Statesman*. Oxford: Oxford University Press, 1961.

———. *Muslim-Christian Encounters: Perceptions and Misperceptions*. London: Routledge, 2013.

———. "The Qurʾān and Belief in a 'High God.'" *Der Islam* 56, no. 2 (July 1979): 205–11.

Wensinck, Arent Jan. "Khuṭba." In *Encyclopaedia of Islam*, edited by P. J. Bearman et al., 4:317–22. 2nd ed. 12 vols. Leiden: Brill, 1960–present.

———. *Muhammad and the Jews of Medina*. Berlin: W.H. Behn, 1982.

———. "Takbīr." In *Encyclopaedia of Islam*, edited by P. J. Bearman et al., 10:119. 2nd ed. 12 vols. Leiden: Brill, 1960–present.

Zahed, Ludovic-Mohamed. "Why I Want to Open a Gay-Friendly Mosque in Paris." *Guardian*. November 26, 2012. https://www.theguardian.com/commentisfree/belief/2012/nov/26/paris-gay-friendly-mosque.

Index

Bold numbering signifies detailed discussion of the term.